READING BETTER STATES

Reading Better States

UTOPIAN METHOD AND ENVIRONMENTAL HARM
IN THE GLOBAL SOUTH

Rebecca Oh

FORDHAM UNIVERSITY PRESS   NEW YORK   2026

Fordham University Press gratefully acknowledges financial assistance and support provided for the publication of this book by the University of Illinois Urbana-Champaign.

Copyright © 2026 Fordham University Press

All rights reserved. No part of this publication may be reproduced, stored in a retrieval system, or transmitted in any form or by any means—electronic, mechanical, photocopy, recording, or any other—except for brief quotations in printed reviews, without the prior permission of the publisher.

Fordham University Press has no responsibility for the persistence or accuracy of URLs for external or third-party Internet websites referred to in this publication and does not guarantee that any content on such websites is, or will remain, accurate or appropriate.

Fordham University Press also publishes its books in a variety of electronic formats. Some content that appears in print may not be available in electronic books.

Visit us online at www.fordhampress.com.

For EU safety/GPSR concerns: Mare Nostrum Group B.V., Mauritskade 21D, 1091 GC Amsterdam, The Netherlands, gpsr@mare-nostrum.co.uk

Library of Congress Cataloging-in-Publication Data available online at https://catalog.loc.gov.

Printed in the United States of America

28 27 26   5 4 3 2 1

First edition

Contents

Introduction: Reading Better States   1

1   Unsettled: Toxicity after Bhopal   25

2   Beyond Petrostates: Oil Pollution in the Niger Delta   59

3   Undoing Apartheid: Water Pasts and Futures in Cape Town   92

4   Making Time: Pacific Futurity and Rising Seas   125

     Coda: Utopia beyond Negative Critique   160

ACKNOWLEDGMENTS   165

NOTES   169

WORKS CITED   193

INDEX   215

READING BETTER STATES

Introduction
Reading Better States

"Instead of dem to address de unemployment and real cause of poverty and crime, dey want to cover it all under one pile of rubbish."[1] So intones Sunday Oke in Chris Abani's novel *GraceLand* (2004). Sunday and his family live in the "swamp city" of Lagos's Maroko slum, surrounded by garbage, starving animals, and other members of the urban underclasses who have been displaced from the countryside.[2] Sunday is buffeted by both poverty and state neglect before being killed by police during a clearance of the slum. But before his death his partner, Comfort, suggests that the state might compensate them for their displacement: "Maybe dem go pay before de bulldoze . . . anything is possible." "Dat is a pipedream," Sunday shoots back.[3] He may mean that compensation is far-fetched or fanciful. But Sunday's statement also gestures to communities in the Niger Delta who have demanded compensation for oil pipeline spills on their land. Not himself a Delta resident, Sunday in his statement nonetheless links the infrastructural neglect, massive pollution, and impoverishment of the Niger Delta with the inequities that have created Lagos's massive slums, including his own Maroko. This example from *GraceLand* neatly captures the twinning of environmental harm and social injustice in Nigeria, where oil wealth's unequal distribution cannot be separated from its unequal environmental costs, and where state redress recedes like a figment of the imagination.

And yet, Sunday and Comfort's conversation also hits upon a paradox. Their future is menaced by the state, but the state is simultaneously invoked as a potential provider, one that might distribute compensatory payment and could or should address social and environmental problems like poverty, garbage, and unemployment. The state is the third party in Sunday and Comfort's dialogue, an imagined interlocutor schismed by experiences of violence and neglect but also desires, however jaded, of provision and care. Despite the pipedream quality of redress, the state is not subject to total condemnation, nor is it held forth as a simple panacea for social ills. For Comfort and Sunday the state is contradictory, and complaint about and desire for the state are two sides of the same coin.

In the face of environmental harms and climate catastrophe, postcolonial states are commonly imagined as they are in *GraceLand*: as plural and contradictory, both bad actors and sites of appeal. In places like Maroko and other zones of environmental harm or climate risk, futurity is materially threatened and hard to imagine. But postcolonial writers and ordinary people alike have not ceded their futures to the bad presents they inhabit. Instead, they envision an assortment of better futures from within the damaged present, and, like Abani's characters, they often do so by turning to the state. *Reading Better States* argues that postcolonial writers and everyday citizens repeatedly construe postcolonial states as powerful actors that might intervene in environmentally destructive processes like global capitalism or provide environmental protections and material necessities. Far from being seen as unidimensional sites of violence and disappointment, postcolonial states are imagined through a range of contradictory roles in places like India, Nigeria, South Africa, and the Pacific, which each ground a chapter of this book. In these places futurity is menaced by pollution, toxicity, drought, sea level rise, or other environmental harms and climate threats. But far from being completely determined by bad futures, in each of these locales, different and better forms of futurity are imagined through possibilities for state action on behalf of vulnerable peoples, lands, and waters.

These imaginaries point up the state as a site of utopic desire in contemporary times. Indeed, *Reading Better States* considers state interventions into the environment as examples of what Marxist philosopher Ernst Bloch called "concrete utopia[s]."[4] For Bloch, concrete utopias were not environmental, but they did name visions of "surplus" or excess that were also forms of resistance or "*counter-move[s] contradicting the badly existing*" in the present.[5] Concrete utopias are steeped in the quotidian and in scales of transformational striving that attach to limited and specific concerns. In this book, concrete utopian imaginings eschew the large-scale dreams of systemic transformation once associated with postcolonial utopia in favor of state-based change that is circumscribed, attentive to local conditions, and focused on alleviating environmental damage, bodily suffering, or material want. Demanding clean water in the midst of pollution, for instance, is at once ordinary and utopic, a most basic necessity and a goal that often remains so elusive it courts the impossible.

In environmental concrete utopias, the mundane and the implausible often coincide. But such visions and desires are no less utopic for being quotidian.[6] *Reading Better States* follows environmental visions of concrete utopia that pursue environmental surplus rather than transformation and make countermoves against the badly existing that do not rise near the scale of revolutionary rupture. Environmental concrete utopias are not coded to the once familiar blazon of midcentury anticolonial revolution or other visions of radical overhaul, nor are they mere abstractions or "wishful thinking."[7] They are more circumscribed and less abstract, pursuing situated forms of environmental change while remaining in touch with particular conditions. They maintain "contact between dreams and life," mired in the present but forever reaching beyond it.[8]

Reading Better States is thus tuned to a minor but persistent scale of utopic imagining in the contemporary global South that responds to systemic environmental devastation with situated, state-based attempts at intervention. Sometimes envisioned by postcolonial states themselves and at other times imagined and demanded by writers, activists, and citizens, the concrete utopias in *Reading Better States* arise in historical conditions of capitalist predation, environmental degradation, and climate catastrophe that threaten imaginable futures from India to Kiribati. Within these conditions, concrete utopias name specific forms of material improvement that might be had through the state. They include bodily care and corporate accountability for pesticide poisoning in India (chapter 1), protection from poverty and corporate oil pollution in Nigeria (chapter 2), access to housing and water infrastructure after South African apartheid (chapter 3) and the ability to remain in place in the face of rising seas across the Pacific (chapter 4). *Reading Better States* attends to the way postcolonial writers and ordinary people use possibilities and desires for state intervention as imaginative tools in their fights for better environmental futures, and sometimes in fights simply for futurity itself. In doing so this book also uncovers instances in which postcolonial states have actively, if sporadically and imperfectly, pursued shared environmental visions, likewise seeking to hold corporations accountable or combat environmental racism and exploitation through legislative acts, policies, and institutions like the courts.

However, it has become profoundly counterintuitive to see postcolonial states as anything but antagonists in these battles. The state-based concrete utopias tracked here have arisen at a time when, in fiction, scholarship, and theory, postcolonial states are predominantly defined through violence and disappointment. Seeing past this obvious negativity also requires, therefore, a utopian method of reading, a way of seeing the state that reads its failures, violence, and inadequacy against the grain for alternative paths and possibilities.

A utopian method allows this book to account for, but to also move beyond, the state's patent brutality and limitations to the positive potentialities within. In *Reading Better States*, the state is Janus-faced. It is a bad actor, but it is also an object of collective desire and a site of concrete utopian hopes, of specific and historically situated visions for improving life in ways that are limited but crucial. Such pluralities come into view by reading utopically for concrete utopian visions shared by states and their citizens, however unevenly. These utopias exist beneath the state's bad surfaces, as do popular desires for intervention that have never disappeared but adhere to the state, waiting to be read. *Reading Better States* therefore argues for the place of concrete utopias in the present and reconsiders the postcolonial state for its interventionist possibilities as well as its violence. It does all this through a utopian method of reading that, like concrete utopias themselves, dwells in the badly existing while looking beyond it, seeking out those visions of surplus that exceed, even if they cannot escape, the damage and disappointment of the present earth.[9]

Janus-Faced: State Violence, State Intervention

Humanists love to hate the state. Critiqued both for its own repressive practices and for its collusions with global capital, violence is central to theories of the state across the humanities. From such vantages this book's claim that postcolonial states are plural, imagined as both bad actors and sites of appeal, and that they are sites of concretely utopian potential, may smack of conservatism or naivete. In part, this is because the most influential critical theories of the state define it through violence. Max Weber famously defined the state as that which claims "the *monopoly* of the *legitimate* use of physical force," while Karl Marx's writings contain countless denigrations of the state as an oppressive tool in the hands of national bourgeoisie.[10] More recently, philosopher Giorgio Agamben has argued that the state exists in a zone of exceptional power, where rule of law or checks upon its violence are suspended and everyone is potentially susceptible to being killed by the state at any time.[11] For Agamben, the capacity to designate which life may be killed with impunity makes the state what it is. Among postcolonialists, political theorist Achille Mbembe forcefully continues this trend. His *Necropolitics* draws on both Agamben and Michel Foucault's biopolitics to stress the state's ability to make die. Mbembe, along with many other biopolitical theorists, reads the interventionist powers of the state as "the work of death."[12] Thus, many theories of the state delineate the state's right to kill as its founding characteristic or exposure to violence as the primary political relationship between states and their citizens.

In postcolonial studies, a particular kind of state violence has moreover preoccupied attention: namely, the exclusions and repressions states practice upon their own national minorities. Theorized as the collision between homogenizing states and the heterogeneous national populations inhabiting them, state repression of ethnic and religious minorities or other nonhegemonic groups has loomed large for both postcolonial critics and authors. Literary and cultural studies scholar David Lloyd suggests that postcolonial states always try to cultivate one particular kind of nationally imagined community while repressing those who do not conform to it, while political scientist Mahmood Mamdani has argued, in a related formulation, that postcolonial states only tolerate their own minorities under the threat of ethnic cleansing.[13] State violence, seen in relation to those parts of the nation it cannot or will not contain, has been central to postcolonial theories of the state. Canonical postcolonial novels have in turn tended to reflect these national conflicts and the state violence they spawned, enshrining a deep suspicion of the state in their depictions of corruption and repression. Salman Rushdie's *Midnight's Children* is, for instance, well known as both an allegory of national fracture and a warning about the closure of Indian independence's magical possibilities at the hands of state authoritarianism. Ayi Kwei Armah's *The Beautiful Ones Are Not Yet Born*, published shortly after Ghanian independence, meditates on the pervasive corruption of Ghanian bureaucracy that strangles the nation as it emerges, and Ngũgĩ wa Thiong'o's *Petals of Blood* and *Wizard of the Crow* foreground state violence, ineptitude, and corruption in Kenya. Anti-statism is as pervasive in postcolonial fiction as it is in theory.

From other vantages, postcolonial state violence is not intrinsic to states so much as it is symptomatic of economic imperialism and the state's capture by global capital. The "development of underdevelopment" instituted by the International Monetary Fund and the World Bank has thus been a major site of postcolonial critique.[14] These institutions perpetuated economic imperialism on newly independent states after decolonization by imposing structural adjustment programs (SAPs) that emptied out states' social and economic capacities. It is by now well established that SAPs mired postcolonial states in debt and high interest rates, handcuffed development money to neoliberal terms, mandated cuts to social spending, and forced postcolonial countries to develop cheap export industries within a skewed global market.[15] The results were political weakness, spiking poverty, and resource exhaustion. But even as postcolonial states were externally hamstrung by global finance, state power was often internally captured by corporate actors who *"shape[d] the formation of the basic rules of the game"* by influencing national laws and regulations in their favor.[16] In such instances of "state capture," corporations insert their profiteering interests into the way the state functions, shaping policy by working with colluding state officials. Captured states become, in short, little more than handmaidens to expropriative market interests.[17] These neocolonial processes of state capture and structural adjustment have worked violence on, but also through, postcolonial states.

Whether considered through histories of violence or complicity with capital, it is easy to see why postcolonial states are such objects of opprobrium. And yet, the postcolonial state has also been understood through another, contradictory model that centers its capacities for positive intervention, care, and social provision. In contrast to figures like Mbembe and Mamdani, anthropologist and political theorist Partha Chatterjee suggests that interventionist states, defined by their capacities for social provision and improvement, are the dominant political form across the global South. Chatterjee notes that "without exception . . . state[s] which promised to end poverty and backwardness by adopting appropriate policies of economic growth and social reform" arose in the wake of midcentury independence movements.[18] For populations in the global South or "three-fourths of contemporary humanity," this "triumphant advance of governmental technologies that have promised to deliver more well-being to more people at less cost" is the version of the state that matters.[19] Intellectual historian Sudipta Kaviraj agrees that after decolonization, "it was the state which almost entirely arrogated to itself the power of proposing, directing, and effecting large-scale social change" and "that is why the state is central to the story of non-Western modernity."[20]

Such interventions belong within the theoretical lineage of state welfare.[21] The ideology of the welfare state contends that states can and should intervene in society to ameliorate the painful effects of external forces like unpredictable markets or cycles in unemployment. Welfare states developed from the recognition that individuals cannot control or account for large-scale processes outside themselves and are therefore "entitled to relief precisely because they could not be held (morally) responsible for the predicaments in which they might find themselves."[22] Western welfare states have been traced back to a number of possible precursors—the eighteenth-century rise of a "social" understanding of the world made by humans and thus subject to human change, the nineteenth-century French Jacobin state, or practices of rationing during wartime in twentieth-century Britain. But welfare states, whatever their origin, are defined by their interventionist character, and more particularly by the need to intervene in circumstances that individuals cannot confront or control.[23] Thus, when decolonization "brought the ideology of welfare to far more human beings than ever before," postcolonial state-makers, often drawing on socialist principles, established welfarist "high capacity states" with an "empowerment to save the public realm from private interests."[24] From the Nigerian and Kenyan Bills of Rights to Nehruvian economic planning and Nyere's socialism, positive large-scale social and economic interventions were central to the early aims of many postcolonial states.[25]

This welfarist tradition means that for some postcolonial scholars, to say that the state is a site of utopic imagining will be both familiar and scandalous. The independent nation-state *was* a horizon of hope and aspiration during decolonization, and new states *were* often seen utopically as vehicles of social justice and material improvement.[26] Yet it is equally true that few would make such claims about postcolonial states today. Since the hopeful decades immediately after midcentury decolonization, states have fallen far short of their earlier aspirations, and postcolonial scholarship has tended to take the contemporary failures and disappointments of the state for granted. Postcolonial historians like Frederick Cooper and Gary Wilder have used that disappointment as an impetus to recover midcentury alternatives to the state like regional federations, and literary critics like Neil ten Kortenaar remind us of the state's former potential at midcentury. These intellectual moves all testify to the way utopianism does not shadow the state now.[27] Likewise, in *Worldmaking after Empire*, political theorist Adom Getachew has traced the rise and fall of postcolonial states' commitments to welfare domestically and as a platform for international decolonization in the 1960s and 1970s.[28] But such visions never fully came to pass, and in the decades since the 1970s, postcolonial projects of large-scale utopian worldmaking have faded.

These disappointments have not, however, meant the obsolescing of state intervention or its total defeat by the more prominent forces of state violence and state capture. If anything, demands for and ideas about state intervention have expanded to encompass new objects. The archive of texts collected in *Reading Better States*, which includes novels, films, court decisions, legislation, poetry, and testimony, reflects demands for state action that are being made in response not only to once-familiar objects of intervention like the economy, but also vis-à-vis environmental damage and, increasingly, in response to climate change. Interventionist states are being called upon not only to rectify long-standing capitalist byproducts like poverty and unemployment but also the environmental effects of global capital, such as corporate pollution and fossil-fueled sea level rise, whose spatial and temporal spans extend across the planet and far into the future.

An environmental lens thus makes visible the persistence of a welfarist role for the postcolonial state and the ongoing importance of state interventions in an era when visions of grand state-based action have waned. The environmental concrete utopias found in *Reading Better States* have arisen after the death or at least the decline of many earlier postcolonial dreams, including ideals of state-driven modernization and autonomy in a new world order where the global South would neither "imitate Europe" nor remain the wretched of the earth.[29] Such large-scale utopic visions have been a general casualty of poststructuralism's turn against comprehensive narratives and the historic collapse of counterweights to the free market. Defined by impulses for world-changing newness that fall short of actual achievements, utopia has always been caught between a sense of the good and a sense of the nowhere, between eutopia and utopia.[30] And today, that gap seems wider than ever. But though postcolonial states have lost much of their former luster, at times they have intervened in the destructive externalities of capitalist profiteering, and they are still called upon to provide social goods and dampen the intensifying effects of anthropogenetic climate change. In the global South, forces like pollution, toxicity, drought, and flood have become part of dynamic political relations and ideas about state power. As this book will go on to show, postcolonial states have at times sought to remediate situations of emplaced material harm that resist transcendence or transformation, with very limited success. But despite these limits, postcolonial citizens and writers have continued to turn to interventionist states to make change where they cannot.

Demands for state intervention thus underscore something basic: that people living under environmental hardship cannot produce the concrete utopias they want, and corporations never will. However much the postcolonial state is constrained by or complicit with the ravages of global capitalism or otherwise experienced as a violent actor, it is crucial to recuperate its buried, forgotten, and disappointed potentials. This is because postcolonial states are also one of the only entities that can substantially mitigate the capitalist processes destroying the environment or produce emplaced social interventions that better the lives of ordinary people. As social justice scholar Raj Patel and geographer Jason W. Moore put it, capitalism "in the web of life" views every form of life as a frontier for extraction and renders all nature "cheap" in a race to the bottom for profit.[31] Individuals and even activist groups in the global South, however robust, cannot match the expanse of corporations' destructive piracy or shut down their frontier ethos. If anyone or anything can contest the scale of capitalist exploitation in the global South, it is the postcolonial state, with its own powerful arsenal of agendas, players, and power.[32] Somewhat like Plato's pharmakon, which can be both poison and cure, postcolonial states perpetuate environmental violence and are time and again called upon to ameliorate it.

Reading Better States does not discount the state's violence. But it will go on to show how, in the past and in the present, postcolonial states have sometimes fought against market forces like extractivism, privatization, and the objectification of human and nonhuman life; they have also fought for environmental protections and corporate accountability, albeit in limited ways. States have enacted corporate regulations and environmental safeguards, attempted to hold companies accountable for producing injury and death, worked to provide infrastructures that combat racial capitalism, and challenged destructive giants like the fossil fuel industry. These fights are painfully rare. And they appear in situated, partial, and often obscured forms in particular places, leaving capitalism as a system intact. Yet, such limited environmental interventions are significant when viewed as concrete utopias, pursuits of surplus that contest, even if they do not overturn, the "badly existing" present. They matter for the imaginative futures they enable, and they matter as actually existing efforts against the ruination wrought by capitalism and climate change across the global South.

In these ways, interventionist states in the global South continue to be sites of desire and expectation, even for those they have harmed. Indeed, for many people in the global South, turning to state intervention is a way of imagining not only material futurity, but also political inclusion and social survival. The environmental demands postcolonial citizens and writers make upon their states frequently form a continuum with desires for other kinds of better treatment from the state. Time and again, postcolonial writers and ordinary citizens imagine states that provide specific kinds of environmental betterment while rhetorically and imaginatively linking these to desires for greater political participation, thicker belonging, or state recognition. Efforts to secure basic resources, bodily care, and different environmental futures affect political life as much as more traditional demands like those for civic participation or legal rights. Treated more like subjects than citizens, the communities examined in this book tend not to experience robust citizenship, either in terms of formal rights or political and social inclusion. Their exclusion from protections and political visibility goes hand in hand with their disproportionate exposure to capitalism's environmental harms and the ravages of climate change; redressing one kind of lack is indubitably tied to redressing the other. Thus, postcolonial states are called upon both to offer better kinds of political life and to address environmental damage that dwarfs individual agency or community effort.

It behooves postcolonial critics, environmental scholars, and humanists to examine the investments and uses that attach to these complex ideas of the state as well as to examine how such imaginaries themselves are produced between states and their citizens. For postcolonial states do not unidirectionally impose concrete utopias such as social provision, environmental protection, or capitalist regulation—they are popularly imagined through and often hailed in precisely these terms. Historian and anthropologist Lisa Mitchell describes this dynamic as the way postcolonial citizens interpellate states while being hailed by them in a "multidirectionality of practices of hailing."[33] And sociologist Pierre Bourdieu noted that we are always "being thought by a state that we believe we are thinking."[34] Though originally couched as a warning about political subjectification, this point also emphasizes how states and citizens constitute each other in imagination. Such mutual imaginings have important effects, effects on the way those under the state's rule are identified, recognized, and treated, but also effects on the way the state itself is described and addressed in cultural objects produced under conditions of environmental damage and climate catastrophe. These objects, which here include protests, testimony, interviews, petitions, novels, poetry, court cases, legislation, and films, record a multitude of conflicting state actions and imaginaries. But crucially, together they reflect collective desires for concrete utopian possibilities that turn, despite all odds, toward the state.

For all these reasons, looking to the environment is central to understanding the significance and place of state interventions in the global South today, where capitalism in the web of life is draining life down to the lees. Ongoing demands for environmental intervention highlight and expand on the postcolonial state's earlier potentials for social provision and its ability to intervene in large systems that individuals cannot confront. And though capitalism's environmental injustices are often abetted by states, they are also central to the kinds of claims postcolonial citizens make *upon* their states. Attending to the concrete environmental utopias envisioned by states themselves and imagined, too, by writers and citizens reveals how postcolonial states are imagined beyond their violence, as agents of desirable change.

Reading Better States insists that postcolonial states must be understood as Janus-faced and plural, divided between their brutality and neglect on the one hand and their positive interventionist possibilities, or what literary and cultural critic Bruce Robbins calls their "caring and rescue functions," on the other.[35] These plural state roles cannot be separated, but shape the contradictory ways in which postcolonial states are experienced and imagined. In *Debt Law Realism*, postcolonial literary scholar Neil ten Kortenaar argues similarly that postcolonial states are dual. For Kortenaar, the state is schismed between violence and the rule of law rather than between violence and positive, concretely utopic interventions. But like *Reading Better States*, his work makes clear that it should be impossible to talk about the postcolonial state as a singular form, to define it by one pattern or equate it with one kind of action, even one as obvious as violence. In fact, political constructivists like Philip

Abrams have long argued that no state can be defined singularly.[36] For Abrams, the state is both an idea and a system, a notion that combines the ideological and material aspects of statehood to suggest that the state must be understood through the interplay of its ideas and institutional effects. It is the dialectic of "state-idea" and "state-system" that for Abrams makes up what we call "the state" at any given time.[37] Like Kortenaar and Abrams, this book attends to how a plurality of ideas and imaginaries shapes what the state is at any particular moment.

Perhaps because postcolonial states have so largely been theorized through a focus on forces like violence, disappointment, and capitalist complicity, postcolonial literary studies has not tended to engage contradictory imaginaries of the state, and the field has often relinquished state-based hopes to illusion—what Abani called "pipedreams." Exceptions like Kortenaar's work are relatively rare.[38] Postcolonial environmental humanists and ecocritics have also yet to interrogate the way desired environmental futures sometimes depend on states' roles in mitigating corporate violence. This holds true even for seminal postcolonial ecocritics like Rob Nixon and Jennifer Wenzel, who largely view postcolonial states through their participation in environmental destruction.[39] These negative tendencies are only particular strands within more widespread forms of anti-statism across the humanities. But this cannot be the only narrative we have about states. It is imperative to theorize states, and especially postcolonial states, through complexity and plurality.[40] For despite its violence, the idea of an interventionist postcolonial state that might provide concrete forms of environmental and social betterment has animated the state's own actions, and it has proven sustaining for those communities and individuals most exposed to capitalist profiteering, environmental damage, and climate catastrophe across the global South.

Utopian Method

Despite their importance, it is no easy task to see contemporary postcolonial states as sites of positive intervention or utopic desire. To bring state-based concrete utopias into view, *Reading Better States* elaborates a version of critical reading called utopian method. This method deliberately resists what seems all too obvious about the postcolonial state and highlights instead the state's imagined plurality, its position as both a bad actor and a site of appeal. Marxist cultural and literary critic Fredric Jameson first coined the term "utopian method" in the essay "Utopia as Method, or the Uses of the Future," to name a way of reading that reads patently negative circumstances against the grain for their positive potentials. For Jameson, utopian method is:

a prodigious effort to *change the valences* on phenomena that so far exist only in our own present and experimentally to *declare positive things that are clearly negative in our own world*, to affirm that dystopia is in reality utopia if examined more closely, to isolate specific features in our empirical present so as to read them as components of a different system.[41]

Jameson's theoretical example was Walmart, that corporate conglomerate of consumptive capital which, from another angle, manages a vast machinery of affordable and consistent products.[42] In his earlier work on utopia in *Archaeologies of the Future*, Jameson distinguished between comprehensive utopian plans and a utopian impulse toward newness that was not limited to particular content. But in "Utopia as Method" he attends to the newness available within present structures, to the ways in which a "whole new world is objectively in emergence all around us, without our necessarily perceiving it at once."[43] If utopian impulse pursues the new, utopian method repurposes the already-existing. My utopian method of reading adopts Jameson's general impetus and refines it through several techniques to reread the postcolonial state. In *Reading Better States*, utopian method is used to read complaints about the state as both catalogues of negativity and demands upon power; to read the state recursively or nonlinearly beyond its present, obvious manifestations; to read the state's unfulfilled promises as future potentials rather than as closures; and to read for alterative versions of the state in aesthetic works as well as in the state's own archives, both past and future.

This book's utopian method reads many kinds of texts for their concrete utopian visions, for the archives of utopia are promiscuous and widespread. Utopic hopes are certainly found in art and literature, but concretely utopian, future-making ideas are not confined to novels or poetry. Indeed, some of the central objects in this book are environmental complaints, which appear across texts fictional and nonfictional, legal and popular. In the *OED*, the meaning of "complaint" ranges from the utterance of grief to the utterance of a grievance, an outcry against injury.[44] It is also a legal text. Indeed, "complaint" may come to mind first as a special kind of legal language, the pleading that starts a civil case. A legal complaint sets forth a jurisdictional basis for the court, names a plaintiff's sense of injury or cause of action, and demands judicial relief.[45] Law and literature scholars have stressed the importance of complaint as a particular kind of legal language, and this tradition has influenced my thoughts on complaint.[46] This book will examine a number of legal documents, including part of the case history surrounding the Bhopal gas disaster settlement of 1989 in chapter 1. This case, settled in India's Supreme Court, began with a legal complaint. However,

Reading Better States generally considers "complaint" within a wider ambit. The basic formal aspects of complaint—naming a sense of wrong and appealing to an authority for redress—are wide-ranging and not unique to legal procedure.[47] Structurally, complaints combine a catalogue of negativity with a demand upon power. When addressed to the state, complaints diagnose what states have done wrong but are also invested in state intervention. The other side of complaint's negativity is desire. Complaints *about* the state are also complaints *to* the state. Complaint, both a verb and a noun, is the naming of a perceived wrong and the expectation of institutional response to it. As such, the complaints assembled here are most important for their rhetorical structure of naming injury and demanding state redress. That is, they are important for the way they concretize and capture the state's dual appearance as both a bad actor and a site of appeal.

Many of the complaints in *Reading Better States* are also a way of assessing what state power should or should not do. This sense of complaint as a kind of "institutional mechanics" that shows the workings of power is central to how feminist scholar Sara Ahmed has used it in her book *Complaint!*, which follows the procedures of blockage and flow around university title IX complaints.[48] So too, when Sunday complained about the Nigerian state in *GraceLand*, he named a sense of injury ("dey want to cover it all under one pile of rubbish") and simultaneously proposed an alternative possibility for redress—a suggestion of what the state should do instead ("address de unemployment and real cause of poverty and crime"). Complaints are a way of assessing state priorities and of making oneself visible in the political landscape. They "[enable] people to construct the state symbolically and to define themselves as citizens," as anthropologist Akhil Gupta puts it.[49] Complaints thus capture and represent the kind of Janus-faced, plural state I argue for in this book as a whole and they reward utopian reading, a method of reading against the grain of negativity for the positive potentials caught in what appears like a negative surface.

No less a thinker than anticolonial revolutionary Frantz Fanon offers an extended example of the two-part structure of complaint—its twinned aspects of negativity and demand—that simultaneously capture two roles for the state. In *The Wretched of the Earth*, Fanon offers a systematic and Marxist-inspired critique of the postcolonial state. Focusing his attention on the parasitic role of the national bourgeoisie, Fanon complains about the entrenched comprador class, which merely seeks to "[take] the place of the colonist."[50] This is elaborated especially in chapter 3, "The Trials and Tribulations of National Consciousness," where Fanon describes how the bourgeoisie have captured state power and set up a state that works in their own interests: "It does not establish a reassuring State for the citizen, but one which is troubling."[51] Fanon diagnoses the postcolonial state as the instrument of a national bourgeoisie that co-opts state bureaucracy and political parties and corrupts charismatic leaders into "the CEO of the company of profiteers composed of a national bourgeoisie."[52] For Fanon, the postcolonial state has too often become a "semicolonial State."[53]

Yet at the same time, with almost every line, Fanon proposes alternatives to the comprador, disappointing states he has seen come into being after postcolonial independence movements. In one rhetorical pairing after another, Fanon lays out what the postcolonial state has done badly but also what it should and could do better. Critique and alternative accompany each other. In short, his complaint about the state he sees is always entwined with complaint for the state he wants. Naming the negativity of the present state is inextricably yoked to visions of a different, future state. Hence, "the State... imposes itself in a spectacular manner, flaunts its authority, harasses, making it clear to its citizens they are in content danger"—"*instead* of inspiring confidence, assuaging the fears of its citizens and cradling them with its power and discretion."[54] Here and elsewhere, Fanon's description of what the state has done badly is conceptualized in relation to what it should do well. Complaint is simultaneously a catalogue of negativity and a demand upon power; the other side of complaint's negativity is desire. These dual aspects cannot be separated but are twinned.

Likewise, toward the end of this chapter, Fanon makes a great call upon the postcolonial state—clearly not the "semicolonial" state he has just described in all its negative qualities, but an alternative imagined state he has also constructed in tandem with this diagnosis, through his complaints. Such a state would "take great strides toward development and progress" and become a state that "govern[s] by the people and for the people, for the disinherited and by the disinherited."[55] This state, which serves the people, is nowhere to be found in the present of Fanon's writing, but it is imagined out of the circumstances of titular tribulation in which he writes and it is fleshed out in close relation to state failures. The state Fanon knows has been a bad actor; the one he imagines might be better, and this better future state is produced in relation to specific historical circumstances, as both a diagnosis of and alternative to them. Though he goes on later in *The Wretched of the Earth* to envision the eventual transcendence of the national state, it is clear that Fanon's complaints about the state are never only a negative catalogue of the bad state but also always an appeal to, and for, a better state. Utopian method involves this kind of reading: reading complaints against the grain of their negative valences for the positive potentials that shadow them. This twofold structure of complaint, which combines a bad present with proposals for a future beyond it, produces also a plural state, one imagined as simultaneously a bad actor and a site of appeal that might support concretely utopian futures.

In addition to reading complaints about the state against the grain, this book's utopian method reads the state against the grain temporally, drawing on postcolonial anthropologist and historian Ann Laura Stoler's idea of recursion. Rather than focusing on a downward trajectory in which states have not lived up to their interventionist hopes or in which state violence will extend inexorably into the future, a recursive and nonlinear orientation toward the state allows us to see how better states are envisioned in complex temporal configurations of past, present, and future. In *Duress*, Stoler describes "'recursive analytics,' or history as recursion" as a history "marked by the uneven, unsettled, contingent quality of histories that *fold back on themselves* and, in that refolding, reveal new surfaces, and new planes."[56] Recursion stresses the nonlinear overlaps, meshings, continuities, and eruptions between historical events and processes: "Recursion is precisely *not* to imagine that social and political processes ever play out in a repetitive and mimetic fashion. . . . Rather, they are processes of partial reinscriptions, modified displacements, and amplified recuperations."[57] This attention to the way past, present, and future may diverge, run parallel, overlap in part, amplify, or interrupt each other is central to my utopian method because it disrupts linear trajectories of state disappointment and slow environmental violence, in which the future will only bring more of the same bad present.

Though not always called recursion, nonlinear heuristics have generally been central to postcolonial studies' temporal sensibilities and the field's attunement to the way past, present, and future in the postcolony have never followed one another in a "Romantic mode of . . . progressive overcoming."[58] From postcolonial historian Dipesh Chakrabarty's work on multiple modernities in India, to postcolonial scholarship on trauma, where the collective past is not past but repeats and interrupts the present, to Indigenous and African cosmologies that foreground cyclicality, nonlinear temporalities have suffused many different aspects of postcolonial thought.[59] Yet a nonlinear or recursive heuristic has not been applied to the postcolonial state and its interventionist potentials. Reading the state recursively, with an understanding that past, present, and future touch in unpredictable ways, reveals complex interweavings of past and future states that interrupt present versions.

Recursion illuminates the way states have contradicted themselves over time and the fact that they are plural not only in imagination, but in practice. The postcolonial state's own recursivity or plurality appears in legislative antecedents and regulations, where states once thought to limit corporate actors or intervene in environmental damage in ways that have come to seem ludicrous today. But recursion gives credence to *"historical roads not taken, to brazen and impossible alternatives* proposed and squashed, to muted dissensions and suspended plans."⁶⁰ As part of utopian method, recursion attends to alternatives to the state's dominant versions that are contained in its own past archives. At earlier moments in time, for instance, the Nigerian state thought about spilled oil and broken pipelines in the Niger Delta as corporate responsibilities, and the Indian state once thought about holding Union Carbide Corporation accountable for the thousands killed and injured by its 1984 factory explosion in Bhopal. In these past moments it is possible to see how the state itself once thought about intervention in ways that align with popular demands still being made upon it today, after decades of ongoing harm. These forms of state action are all but invisible in a present dominated by civilian suffering, cynicism about the state, and unchecked capitalist expansion. Though these protective visions have been repressed, forgotten, or ignored, utopian method's recursive orientation highlights their existence in the state's own past and in turn the way they pluralize the state. Such antecedents cannot be dismissed just because they have not produced new outcomes.

Likewise, utopian method attends recursively to proposals for alternative future states. While the first two chapters of this book excavate suppressed legislative antecedents that pluralize the Indian and Nigerian states from the past, the last two chapters consider "novel contingent possibilities" that arise from future states imagined in the face of climate change.⁶¹ In chapter 3, writer Alistair Mackay proposes a new South African state that might take drastic climate action, and in chapter 4, the Pacific state of Kiribati offers a creative, speculative version of statehood to resist predictions of inundation and climate displacement in the face of sea level rise. Within utopian method such future alternatives are not dismissed because they have not come to pass or because they push the boundaries of imagination. Instead, alternate future states, like their past antecedents, can be read for the potentials they articulate against the grain of an environmentally damaged and politically disappointing present.

Finally, a utopic and recursive orientation toward the state shapes the way this book reads state promises of intervention that remain unfulfilled. Time and again, postcolonial citizens and writers draw upon the language of state interventions to populate their own demands for what counts as a better future. In making such demands, they treat state interventions as promises that might one day come to pass, participating in what political theorist Seyla Benhabib has called a "politics of fulfillment."⁶² In a politics of fulfillment, "the society of the future attains more adequately what present society has left unaccomplished" and utopia consists of "what ought to be, but is not."⁶³ For Benhabib, a politics of fulfillment pursues "the implicit but frustrated potential of the present."[64] Like Bloch's concrete utopias, Benhabib's politics of fulfillment is not about radical newness but about situated and historically recognizable goals. Healthcare after poisoning. Water for all citizens. A politics of fulfillment suggests that utopia can adhere in what is known and desired but absent.[65] In contexts of environmental harm where states have publicly articulated specific interventions but failed to implement them or where political and material rights have been named but are not enforced, concrete utopias and a politics of fulfillment illuminate visions of change that pursue the familiar rather than the extreme. A politics of fulfillment situates the damaged now within a trajectory of possible improvement. It casts the present as fluid rather than ossified or suspended forever in the temporal distention of a harmful status quo. And while a politics of fulfillment might seem bound to linear trajectories—the future will achieve what the present has not—this smooth linearity is clearly missing in the sites central to this book. Instead, a politics of fulfillment emphasizes the possibility of achieving "what ought to be, but is not" from within what looks and feels like stasis.

These techniques of reading are all central to the utopian method of *Reading Better States*. Reading complaints about the state against the grain, reading states recursively, through a politics of fulfillment, and through both past antecedents and future alternatives, reveals how and how often postcolonial states have been viewed as sites of concrete, particular change in zones of enduring material damage. This is so even when they have been unable to undo that damage or had a hand in producing it. And this means, finally, that utopian method is also the methodological corollary of what Bloch, in the essay "Can Hope Be Disappointed?," has called *"well-founded"* or *"educated"* hope.[66] For Bloch, however much it is marred by disappointment or caught between what "has not yet been defeated, but likewise has not yet won," well-founded hope is that which acknowledges that "disappointment over realization's 'minus' finally counts toward the credit of well-founded hope."[67] For Bloch, moving toward an unrealized goal is still movement, and the disappointment that accompanies what has not yet been won is intrinsic to hope. Jameson and other scholars of utopia have described this lacuna as the way utopian desires always exceed utopian achievements. From this angle, utopian desire will always be dissatisfied, and perhaps nowhere has this been borne out more bitterly than in the aftermaths of anticolonial liberation. But this also means it is something of a misrecognition to call that disappointment a symptom of failure, to not see it as part of the structure of having hope, intrinsic to and a consequence of pursuing better futures. Because hope is "something that does not, in spite of all, make peace with the existing world," well-founded hope is always disappointed with the world in which it finds itself but credits progression even when telos has not arrived.[68] Therefore, Bloch suggests that we must dwell in the kind of well-founded hope that registers both failing and change. The other side of hope is disappointment, just as in utopian method the other side of complaint is desire. One is not the lack or failure of the other, but part of occupying an imperfect world that must be *"judged by* the latency hidden within tendency."[69] For well-founded hope and for utopian method, pursuing and imagining better futures depend on reading for the positive potentials within the negative valences of what exists.

Environmental Justice and Slow Violence

Reading Better States' concern with environmental futurity and concrete utopias is informed by two frameworks that have been especially influential in the environmental humanities and postcolonial ecocriticism: environmental justice and slow violence. Environmental justice foregrounds the need to diagnose and correct environmental racism. Environmental racism names the unequal concentration of environmental harms like pollution and resource scarcity, and the unequal hoarding of environmental goods like clean air and water, as these fall along lines of race and class.[70] As a term, environmental racism was formally coined in the United States by activists of color in the 1980s, but it is reproduced and intensified globally.[71] Indeed, the way former president of the World Bank Lawrence Summers once described Africa is almost a caricature of environmental racism: "I've always thought that countries in Africa are vastly under polluted . . . shouldn't the World Bank be encouraging more migration of the dirty industries to the Least Developed Countries?"[72]

For postcolonial environmental humanists, it has long been clear that environmental racism and the corresponding need for environmental justice are not just contemporary concerns but as old as empire. In fact, environmental racism's uneven material geographies have been central to how postcolonial environmental humanists like Elizabeth M. DeLoughrey and George B. Handley theorize colonialism itself: as foundationally a project of expropriating nature.[73] Summers's comment only reproduces the kind of racialized sacrifice zones and regimes of disposability that have underpinned colonial projects of extraction, displacement, resource appropriation, and terraforming across the global South for centuries.[74] For postcolonial environmental humanists, the campaigns of material ruination central to colonialism, neocolonialism, and global capitalism mean that the environment has always been an arena of "social conflicts" inseparable from human struggles.[75] Environmental criticism is in turn an "aesthetics committed to politics," and combating environmental racism and pursuing environmental justice on a global scale remain two of the most urgent shared challenges of postcolonial environmental humanities work and the environmental humanities field as a whole.[76]

The long lives of environmental racism and environmental injustice dovetail with another framework that has become equally important to the environmental humanities and this book: slow violence. "Neither spectacular nor instantaneous, but rather incremental and accretive," slow violence exceeds the flash of media headlines and challenges narration with its scale.[77] When postcolonial environmental humanist Rob Nixon coined the term "slow violence" in *Slow Violence and the Environmentalism of the Poor*, he could not perhaps foresee the way this concept would revolutionize the fields of ecocriticism and the environmental humanities. But now environmental violence, for Nixon and nearly everyone else in these fields, is violence that accumulates across vast scales of time and space. Slow violence has come to encompass environmental damage across the planet, from the long-term effects of poisons and pollutants in human and nonhuman bodies, to creeping desertification and food scarcity, to heat deaths and freshwater salination.

Nixon was concerned with the representational challenges posed by slow violence and the need to link instances of slow violence with their distant origins in environmental racism and corporate piracy. *Reading Better States* shares these concerns but is most interested in slow violence for the way it puts its finger on the temporal span of environmental damage's material consequences. Extending from the past into the conceivable future, the temporal drag of slow environmental violence threatens to subsume imaginable futures into more of the same bad present. Slow violence is significant to this book because it begs the question of how futurity is imagined at all from within the material intransigence it names. It is from within the unending duration of slow violence that the concrete utopias of *Reading Better States* must emerge to posit different futures. By unpacking the way postcolonial subjects envision better ecopolitical futures through the state, this book illuminates struggles for futurity against slow violence's cannibalization of the future. Concrete utopias must persist in slow violent times.

These framing concerns play out in the book's primary cases, which include the long aftermath of Bhopal's 1984 pesticide poisoning at the hands of American chemical company Union Carbide, the decades-long oil pollution of the Niger Delta by a range of oil companies such as Shell, BP, Chevron, and ExxonMobile, Cape Town's feared water cut-offs in 2018 and their intersection with the legacies of South African apartheid, and the increasing threat global fossil-fueled sea level rise poses to atoll nations in the Pacific. In each of these contexts, where capitalism's environmental damage and inexorable environmental catastrophes threaten to subsume the future, interventionist imagined states appear at every turn. Across the global South, the desired interventions and contradictory roles of plurally imagined states are vehicles for pursuing concrete utopian ideas, more just presents, and better environmental futures from within the accumulated slow violence of the present.

Chapter Overview

Reading Better States has four body chapters. Across them all, literary and nonliterary texts appear horizontally as I mine them for the "common dimension" of their plurally imagined states and concrete utopian visions.[78] The beginning of each chapter attends to the way postcolonial states have directly produced or indirectly abetted environmental harm, for these negative narratives capture part of the historical and aesthetic experience of environmental violence and climate change. But the dominance of these negative narratives has also obscured how the state is imagined in other ways. Therefore, each chapter then turns to how postcolonial states, even those most obviously imbricated in violence, have never been imagined only in these terms. Multiple, cross-cutting versions of the state are always at work, mediating how postcolonial writers, activists, and ordinary people envision their ecopolitical futures.

The first two chapters consider two cases of environmental slow violence that have become exemplary instances of environmental racism and state injustice among postcolonial environmental humanists: the 1984 Bhopal gas explosion and the oil contamination of Nigeria's Niger Delta. These are instances where the state has been considered solely for the way it aided corporate profiteering and repressed the needs of injured and vulnerable citizens. In Bhopal and the Niger Delta, we first must consider the dominant narratives of environmental, state, and corporate violence that make up the everyday lives of residents and have framed how scholars write about these places. But we then consider, in counterpoint, the way writers and residents of Bhopal and the Niger Delta have at times turned to the state to imagine futures beyond the contaminated present.

Chapter 1 occupies the grounds of Union Carbide Corporation's abandoned pesticide factory in Bhopal, the capital of Madhya Pradesh. Union Carbide's factory exploded in 1984, releasing tons of poisonous gases into the surrounding city. Damages between the American chemical company and the Indian government were legally settled in 1989, but toxic remnants from the explosion continue to poison city residents and the environment. This chapter reads

Indra Sinha's novel *Animal's People* (2007), which fictionalizes the aftermath of the 1984 factory explosion, alongside a selection of court documents and legislation that preceded the settlement the Indian state reached with Union Carbide in 1989. Sinha's novel critically interrogates the role of legal justice as well as corrupt state ministers and officials, and other scholars have examined the final settlement for its many inadequacies and the hypocrisy of American courts that refused to try Union Carbide. But this chapter focuses on aspects of the case once it was taken up in India, for though the final settlement eventually offered legal closure and minimal penalties for Union Carbide, at earlier moments in the legal process, the Indian state accused Union Carbide of total negligence and liability. In an early piece of legislation, the Bhopal Gas Leak Disaster (Processing of Claims) Act (1985), the state also envisioned robust, multifaceted forms of care for victims. The potential fulfillment of these kinds of state interventions is central to the fantasy of state justice that haunts the plot of *Animal's People*, despite its critiques of the state. The persistence of similar demands against Carbide and for greater state care, especially in relation to bodily pain and multi-generational injuries, are also chronicled in survivor testimonies and Bala Kailasam's documentary *Where Do the Children Play?* (2019). Despite the legal closure of the settlement, these texts show how the Indian state has been imagined as a potential provider and interventionist actor in Bhopal's aftermath, a contradictory and Janus-faced agent that could mitigate the very harms it had a hand in perpetuating.

Chapter 2 moves east, to the oil-soaked Niger Delta in Nigeria's southeast, where decades of oil spills, gas flares, and negligence by foreign corporations have made the Delta one of the most polluted places on earth. This chapter considers a range of Niger Delta texts that respond to the entwining of oil pollution, corporate profit, and political inequality in Nigeria. The chapter considers how the Nigerian state institutionalized corporate regulations and protection from oil spills in an ur-text of Nigerian oil legislation, the Oil Pipelines Act (1956). The act supported oil drilling but also understood pipelines as liable to breakage and spillage. It required corporations to keep their pipelines in good order and allowed communities to seek compensation for spills. This complex consideration of oil as both profit and pollution has become almost unthinkable in the petrodollar-driven present that dominates Nigeria today, a view confirmed in novels like Isidore Okpewho's *Tides* (1993). Yet this dual understanding of oil's benefit and risk has been echoed in demands Delta residents like the Ogoni made to the state in their Bill of Rights (1990) and during the Movement for the Survival of the Ogoni People, spearheaded by Ken Saro-Wiwa before his death. Saro-Wiwa may by now be better known for his international campaigning and for the way he pioneered an environmental activism that was keyed to pollution instead of conservation. But the Ogoni Bill of Rights he coauthored is also deeply engaged with state promises of provision and protection. African novelists, by contrast, have sometimes approached the pollution of the Delta by positing alternatives states. Chinua Achebe's last novel, *Anthills of the Savannah* (1987), interrogates the condition of Nigerian leadership and critiques resource violence while calling for a new democratic polity, while Imbolo Mbue's more recent novel *How Beautiful We Were* (2021) considers a range of responses to oil pollution, including armed resistance. But it too suggests that oil's environmental harm must be addressed through state reform.

Chapters 3 and 4 shift from long-term environmental toxicity and pollution to the uneven effects of climate change. These chapters consider the role the state is imagined to play in mediating catastrophic climate effects like water scarcity and rising sea levels that are in many ways unstoppable. Indeed, a postcolonial understanding of the environment as a place of "social conflicts" has only reached new heights in the Anthropocene, the term popularized by scientists Paul Crutzen and Eugene Stoermer in 2000. The Anthropocene names a new geological epoch in which humans have moved beyond manipulating and contaminating the environment to affecting the climate systems of the planet as a whole. The disastrous effects of human-induced climate change are arriving at uneven speeds, and the most severe climate effects are being visited first on postcolonial countries that have relatively few resources and at least until recently have done little to drive climate change.[79] In the global South, climate futures like torrential flooding, intensified storms, increasing drought, crop failure, desertification, and their social consequences are already here and layered on top of preexisting histories of resource extraction, pollution, displacement, or other forms of slow violence. This confluence of unequal causes and unequal victimization have led many, including Indian author Amitav Ghosh, to argue that the origins of climate change lie in colonialism and that climate change can even be considered colonialism by other means.[80]

In chapters 3 and 4 the interventionist role of the postcolonial state is more easily visible and not as difficult to separate from narratives of violence or disappointment. Chapter 3 considers Cape Town before and during its historic 2015–18 drought, which was anticipated to culminate in "Day Zero." Day Zero named the day the city would run out of water and private taps would be turned off throughout the city, leaving residents to queue at public collection points for water. While Day Zero provoked a kind of apocalyptic rhetoric, I consider it an example of positive state intervention, as Cape Town's government worked to prevent a dry future for the city. Capetonian leaders deployed many disciplinary measures, largely aimed at upper- and middle-class white consumers, to curb high water consumption and prevent the actual arrival of Day Zero. Day Zero is also, however, an example of an "Anthropocene conjuncture" in which impending climate challenges met and overlapped with historic environmental injustices that remain in the present from colonialism and apartheid. Chapter 3 reads the state's Day Zero policies alongside a series of South African novels: K. Sello Duiker's *Thirteen Cents* (2000), Henrietta Rose-Innes's *Nineveh* (2011), and Alistair Mackay's *It Doesn't Have to Be This Way* (2022), each of which probe the disappointments of the post-apartheid transition. *Nineveh* and *Thirteen Cents*, though, also acknowledge the provisionary role the state has taken in rectifying the water inequalities it inherited from apartheid, and *It Doesn't Have to Be This Way* suggests that the state might implement social transformations to fight climate change that rival the historic scale of transition from apartheid.

Chapter 4 attends to a group of low-lying Pacific atoll nations, Tuvalu, Kiribati, and the Marshall Islands, most at risk from rising seas. This chapter considers the unprecedented threat sea level rise poses to these small island states and the efforts of writers and state leaders to combat narratives of inevitable climate refugeeism and displacement that have been imposed on them by the international community. These efforts are spotlighted in a cluster of climate documentaries, including Andrea Torrice's *Rising Waters: Global Warming and the Fate of the Pacific Islands* (2000) and Matthieu Rytz's *Anote's Ark* (2018). Struggles in the arena of international climate diplomacy are complemented by widespread national efforts to adapt in-place, exemplified in Tuvalu's climate adaptation policy *Te Kaniva* (2012–21), which refused to plan for climate migration. The chapter pairs these national and international policy efforts with Marshallese poet Kathy Jetñil-Kijiner's debut collection *Iep Jāltok: Poems from a Marshallese Daughter* (2017), which situates Pacific sea level rise as livable history rather than the end of the future. Former Kiribati president Anote Tong's policy "Migration with Dignity" offers an exception to these trends. During his tenure as president, Tong accepted scientific predictions that sea level rise would swallow his nation's islands and advocated sending his population abroad before this happened under the policy "Migration with Dignity." "Migration with Dignity" was a complex policy that tried to provide a variety of futures to Kiribati citizens, but it also implicitly challenged the existing system of international statehood with a new speculative kind of state, one that does not yet exist. The conclusion of the chapter briefly considers Maori New Zealander Keri Hulme's short story collection *Stonefish*, which critiques climate inaction and denialism while calling for an ethics of adaptation in a climate-changed world.

Reading Better States illuminates the way interventionist imagined states continue to have a great deal of purchase in the global South, not only in the minds of elites or those who have manifestly benefited from state interventions, but precisely for unimagined and environmentally vulnerable communities, where one would not expect to find such investments.[81] Far from dying out, visions of state-based intervention have proven surprisingly tenacious as they have been remobilized and rearticulated to address capitalism's environmental ruination and newer, but equally devastating, climate changes. These demands for situated forms of state intervention into the environment have emerged even as other large-scale visions of postcolonial utopia have faded. The concrete utopian archives assembled in this book reveal the limits but also the prevalence of interventionist state visions in the global South and they contradict the anti-statism in humanist theory and scholarship. *Reading Better States* instead reveals how desires for the postcolonial state facilitate visions of ecopolitical futurity against the ravages of capitalism, environmental damage, and climate catastrophe that threaten futurity in the global South and, indeed, across the earth.

1
Unsettled
Toxicity after Bhopal

On August 12, 1985 in Institute, West Virginia, a chemical plant run by Union Carbide Corporation, headquartered in Danbury, Connecticut, sprang a gas leak and injured scores of residents. "This stuff makes my head ache and my skin itch. . . . I guess it means we all have to move out of here if we want to be safe," one woman told *New York Times* reporters in the wake of the leak.[1] Union Carbide, which specialized in manufacturing a range of chemical products from pesticides to batteries, cut corners in Institute. It did, however, also spend $5 million to implement a new safety system at its West Virginia plant after the leak, and it vehemently denied that methyl isocyanate (MIC), a common pesticide component, was part of the gases affecting West Virginians.

Methyl isocyanate was on everyone's minds. Just eight months earlier, shortly before midnight on December 2, 1984, Institute's sister plant in Bhopal, India, also run by Union Carbide and used to manufacture large quantities of MIC, had exploded. The Bhopal gas explosion was and still is considered the world's worst industrial disaster. It killed thousands of people overnight and left tens of thousands more seriously ill, injured, or disabled from toxic exposure. In August 1985, victims of the Bhopal explosion were in the process of seeking compensation and liability from Union Carbide, but they would achieve little of either. Unlike its factory in the United States, Carbide simply shut down its Indian plant. Today the Bhopal plant gathers rust, its pipes and tanks slowly deteriorating. Abandoned papers and bottles of chemicals litter the floors, left where they fell on what survivors call "that night."

In the decade after Bhopal, there were more than one hundred serious industrial disasters worldwide.[2] Again and again, with almost generic repetitiveness, in the wake of deadly industrial disasters that menace human and nonhuman life, corporations have absconded with their profits and left misery in their wake. Time and again, dangerous industries have failed to contain the materials they produce or shield workers and local residents from their adverse effects. Explosions, leaks, hazardous exposure, and other "accidents" of all kinds are virtually manufactured through a confluence of neglected safety measures, lax training, failure to implement best practices, and environmental racism that discounts the lives of laborers, minority and indigenous communities, and people of color the world over. In Bhopal, activists and survivors burn effigies of Union Carbide's former CEO Warren Anderson every December and continue to demand justice for the explosion. But Union Carbide and other corporations, motivated by profit myopia and justified by market logics of cost-cutting and value accumulation, do not hold themselves accountable for the lives and environments they sacrifice to the bottom line. And civilian pressure groups, especially those mobilized by poor or marginalized communities in the global South, have limited clout and resources. What chances are there, then, for holding large companies responsible for the death and harm they cause?

Facing off against multinational corporations requires larger players and more powerful actors. It requires, more often than not, state intervention, which can enforce victim claims, corporate liability, and environmental remediation at scales far beyond that of ordinary citizens. Only states have the resources to take on multinational corporations at scale, bringing their own array of regulations, judicial rulings, sanctions, investigations, and public relations campaigns against the lawyers, image gurus, and deep pockets of large companies. The history of the Bhopal gas explosion of 1984 reveals that at times, states have done just this and emerged as powerful interventionist actors in the lives of citizens injured by corporate violence. In the early years of the Bhopal explosion's aftermath, the Indian government went after Union Carbide. It charged the American chemical company with full liability for its factory explosion and sought to hold it accountable for a huge range of physical, emotional, and financial losses suffered by the gas victims. It situated Carbide's responsibility in a long view of toxic effects that spanned generations, took account of intensified poverty, and included environmental containment. In doing so it positioned itself as an agentive actor in the lives of Bhopal's residents, one that could be called upon to provide relief and welfarist interventions. Decades later, when it turns out that none of these interventions have been realized, survivors and culture-makers alike continue to turn to the state to imagine futures from within Bhopal's toxic aftermath. Despite its failures, they demand better forms of care and recognition from the Indian state, especially for ongoing bodily pain, and they continue to demand state-based accountability for Union Carbide.

Such a complex narrative is not, however, one postcolonialists and environmental humanists usually tell about states in general or the Indian state in particular. Not only do many multinationals like Carbide routinely flout the regulations of the countries in which they operate or set up shop where such national regulations are lacking, states themselves frequently collude with corporations to boost the national economy, trading protections for growth. State complicity is as much a factor in industrial disasters as the practices of corporations themselves, and the story of Bhopal told by scholars, journalists, and activists is dominated by both the corporate violence of Union Carbide and the violence of the Indian state, which ultimately settled with Carbide for a paltry sum in 1989. Demanding only money, the state relinquished its earlier goals of multi-generational care, corporate accountability, and environmental cleanup. The Indian state failed to achieve the kinds of protection and redress it once pursued, and so it has been primarily viewed through the lens of betrayal. Bhopal's survivors have been left to waste away in pain and poverty, and their unrelieved suffering has in turn shaped discourses about the state in Bhopal, with good reason. And yet, the place of the state in Bhopal's aftermath is far from straightforward. Indeed, looking at how the state has been imagined in Bhopal's long aftermath and its own early actions toward Carbide reveals a plural, Janus-faced state at work in Bhopal, one that has been both a bad actor and a site of appeal.

How can we account for these yawning gaps and contradictions? In the wake of such an enormous disaster, when the state badly shirked its duty to protect its citizens and appears all too much like a corporate crony, why have survivors turned to it as a site of redress at all? This conundrum can only be unraveled by considering the twinning of state violence and care in Bhopal, where toxicity has been legally closed but remains a potent and ever-pressing concern in the everyday lives of city residents. Tracking the plurality of the Indian state's actions in Bhopal reveals the way the state offers grounds for imagining futurity in the explosion's toxic aftermath despite and alongside the way it has facilitated certain kinds of closures. Despite all its limits and disappointments, state interventions undergird the way survivors, filmmakers, and writers imagine futurity in Bhopal's enduring history of pain. In particular, desires for state-based legal accountability and bodily care emerge as what Bloch called concrete utopias, or circumscribed and specific forms of "surplus" that resist the "badly existing" of the Bhopal explosion's wake.[3] These concrete utopias come into view by reading the state for the plural and contradictory ways in which it is imagined, as its interventionist potentials persist and coexist alongside its violence in the many cultural objects that have been produced since the disaster.

Reading the Indian state this way draws on and enacts what *Reading Better States* calls utopian method, a way of reading that sees beyond negative surfaces for the positive potentials within them. Reading the Indian state utopically means taking seriously the early if unrealized interventionist potentials the state once had in Bhopal, and it means following the way survivors and writers have continued to turn to the state, despite its disappointments. Complaints about the Indian state's unfulfilled promises, along with proposals for alternative versions of the state, all produce a sense of plurality and nonlinearity around the state that responds to but also unsettles its obvious violence in Bhopal. This utopian method of reading the state reveals the way concrete utopias of legal accountability and bodily care are imagined through what the state might still do since "that night" in Bhopal.

The Afterlives and Prelives of Toxicity

Before we can understand the plurality of the state in Bhopal, we must first attend to the entwined corporate and state violence that have by now become synonymous with the Bhopal gas explosion. Because the violence of toxicity is so widespread and so obvious, narratives of corporate exploitation and state complicity have rightly dominated how Bhopal and its aftermath are written about by environmental and postcolonial scholars. When the Indian state settled with Union Carbide in 1989, it minimized victim claims and attempted to contain an event that could in no way be confined neatly in time or space. The settlement did not acknowledge the extensive physical needs of victims or the long life of toxicity in the environment, and the flipside of its myopia was a paltry fee for Carbide, which ramped up India's appeal to other overseas corporate investors. These hierarchies are built into the settlement the Indian state brokered with Carbide but also extended before and after it. Before we can turn to the Indian state's potentials and desired interventions, this first section lays out the twofold story of civilian silencing and corporate coddling that are so apparent in the settlement and that have undergirded critiques of the state in Bhopal. It is from within these sacrificial exchanges that better and different imaginaries of the state must struggle to emerge and become legible. But emerge they do, and the rest of the chapter develops a utopian reading of the state that troubles these dominant narratives—not to invalidate them, but to reveal those aspects of the state and of futurity that have been obscured by the prevailing discourses of environmental injustice, state violence, and corporate greed that surround Bhopal.

When Union Carbide Corporation's pesticide factory exploded in Bhopal, the capital of Madhya Pradesh in central India, it released at least forty tons of poisonous gases into the city. The exact composition of the poison cloud has never been identified but included methyl isocyanate (MIC), a volatile and deadly chemical used to manufacture pesticides like Sevin, and possibly cyanide. By the Indian government's count, 1,754 people died that night and a further 200,000 were injured in the leak. These numbers are dwarfed by activist and scholarly estimates that place the number of dead at 3,000–10,000 and the number of injured at 300,000–500,000, around half the total city population of 800,000–900,000.[4] Since then Bhopal's soil and groundwater have also been contaminated with toxic residues, leading to long-term illnesses and toxic exposure across multiple generations of the city's populace.

The actual effects of the pesticide explosion have seeped outward in time and space, across bodies and materials. But the Indian state's response to Bhopal took the opposite track: closure and containment. The Indian government reached a settlement with Union Carbide in February 1989 that is very brief in both form and content. In order to alleviate the "enormity of human suffering occasioned by the Bhopal Gas disaster and the pressing urgency to provide immediate and substantial relief to victims of the disaster," the settlement ordered Carbide to pay $470 million "in full settlement of all claims, rights and liabilities related to and arising out of the Bhopal Gas disaster."[5] This singular sum, attributed only to the relief of immediate suffering, subsumed all further claims and lawsuits.

The inadequacy of this compensation cannot be overstated. From the $470 million, victims recognized as permanently disabled would receive only $5,200 each, those temporarily disabled were allotted $3,215 each, and families where a member had died would receive approximately $14,500.[6] The remainder of the funds were kept for claims to property damage, minor injuries or other incidentals, and general medical treatment, the latter of which has repeatedly been shown to be deeply inadequate when not simply absent. Additionally, bureaucratic requirements, like proof of identity or needing to be designated within particular categories to receive benefits, make it very difficult for victims to claim whatever money they have been granted.

The Bhopal settlement's limited logic of monetary compensation was premised on an attenuated, atomized version of the body and a truncated temporal view of toxic effects. As science and technology studies scholar Kim Fortun explains in her ethnographic work *Advocacy after Bhopal*, the official number of victims and the amount of settlement compensation negotiated in 1989 were based on a medical schema that sorted victims into categories that overlooked many victims completely or distorted the actual damage they suffered.[7] The data was based on a scoring method that ranked bodily systems and categorized victims according to degrees of injury and disability. But separating bodily systems falsely quantified and isolated toxicity's multisystem spread, and it utterly bypassed many collateral consequences of bodily injury, such as losing the ability to work. The official count partitioned bodies into damaged organs rather than considering the body as an integrated unit. It also failed to account for the transcorporeal, transgeographic, and transtemporal nature of toxic effects. It "[subordinated] complexity into categories with which bureaucracy could work" in the name of delivering expedient justice to the victims.[8] Many victims, especially those not diagnosed in the first few days after the explosion, were deemed unaffected, even if they were treated in the MIC ward of Bhopal's local Hamida Hospital or exhibited known symptoms of exposure to the gases.

Meanwhile, in 2001, twelve years after the settlement, Union Carbide disappeared as a legal entity. Bought by Dow Chemical for $11.6 billion, its toxic legacy or "foreign burden" endures as Bhopalis continue to be poisoned.[9] The Carbide factory has not been cleaned up, since the settlement made no demands or provisions for environmental restitution, and pesticide materials that were left in the factory or dumped in Bhopal's lakes make their way into the bodies of city residents. Children are born with serious physical and mental disabilities while adults die of numerous illnesses, including lung and uterine cancers. Many survivors complain about being unable to breathe, run, or work; they suffer breathlessness, nausea, and terrible pain. While hospitals for gas-affected victims have been set up, the Indian Committee for Medical Monitoring reported as recently as 2021 that these hospitals do not have specialists, quality medications, diagnostic equipment, monitoring systems, or standardized treatment.[10]

These inadequacies are not, however, only a product of corporate negligence or state failure. The temporal, bodily, and legal containments exemplified by the 1989 settlement must also be understood as part of the Indian state's turn to prioritizing the global market. Prime Minister P. V. Narasimha Rao's 1991 economic reforms are usually seen as the watershed in India's economic embrace of global capitalism after earlier policies of trade protectionism. But India's economic pursuit of international investment arguably began with the liberalization of trade in the late 1970s, initiated by Indira Gandhi during her second term and in the so-called "New Economic Policy" of Rajiv Gandhi's government in 1985. Indeed, since the 1970s, India's economic policy has gone through distinct waves, each more liberalizing than the last.[11] Union Carbide received its license to manufacture pesticides on-site at its Bhopal plant in 1974, amidst this first wave of deregulating changes. It was given incentives from the state like automatic license renewals and cheaply rented land in Bhopal, where it leased its factory ground for 500 rupees ($40) an acre.[12] The 1980s also saw other piecemeal reforms that encouraged market growth, especially in 1988 and 1989.[13] With all these moves the Indian state sought to exchange one thing for another: slow economic growth for faster growth, a relatively closed economy for a more open one, and local economic protections for international investments in Indian markets and labor. An event like the 1984 Bhopal gas explosion and its aftermath did not check India's intensifying priorities of openness to overseas corporate actors. Indeed, Bhopal was in many ways sacrificed to and symptomatic of these changing state priorities.

Those who survived the explosion are bitterly aware of these hierarchical logics. As one survivor, Champa Devi, said in an interview, "First the company tried to minimize the number of those affected, then the government joined them in speaking the same language. You would think the government is for us—the people—but living through that night made it very obvious who is with us and who is against us."[14] Anthropologist Veena Das, in a characteristically suspicious reading of the 1989 settlement, likewise asserts that the government "compromise[d] the rights of victims by unilaterally arriving at a settlement and granting immunity to Union Carbide against the expressed wishes of the victims."[15] In these views, Bhopal provided an opportunity for the Indian state to display its commitment to marketized exchanges. The settlement was set deliberately low to signal the Indian government's friendliness to overseas corporations looking to invest in India, where even death would be cheap. Such critiques are premised on the settlement's limited monetary scope and temporal containment, as well as its minimization of corporate liability; they are also no doubt shaped by victims' suffering and neglect in the settlement's wake.

However, even before the explosion and subsequent settlement, Union Carbide was allowed to maximize its profits by minimizing its costs in Bhopal. Thus, in failing to punish Carbide for the explosion itself and its aftermath, as well as the prelife of the disaster, the Indian state enabled and abetted an extensive chain of cost-cutting that rendered Bhopal's residents disposable long before "that night" in December 1984. The corporate negligence that led to the plant's final explosion has been the subject of cinematic representations of Bhopal like the feature films *Bhopal Express* (1999), directed by Mahesh Mathai, and more recently, *Bhopal: A Prayer for Rain* (2013), starring Hollywood heavyweights like Martin Sheen and Kal Penn. Extensive journalistic and nonfiction accounts have detailed how Carbide blatantly overlooked accidents when they occurred, fired plant employees including engineers familiar with the MIC unit, cut education requirements and training levels for operators, neglected routine maintenance, and failed to replace critical safety equipment like broken pressure gauges, thermometers, refrigerant, and leaking valves. These factors all contributed to the factory's runaway explosion on the night of December 2–3, 1984.[16]

Exposés written shortly after the explosion, like Larry Everest's *Behind the Poison Cloud* (1985) and Dan Kurzman's *A Killing Wind* (1987), also detail how cost-cutting measures were built into the original Bhopal plant design. Warren Anderson, then Union Carbide's CEO, claimed that the Bhopal plant had the "same equipment, same design, same everything" as its sister factory in Institute, West Virginia.[17] But the Bhopal plant was in fact not run with the same standards of design, staffing, safety, or expense. In Bhopal, the plant's safety systems were manually operated and could not be monitored from the plant's control room, and detection of gas leaks was done by workers, even though detecting gas through physical responses, such as stinging of the eyes, indicated MIC exposure already at much higher levels than considered safe.[18] Union Carbide's MIC plant thus exploded after a slew of environmentally racist double standards that prioritized production costs over the safety of Bhopali workers and the surrounding environment. With the 1989 settlement, the Indian state punished Carbide minimally for both the afterlife and prelife of the explosion.

Concrete Utopias: Before and Beyond the Settlement

The 1989 settlement between Union Carbide and the Indian government made Bhopal a posterchild for environmental injustice, state collusion, and corporate negligence.[19] It closed down further substantial forms of legal action and left victims mired in pain and poverty.[20] It sacrificed Bhopal's soil and water to overseas investments. Given the way the state facilitated corporate profiteering and ongoing toxicity, could it ever be viewed as more than a bad actor in Bhopal? Could the state do more than bow before the altar of market interests? Though it may be hard to believe, in fact it could. For the state's role in the Bhopal explosion's aftermath is not as straightforward as it seems. In brokering the settlement, the state indisputably worked against the needs of victims and produced a legal result favorable to Union Carbide. And yet, this is not all the state has done in Bhopal: it has also taken on other, contradictory roles.

In the immediate aftermath of the Bhopal explosion, years before the 1989 settlement's conclusion, the Indian state sought to hold Union Carbide accountable for producing the world's worst industrial disaster. This occurred in two astonishing antecedents to the settlement that recognized the complexity of victim needs and the huge range of harms Carbide caused before, during, and after the factory explosion. These antecedents were the 1985 Bhopal Gas

Leak Disaster (Processing of Claims) Act and *Union of India v. Union Carbide Corporation*, the original civil suit for damages filed against Union Carbide in Bhopal's district court on September 5, 1986.[21] Both these antecedents profoundly contradict the closures imposed by the later settlement in ways that seem almost fantastical in their scale and ambition. Yet they are not hypotheticals or fictional proposals. They are actually existing texts within the Indian state's own legal and legislative archive. Buried in the state's own past, these early texts belie the bad version of the state that was institutionalized later, in the settlement. In Bhopal, the state once tried to secure many kinds of care for victims and to hold Union Carbide liable for an immense range of wrongs: negligence, irresponsibility, duplicity, emotional anguish, serious injury, and loss of life.

The Processing of Claims Act and Bhopal's original civil suit pluralize the Indian state from the aftermath's early days, and they reveal that the settlement was not the only outcome envisioned for Bhopal's victims. The Processing of Claims Act was one of the Indian state's first responses to the Bhopal explosion. Passed in reaction to what it called the "highly noxious and abnormally dangerous gas" released from the pesticide factory, the Processing of Claims Act named the state's power to act on behalf of those injured by Carbide's poisons, most of whom were poor.[22] To this end it stipulated that the state could secure compensation for a capacious range of victim claims. These included items like, in section 2b on the definition of a claim:

(i) . . . compensation or damages for any loss of life or personal injury which has been, or is likely to be, suffered;
(ii) . . . damage to property which has been, or is likely to be, sustained;
(iii) a claim for expenses incurred or required . . . for containing the disaster or mitigating or otherwise coping with the effects of the disaster;

and other claims including those from loss of business or employment.[23] It also specified that in the case of deaths caused by the disaster, claims might be made for the benefit of spouses, children, and children in the womb.

The Processing of Claims Act acknowledged a long view of toxic effects that might encompass future generations, injuries that developed in the future even if they were not manifested at the time of the writing of the act (i), loss of property (ii), and potentially cleanup of the environment as part of the disaster's containment (iii). It is within these provisions and directives for human and nonhuman victims and human victims present and future that the state first claimed the right and the duty to represent those affected: "Subject to the other provisions of this Act, the Central Government shall, and shall have the exclusive right to, represent . . . every person who has made, or is entitled to make, a claim."[24] These claims are a far cry from the language of containment, minimization, and closure found in the settlement.

Because the 1989 settlement is the final outcome of the 1985 Processing of Claims Act, the act has been interpreted as inflicting the same violence upon survivors as its later counterpart. Activist and English literature teacher Suroopa Mukherjee has said, in a typical assessment of the Processing of Claims Act, "The Claims Act was the ultimate red herring used by the state and the corporation to hide its need to 'settle' matters with each other while claiming to act on behalf of the people."[25] Such assessments adhere to a linear perspective rather than a utopic one, where the Bhopal disaster's ultimate outcome, the settlement, is seen to arise in a straightforward way from the Claims Act. However, examining the language of the act separately from the settlement that was its eventual outcome reveals remarkable discrepancies in the state's earlier approach to and understanding of victim needs.

The original civil suit filed in Bhopal's district court in September 1986 is even more surprising. It went far beyond acknowledging "immediate suffering" from the disaster as the basis for its claims against Union Carbide. Suffering instead spread out across bodies and materials, time and space. Suffering in the original civil suit was multiform and enormous. The original suit wove together a complex and comprehensive account of the many kinds and scales of suffering produced from the explosion. As "direct and proximate result of the conduct of defendant Union Carbide," it charged that "numerous innocent persons in Bhopal, the adjacent countryside and its environs suffered agonizing, lingering and excruciating deaths, serious and permanent injuries."[26] And, it charged that survivors suffered not only physical injuries like respiratory distress and blindness, but *witnessing the virtual destruction of their entire world*, have suffered and will continue to suffer severe emotional distress."[27] Agonizing death, permanent injury, emotional anguish, and nothing less than the end of their world. These were only some of the wrongs Union Carbide was accused of in the original civil suit.

The suit went further: the families and relatives of those who died "suffered, and will continue to suffer, from the loss of support, aid, comfort, society, and companionship of the deceased."[28] These charges spanned an ongoing temporality of loss and acknowledged the many material, social, and affective ties that were severed with physical death. The suit's list of accusations proceeded to include damage to businesses, commercial property, government revenue in Bhopal, and the environment. Union Carbide was declared "strictly liable" for all these losses; they were "damages caused or contributed to by the escape of lethal gas from MIC storage tank at its plant."²⁹ These bases of suffering were first articulated in the 1985 Bhopal Gas Leak Disaster (Processing of Claims) Act and then carried out in expanded detail in the original suit. It was to redress this capacious range of victims and multiple scales and sites of harm that the state filed its original civil suit and originally claimed the right to represent the interests of Bhopal's victims. Grounded in and expanding upon the Processing of Claims Act, the original civil suit sought redress for intergenerational victimization, physical, emotional, and economic losses, threats to health and well-being, and injuries to persons, property, and the environment both present and future.

In addition to these charges, *Union of India v. Union Carbide Corporation* argued that Union Carbide was liable due to negligence, breach of warranties, and "wanton disregard of the right and safety of the citizens of the Union of India."³⁰ In the suit, Bhopal's district court argued that Union Carbide had had a duty to design, maintain, and operate its plants safely and adequately train its operators and technical personnel. It declared the company's negligence at its Bhopal plant "unlawful, wilful, malicious and reprehensible."³¹ In the original suit, the state moreover accused Carbide of failing to abide by its own assurances to the federal government of India that, as a pioneer in pesticide research with cutting-edge information about processing, manufacturing, and storing MIC, its technology was the safest and most advanced available.³² This latter charge of misrepresenting itself to the government even put the Indian state on the side of the victims, as having been duped by the company. The original civil suit, in other words, declared that Union Carbide was liable and responsible for a stunning matrix of egregious harms.

In the 1985 Processing of Claims Act and original 1986 civil suit, it seemed that Union Carbide would pay the price for its corporate irresponsibility. The many losses experienced in Bhopal would be balanced at least in part by losses imposed on Carbide. The gains the company had made could not possibly be one-sided; given the many wrongs of which Carbide was accused, some recognition and benefit would go to the victims, the city of Bhopal, and the Indian government in proportion to Carbide's actions. Both texts evidence a state very different from the one that authored the settlement, a state that did not see corporate dollars as worth more than the lives of poor laborers, and one that recognized how extensively those affected by the gases would suffer.

It is only in the language of the final settlement that the Processing of Claims Act's considerable earlier directives for government representation and protection were truncated and made equivalent to vague duties about "the enormity of human suffering."³³ And it is only in the final settlement that Union Carbide was let off the hook for the complex, multi-generational suffering—indeed the world-ending harm—it caused survivors and for the racist negligence, double-standards, and cost-cutting at its plant in the lead-up to the night of the explosion on December 2, 1984. In the final 1989 settlement, in contrast to the original civil suit, only humans are considered victims, and only human suffering in the present, which may be addressed by "immediate" relief, are considered grounds for compensation.[34] The extensive forms of bodily and emotional pain, transgenerational toxic effects, losses to property and livelihood, and the need for environmental containment originally recognized in the Processing of Claims Act and the original civil suit against Carbide were all practicably erased in the final settlement. How can we understand these aborted antecedents and their final successor, shorn of so many earlier ambitions and accusations? Can such state precursors only be considered the casualties of political complicity or neoliberal triumphalism? Are these aspirations totally invalidated because they did not come to pass? A utopic reading of the state suggests otherwise.

Both the Processing of Claims Act and the original civil suit interrupt, rather than lay the ground for, Bhopal's slow violent present. These texts provide buried instantiations of concrete utopian visions. They are evidence of a better version of the Indian state, one that pursued forms of victim care and corporate liability. This version of the state has, technically, been closed down and overshadowed by the settlement. But in a utopian method of reading, the state is never singular, and the future is never easily determined by the past. These versions of a better state remain in the Indian state's archive even if they are historically unrealized and suppressed within the version of the state that has, for now, come to be. Such past antecedents make the state a site of utopian surplus; they enact and record a pluralized version of the state that remains in excess of its current iterations. A utopic view emphasizes the fluidity, collision, and divergence of past, present, and future. Taking a utopian view of the state in Bhopal gives credence to these antecedents despite the settlement's closures. The state once thought very differently about the Bhopal explosion's aftermath, and it could do so again.

In other words, the futures of the Processing of Claims Act and the original civil suit lie astride the inadequate present. They offer visions of concrete utopia that actually exist in the state's own archives, were once pursued by the state itself, and might be resurrected or brought closer to fulfillment in the future. These alternatives have not been invalidated because they were superseded by later developments. Overshadowed by the settlement, they are nonetheless not erased by or coterminous with it. It is only within schemas of linear progression and supersession, where the latest version cancels all others, that these divergent and unrealized futures, inaugurated but not completed in the original civil suit and the Processing of Claims Act, can be discounted. Taking a utopian view of the state here contests such linear perceptions, which reinforce a blinkered present. Utopian method suggests instead that, as Jameson put it, "that which is currently negative can also be imagined as positive in that immense changing of the valences that is the utopian future."[35] However disappointing it is now, utopian method denaturalizes and critiques the force of the state's dominant actions to reveal the potentials and alternatives around them. Utopian method is not bound to the linearity of legal rulings or to legal practicality but promotes a recursive view of the state that unmoors it from its present forms, to make it visible once again as a site of possible interventions and concrete utopias.

Survivors and State Promises

What would Bhopal look like if the concrete utopias of multigenerational bodily care and environmental containment proposed in the Processing of Claims Act had been enacted? Or if Carbide had been held liable for the huge range of atrocities described in the original civil suit? Would Bhopal's residents be free of pain and able to breathe more easily? Would they have access to effective medical treatment or be able to move on from "that night"? It is impossible to say, but in the unsatisfying residuum of the settlement, survivors have continued to turn to the state to imagine their own futures. Despite its obvious violence and failures in Bhopal, the Indian state must be understood not through the finality of the settlement but through the complexities of its earlier antecedents and the contradictory imaginaries that have surrounded it in the years since, which cluster around both violence and provision.

In fact, shortly after the 1989 settlement, the Indian state reaffirmed an interventionist role for itself. This occurred in the case *Charan Lal Sahu v. Union of India*, which set out to judge the constitutionality of the state's role as *parens patriae*, or legal guardian and representative, of the victims during the Bhopal settlement proceedings. In December 1989, ten months after the furor and dissatisfaction of the settlement, *Charan* upheld the legitimacy of the state's representation of Bhopal's victims against a number of contestations. Doing so did not fix or reopen the settlement. But like the Processing of Claims Act, it did affirm the state's role as an interventionist actor. *Charan* acknowledged the state's need to alleviate suffering, but its understanding of *parens patriae* in Bhopal more importantly drew upon a capacious sense of government provision that was itself interpreted as the sine qua non of Indian state legitimacy. *Charan* measured how and whether the state's representation of victims during the Bhopal proceedings accorded with interventionist governing principles the state had mandated to itself before the case. It did not locate these in the 1985 Processing of Claims Act but in the Indian Constitution. In short, it measured the state's role in the settlement against a national interventionist frame that preceded the case and in which the case itself was embedded.

Charan based its judgment on a general interpretation of state duty to protect and guarantee the welfare of the nation's citizens. Section 3.2 of the Headnote, on the meaning of *parens patriae*, specified citizen welfare as an obligation and responsibility enshrined in the Constitution:

> Conceptually, the parens patriae theory is the obligation of the State to protect and take into custody the rights and privileges of its citizens for discharging its obligations. Our Constitution makes it imperative for the State to secure to all its citizens the rights guaranteed by the Constitution and where the citizens are not in a position to assert and secure their rights, the State must come into [the] picture and protect and fight for the right of the citizens. The Preamble to the Constitution, read with the Directive Principles contained in Articles 38, 39 and 39A enjoins the State to take up these responsibilities. It is the protective measure to which the social welfare state is committed.[36]

The Constitutional articles referred to in this section fall under the "Directive Principles of State Policy," all of which are premised by a general directive article: "The provisions contained in this Part shall not be enforceable by any court, *but the principles therein laid down are nevertheless fundamental in the governance of the country and it shall be the duty of the State to apply these principles* in making laws."[37] Directive principles are not formally binding, but they do lay out important guidelines and aspirations for state action. The court here identified three directives that explicitly burden the state with civilian welfare. Of these, Article 38 pertains to "promoting the welfare of the people" in general, and the case went on to elaborate this article as foundational to the state's overall raison d'être:

> What the Central Government has done in the instant [sic] case seems to be an expression of its sovereign power. This power is plenary and inherent in every sovereign state to do all things which promote the health, peace, moral [sic], education and good order of the people and tend to increase the wealth and prosperity of the State. . . . This power is to the public what the law of necessity is to the individual. It is comprehended in the maxim salus populi suprema lex—regard for public welfare is the highest law.[38]

Charan conceived of the welfare of the people as the state's "highest law," and in doing so, the Supreme Court publicly affirmed a provisionary and interventionist role for the state in the wake of the settlement. This role has, in turn, been hailed by many of Bhopal's survivors as an unfulfilled promise or "frustrated potential."[39] Suroopa Mukherjee, a literature teacher who forsook the classroom to conduct fieldwork for her monograph *Surviving Bhopal*, recorded many complaints from survivors that testify to the way they imagine futurity through the Indian state's interventionist promises. She sums up a "deep sense of hurt and anger" many orphaned children voiced "at being let down by the state government."[40] As one man, Shahid Noor, told her, "We were promised education, jobs, and protection by the state but none of the promises were kept. We feel truly orphaned."[41] For survivors like Shahid, the state is a powerful interventionist actor that has not done what it said it will.

Activist groups have also published numerous pamphlets and collections of testimony that publicize the experience of survivors. In one of these, "Voices from the aftermath (1985–1990)," Chander Singh, an auto-rickshaw driver from Karimabaksh Colony says:

> I have given six applications to the Collector, six to Chief Minister, six to the Commissioner, Gas Relief. I also wrote letters to the Prime Minister and the President about the poor conditions of my family. In my letter to the Speaker of the legislative assembly I asked permission to immolate myself along with my family. I was so desperate.[42]

Singh's desperation is clear in the content of his testimony and in the fact that he wrote more than eighteen letters to various state officials. Desperate for relief, he appealed to the state repeatedly to intervene in the "poor conditions" of his family or, conversely, for its permission to escape pain through death. While on their surface these kinds of testimony trace the deep and unrelieved suffering in Bhopal, they are also premised on a certain interventionist imaginary of the state, and they demand from the state specific kinds of relief like education, jobs, and protection. The *Charan* case, alongside the testimonies of Mukherjee's interviewees and collections like "Voices from the aftermath," show how state interventions have been publicly affirmed after the explosion and are in turn taken up by Bhopal's survivors for their own ends, particularly to address ongoing bodily pain. What is most significant here is that survivors draw on the state's promises of intervention to envision their own possible futures.

Bhopal's victims have thus never accepted the endless continuity of their toxified present or the finality of the settlement. Instead, they demand the fulfillment of state promises, and in doing so they articulate futures beyond the contaminated now, futures that do not relinquish the state to the role it took in the settlement. The state's languages of welfare, provision, and intervention offer grounds for the kinds of claims survivors continue to make upon the state in Bhopal's aftermath. These dynamics can also be seen in a few examples from "Voices of Bhopal, 1990," another collection of victim testimonies:

> My husband's name was Dukhishyam. He got a lot of gas in him. . . . Twice he was admitted to the hospital. The second time he was admitted, he never came back. He died in the MIC ward. I gave an application for Rs 10,000 [$400] in interim relief, but they haven't done anything about it yet. . . . I stay sick. I have come back from the hospital on 13th of this month [November 1990]. I was there for one and a half months. I never got breathless before the gas; I used to work as a laborer. Now I get badly breathless and my chest pains.—Natthibai, age fifty-five, resident of Rajendra Nagar

> I used to work as a porter for transport companies. Since the gas, I have not been able to work for a single day. The gas killed my daughter; she died in the morning after the gas leak. I am breathless all the time and I cough badly. My eyes have become weak, too. I have been admitted to the MIC ward more than 5 times since 1987. Last year, I was there for 9 months at a stretch. This year, I have come home after eight months.—Chhotelal, age fifty, resident of Barkhedi

> This is the sixth time I have been admitted to the MIC ward. I have been here since the last month of 1985. When I feel a little better, the doctors send me home but I can't stay there for long. My breathlessness becomes acute and my husband has to bring me back to the hospital. . . . Before the gas, I had never seen the insides of a hospital. And now, I have spent most of the last five years on this hospital bed.—Narayani Bai, age thirty-five, resident of Mahamayee Ka Baug[43]

In Bhopal, survivors have based their relationship to the state and their demands for care and recognition on their injured bodies. Like most survivors of the disaster, the memories and experiences of these individuals are bifurcated into "before" and "after," and their conceptions of self revolve around the ways in which their bodies have changed, weakened, and sickened after the gas leak. In articulating their bodily injuries and the way physical limitations impact work, leisure, and everyday life, these survivors unsettle the view of the body found in the settlement and confront the state with its ongoing work. In continuing to pursue state care and provision, Bhopal's victims participate in a drama with the state by taking up its terms. "Relief for enormous suffering" has not been had, but ongoing calls for state intervention appear in Singh's letters, Natthibai's applications, and Chhotelal and Narayani Bai's stays in Hamida Hospital's MIC ward. Survivors like Chhotelal and Narayani must go in and out of the hospital because whatever treatment they received could not cure their ailments, yet they return to this state institution again and again for whatever limited relief can be had. Singh's multiple missives mentioned earlier and Natthibai's application for interim relief here adhere to government procedures and follow the welfarist role the state affirmed for itself in the *Charan* judgment. Singh and Natthibai do not assume in advance that their applications will go unanswered or forever unfulfilled. Following the state's procedures is painstaking and laborious, often requiring multiple visits to different offices, hours spent on transport, bribes for paperwork, and other hurdles. Such efforts to secure care cannot be dismissed as exercises in futility but underscore how much survivors want what the state says it should provide.

In the wake of the Chernobyl nuclear explosion, which occurred less than two years after Bhopal, anthropologist Adriana Petryna called this kind of relation one of "biological citizenship": a kind of political recognition where "the damaged biology of a population has become the grounds for social membership and the basis for staking citizenship claims."[44] Petryna describes the way biological citizenship in Ukraine was constituted by both "massive demand" and "selective access" to "a form of social welfare based on medical, scientific, and legal criteria that both acknowledge biological injury and compensate for it."[45] Access to such care was pursued in the face of "fundamental losses," just as it is in Bhopal.[46] Thus after Chernobyl and after Bhopal, state redress has been mobilized as a bulwark against further loss, however faulty. In the face of egregious inadequacy, victims of these and other industrial disasters have drawn on a framework of state intervention to interpret their own bodies and what might happen to them.

Complaints about inadequate care participate in a particular idea of the state. They testify to how much the state has failed *and* the way the potential for state relief from bodily suffering is central to how survivors imagine the future. In Bhopal, according to both the courts and the explosion's survivors, the state should protect and care for those affected by the gases. The force of these state promises is most often felt in their violation, but this means that state interventions must be understood through both their absence and their allure as desired objects. In the long life of toxicity, the Indian state has been seen simultaneously as a bad actor and a site of appeal. Bhopal's aftermath seems to throw forward a future that will only be a continuation of the slow violent present. Yet the very aspects of toxicity that most plague the city's residents—ongoing bodily pain, water contamination, genetic mutations, and intensified poverty—also undergird the complaints survivors have made *to* the state and the better ecopolitical futures they imagine through it.

In the wake of Bhopal's settlement, when further legal redress is no longer an option, complaining about the failure of state duties and promises of care is one way of using what is to hand, of mobilizing available languages to pursue ends that have not been met, and of remaining politically visible. Stuck in time in many ways, Bhopal's gas survivors nevertheless imagine change, and they do so, at times, by turning toward the state despite its limits. Survivor complaints are far from reopening the case or producing different practical outcomes. Yet, victim complaints confront the state with ongoing needs, and they testify to the way state interventions promised decades ago are still desired in the present. As vulnerable and injured Bhopali citizens constantly evoke the state outside the parameters of their actual experience, they situate the state in an unruly sense of political time, where the state is never coterminous with or subsumed by its present and dominant versions. In this context, where the contaminated present distends so obviously into the imaginable future, utopian method reveals the way those most injured by the Bhopal explosion imagine futurity through the state and have never been resigned to living only in the settlement's nihilistic and singular time.

Promises of Care in *Where Do the Children Play?*

Concrete utopias of state intervention also appear in aestheticized representations of the state. Indian writers and filmmakers have imagined alternate versions of the state in Bhopal, ones that might attend to the needs of gas survivors even after the settlement. Across Bhopal's cultural archive, in testimony but also, as discussed shortly, in film and fiction, the concrete utopian visions of legal accountability and bodily care once pursued by the state consistently emerge and remerge to frame survivors' imagined futures. These concrete utopias are especially apparent in Bala Kailasam's documentary *Where Do the Children Play?* (2019) and Indra Sinha's novel *Animal's People* (2007), both of which address the aftermath of the gas disaster. In these texts, state interventions are treated as promises that might one day be fulfilled. Refusing the closures of the settlement, these texts draw on the state's own affirmations of civilian support to pursue what Seyla Benhabib called a "politics of fulfillment" and to demand what "ought to be, but is not" in Bhopal.[47]

Bala Kailasam was a prolific Indian director and producer, working in both mainstream television and documentaries. An early documentary on architectural heritage, *Vaastu Marabu*, won Best Film on Art and Culture in Indian's 1991 National Film Festival. His later documentary *Where Do the Children Play?* follows a *padayatra* or political march from Bhopal to the prime minister's residence in New Delhi.[48] One hundred and fifty people began the

800-kilometer march on February 20, 2008, and arrived in New Delhi about a month later. The *padayatra* was undertaken as a protest to then–prime minister Manmohan Singh to demand that the state meet with the people, hear their demands, and intervene in Bhopal's ongoing suffering. Like the aforementioned survivor complaints, this film exemplifies the way state promises continue to shape how bodily futures are imagined, even thirty years after the disaster.

The opening scene of *Where Do the Children Play?* depicts walkers emerging slowly from white early morning fog. To a soundtrack of ominous and repetitive piano chords, this disconcerting and bewildering scene mimics the circumstances of "that night" in 1984, when victims ran through white clouds of methyl isocyanate gas. The documentary creates a visual repetition between that 1984 night in Bhopal and the morning of the 2008 march, between the terror of that night and the ongoing quest for state redress that has motivated the march decades later. This opening scene contests the containment of Bhopal that was imposed by the settlement and represents the unsettled and ongoing quality of the explosion's aftermath in its visual echo.

Shortly after this opening scene, the film offers a series of interviews from survivors. They are all adults and mostly women. They testify to different aspects of their experience on the night of December 2–3, 1984, including the chaos of running through the gas. But the interviewees also talk to and about the state. Haazra Bee, the first interviewee, opens by addressing the prime minister directly: "Mr. Prime Minister, my name is Haazra Bee."[49] She describes the way the children affected by the Bhopal explosion waste their childhoods in the hospital, cannot get an education, and are too physically weak to fend for themselves. She then makes a claim for intervention: "You are the ruler (Rajah) of the whole country. It is your duty. Your one word, one gesture can bring about justice for the victims."[50] Haazra Bee situates her demand for justice not just within state duty but within a mode of supplication; in her imaginary the prime minister is such a powerful figure that one word or gesture can produce change. In using the word "rajah" she also situates her petitioning in relation to older traditions of courtly petitioning found in Mughal India but still used in the present.[51] The prime minister does not of course have the unbridled power of a monarch, but Haazra Bee's imaginary of the state draws on an image of almost princely power, which might be benevolently deployed to "bring about justice." In her interview the state is rhetorically evoked as a powerful and interventionist actor in the lives of Bhopal's gas survivors.

Other interviewees also make demands on the state and likewise call for its intervention. But if Haazra Bee takes on a mode of tearful supplication, Tulsa Bai and Jhulekha Bee are angrier. Jhuleka Bee complains directly using the language of promises: "Where are all those (false) promises? Not a single one has he fulfilled."[52] Though she does not name anyone, the single male pronoun here suggests that, like Haazra Bee, she means Manmohan Singh, and like Haazra Bee, she also attributes to him a wide scope of power. Tulsa Bai, whose anger and frustration are the most apparent, exclaims, "What has the PM done for us? Nothing! . . . We water victims get no treatment at all."[53] She later reiterates, "The PM might think we have come to beg. But we are no beggars. At least give us what is our right!"[54] Though Haazra Bee might come close to begging and Tulsa Bai addresses the prime minister through an angry demand, both these women call upon state intervention.

Noting the language of such appeals is not a claim to knowing how any of these survivors truly feel about the state. It is difficult to know whether their external articulations are earnest reflections of their levels of investment in the state; indeed, at another moment, Jhulekha Bee declares, "Actually we have absolutely no desire to meet with such a minister. But we have no choice."[55] Nonetheless, all these women address the state through a rhetoric of state intervention and, in particular, in their references to the prime minister and his capacity to act in their lives. Tulsa Bai references the way victims of Bhopal's contaminated water have received "no treatment," and other interviewees, who do not mention the PM directly, also testify to how they have not received any medical treatment from state-run hospitals or other state institutions. These imaginaries of the state are all shaped by ideas of "what ought to be, but is not" and more specifically by unfulfilled promises of medical care that could address the pain of survivors' bodies.[56]

The women and other interviewed adults especially appeal for medical treatment for children, who though born after the explosion often bear some of its most severe physical consequences. Shanti Bai explicitly situates survivors' demands as the pursuit of different and better futures for their children: "Our real sorrow is that not only is our life destroyed but that of the children as well."[57] The next speaker is again Haazra Bee, who recounts how on "that night" she found her young son unconscious on a handcart. Now twenty-eight, he is "desperate to get on with his life. Where does he go for any kind of help?"[58] As she speaks about his desire to move on, she becomes visibly upset; her voice breaks and tears trickle down her cheeks. And though she doesn't say exactly what condition her son is in now, her pain suggests that he cannot "get on," no matter how badly he wants to, in part because he has not received the help he needs from the state. For Haazra Bee and the other parents marching in the *padayatra*, the better futures they seek are premised on state aid. Starkly absent and unfulfilled, they march to make specific kinds of claims and demand the fulfillment of specific promises from the state. The disappointing past does not determine the future in a linear or straightforward way here; why march, otherwise? Pursuing better futures by complaining to the state is the affective and political core of this film.

These early interviews precede and frame the marchers' eventual demonstration in front of the prime minister's residence in New Delhi, and their emotional testimonies offer context and highlight the stakes of the march, which is itself only one of many protests that have been made over the decades since 1984. Toward the end of the film the survivors reach New Delhi and congregate at Jantar Mantar, where public protests are typically held.[59] These closing scenes, as the marchers reach the site of protest, only underscore how unfulfilled state promises have both driven the survivors here and shape their imaginaries of the future. As they near Jantar Mantar, cries of "Fulfill! Fulfill!" fill the soundtrack.[60] Eventually, a government worker comes to the protestor's tents to make a statement:

> The Prime Minister has authorized me to say that the demand for setting up a specially empowered commission to carry out medical, economic, social and environmental rehabilitation of the Bhopal gas victims [sic]. The central government is, in principle, in agreement with this demand. The central government will take the initiative in speedily working out the modalities of setting up such a commission by including various communities in different rehabilitation aspects set up by the Supreme Court, the government of India, the government of Madhya Pradesh, and the High Court of Madhya Pradesh.[61]

This statement contains in microcosm the dynamics of grand state intervention, victim neglect and obscuration, and potential fulfillment that have characterized survivors' experiences and imaginaries of the state after the explosion. On the one hand, something concrete has happened. An actual government worker has come to meet with the protestors and affirm their general demands, and the government agrees to set up a commission. But almost immediately, in the move from general declaration to detailed action, the statement devolves into bureaucratic gibberish and labyrinthian language about "speedy modalities" and vague references to "various communities," when it is in fact the very particular communities of gas-affected wards and gas survivors who must be accounted for. This run-on speech takes a minute of this hour-long film, and while bookended by specific state players, its middle portion, where it details what the state will do for survivors, is ambiguous and confusing. Its rhetoric replicates the circuitous routes victims have had to take in their pursuit of care. Indeed, the victims become almost invisible, lost within the winding description and overshadowed by lists of state

Figure 1. Bhopal marchers celebrating in Bala Kailasam's documentary *Where Do the Children Play?*

bodies, from the prime minister at the outset to the Indian Supreme Court at the end.

At the same time, while the statement is being read, the marchers are shown on screen, their faces clearly overjoyed (Figure 1). They hug and slap each other on the back as they listen, grinning, laughing, and nodding at the speaker's words. Such actions speak to a level of attachment and investment in state responses, however imperfect. Yet the omissions and distortions in this yet-further promise of action cannot be overlooked, either. This scene starkly illustrates the uneasy mixture of imperfect, partial state action typical of Bhopal and the investments that are produced through, and in spite of, these limits.

The very last words spoken in the film are given to Shameer, a young boy who makes the trip to New Delhi carried on his father's shoulders. He is a concrete individual who elicits compassion from viewers. Indeed, he is shown curled up on his father's shoulders, asleep, a wrenchingly fragile and innocent figure. He embodies the reasons for the march, and he stands in for the many other children who did not go on this march but remain in Bhopal, menaced by its uncleaned factory and its seeping toxicity. Viewers are chillingly reminded of this as Shameer is shown chugging from a water bottle before he speaks. While it is unclear where this water is from or if it is clean, viewers are aware that the water in Bhopal itself is contaminated and that Shameer is in all likelihood being exposed to heavy metals, toxins, pesticide runoff, and other dangerous chemicals all the time. A lively and vivacious boy with powerful lungs, this act of drinking, of bringing the contaminated world in, makes visible the way futures like Shameer's are being foreclosed every day and moment by moment as promises of clean water and other forms of government provision go unfulfilled.

It is only too appropriate then that the film's last words are given to this boy. He repeatedly yells out, "Manmohan Singh, keep your promise!"[62] Eventually his voice dies down and, cradled in his father's arms, he repeats softly, "Manmohan Singh, keep your promise."[63] From a loud demand to a quiet plea, like the interviewees' statements early in the film, Shameer underscores how hopes for the future are premised on the potential fulfillment of state interventions. Experienced only as unfulfillment after the settlement and again in this moment on the march, *Where Do the Children Play?* illuminates how much state promises have failed in Bhopal *and* how much they continue to matter.

Ever receding but kept alive each time a demand is made, the state's interventionist promises saturate and configure survivors' imaginings of futurity for themselves and their children. As Kailasam's film closes, Shameer's future stretches before the viewer. Already contaminated by Bhopal in some ways, his future is not yet foreclosed, and how it might go, whether he keeps or loses his powerful voice and working lungs, cannot be known at the film's end. At its close, future state interventions are not confirmed, and *Where Do the Children Play?* formalizes the temporal dualities of deferral and desired fulfillment in which Bhopal's victims have lived since December 1984. This condition of suspension, however pessimistic, has not been allowed to ossify into simple closure. Shameer's future might still be better, and the futures of Bhopal's other children too, if the state does what it says it will. As simple as this sounds, such complex state possibilities and investments in state intervention have been largely overlooked by postcolonial ecocritics and environmental humanists who have written exclusively about the injustices of the state in Bhopal. In contrast, Kailasam's documentary records the way state-based care is a concrete utopia envisioned through possibilities of future state action in Bhopal.

Courts and Bodies in *Animal's People*

Like *Where Do the Children Play?*, Indra Sinha's novel *Animal's People* concentrates on survival in Bhopal's aftermath. *Animal's People* is Sinha's second novel, written after *The Death of Mr. Love* and a memoir about early internet culture called *The Cybergypsies*. *Animal's People* has become something of a new canonical novel for postcolonial environmental humanists, and it was shortlisted for the Man Booker Prize in 2007 before winning the Commonwealth Writer's Prize for Europe and South Asia in 2008. *Animal's People* is set in a fictional city named Khaufpur, Urdu for "city of terror," that replicates many of the conditions of Bhopal. Like Bhopal, the city has been poisoned by an American "Kampani" that stands in for Union Carbide. And through the lives of his characters, Sinha represents the many kinds of neglect and pain that have affected Bhopal's residents in the real explosion's aftermath. Like Bhopal's residents, Sinha's characters are time and again ignored by the state. Captured most overtly by a quip from a government doctor that "this is not my department," Sinha illustrates how environmental harm and survivor suffering are exacerbated through state withdrawal and endless bureaucratic deferments.[64] Indeed, state doctors "barely [look] at you," and Animal, the novel's eponymous anti-hero and protagonist, has never received medical treatment even though he must move around on all fours after his spine is twisted by the gases.[65]

Likewise, the novel emphasizes the saturative quality of bodily pain and environmental contamination. In *Animal's People* the spread of poison throughout the environment and people's bodies is presented as an inescapable fact: "'Everything here is poisoned. If you stay here long enough, you will be too,'" a "village [type]" woman from the rural areas outside the city tells Elli, an American doctor newly arrived in Khaufpur.[66] Even living outside the city, this woman's breast milk has become contaminated. Khaufpur's toxins, like Bhopal's, have proven to be especially damaging to children and pregnant women, and Elli and the village woman first meet because the woman refuses to "'feed [her] kid poison'" by breastfeeding.[67] In addition to Animal's own damaged body, a web of minor characters makes the pervasiveness of poisoning and its consequences painfully clear. The "singing breath" of Somraj, a once nationally renowned singer, has been destroyed by the gases, Animal's friend Aliya suffers coughing and fever before eventually dying, and Shambu, whose body is described as "a sack of pain," must drink poisoned well water.[68] Having survived while many around him have died, at the end of the novel Animal declares, "We are the people of the Apokalis. Tomorrow there will be more of us."[69] While this line has many valences, one way to read it is as an index of toxicity's slow and inexorable spread into the future. Tomorrow there will be more suffering bodies. After the fast killing of the explosion's immediate aftermath, Khaufpur's survivors, like Bhopal's, linger in pain, poverty, and slow death.

But like Kailasam's documentary, Sinha's novel tracks investment in the state as much as it records disaffection. This plurality is especially concentrated in the way the novel portrays state promises. Promises first show up in the negative, in complaints. Indeed, the residents of Khaufpur struggle against neglect by the Chief Minister (CM), a state official charged with taking care of gas victims while activists, led by an intellectual named Zafar, have agitated for years for the Kampani to be tried in Khaufpur's court. Despite his mandate, the Chief Minister is represented as an especially dubious and corrupt figure who has done nothing to help poison victims. In response to his statement that "NO DECISION WILL BE TAKEN THAT IS NOT IN YOUR BEST INTERESTS," a crowd asks, "Yes, of what use are your promises? . . . Was it three or four years ago you promised us clean water?"[70] Water is in fact a long-standing, everyday concern. Since the factory's explosion decades prior, the city's residents have had to drink and wash in poisoned water as a result of the inaction of government workers like the Chief Minister. Given this history of failed care, city residents are surely right to congregate on the minister's lawn to ask, "Of what use are your promises?"

Yet like the parents interviewed in *Where Do the Children Play?*, these people still address their anger and their sense of grievance to a figure imbued with both the responsibility and the power to intervene. Their complaints about broken promises are also demands upon power. That the CM and the Indian state more generally have failed to act is one of the novel's primary political critiques. But this scene importantly underscores how, despite its repeated failures, popular complaints index what the state should do. On the surface, the crowd's complaints seem to only reinforce the state as a bad actor, to reinstall perceptions that the state does little in the "best interests" of the people. Yet, as the novel details the myriad ways the state has failed, it also invests in state redress and provides a vision of what a better state could be like. Utopian method reads the state this way, flipping the valences of existing institutions and structures and reading them for the potentials they describe. Utopian method reads complaints beyond their negativity, imagines how bad state responses could work well, and views failed promises not as closures but as frustrated potentials. On the CM's lawn, promises and complaints point to the incompletion of the present, and political failures offer maps to what could be.

The novel's utopic investment in state promises comes through most clearly, though, in the legal campaign that drives much of the plot. It is structured by a temporality of deferral that is simultaneously a temporality of possible future fulfillment. The courts in Sinha's novel encourage, even seem to require, a utopian method of reading. This is because the novel's investment in legal redress rests on a crucial difference between its fictional representation and the historical context of its real-world referent. In Bhopal, the settlement has already occurred. But in Khaufpur, the people have not yet had their day in court. Unlike the real Bhopal, where further legal redress has been technically closed by the settlement, in *Animal's People* the case is consistently delayed. The novel can therefore experiment with what better kinds of justice might look like in Bhopal's aftermath, ranging beyond the settled circumstances of the real city. Yet *Animal's People* still ends up imagining better ecopolitical futures through the state, and especially through the potential fulfillment of "*rights, law, justice*" that work for survivors rather than corporations.[71]

The novel's legal campaign is led by Zafar, who "had given up everything in his life for the poor."[72] Thin and bespeckled like a Muslim Gandhi and "robed in the sweet odour of sainthood," Zafar at one point undertakes a hunger strike to persuade the Kampani to act.[73] It is through him that the text remains most explicitly attached to state institutions. His legal campaign is the most obvious way in which the state and its courts are situated within a utopic politics of fulfillment where better futures are not linearly foreclosed by past failures. The campaign's constant petitions, demonstrations, and court appearances assume that the status quo can change. Indeed, Zafar says, "One day something must surely happen, why not today?"[74] Zafar casts legal change not as radically new or unlooked-for but as a familiar and unfulfilled promise. A change in the case against the Kampani would simultaneously be a stark departure from the previous twenty years of waiting and a fulfillment or confirmation of his expectation that "*one day something must surely happen.*"[75] And in fact, during the course of the story something does happen: the most recent judge to hear Zafar's plea decides to summon the Kampani to court. For Zafar the court's past actions have never foreclosed its future potential. Past failures have never dictated what might happen in the future. The legal campaign itself thus exemplifies a utopian method, situating state courts in a recursive or nonlinear sense of time in which past and future do not relate in a determined way but might diverge from one another.

A different version of this struggle for state-based futures occurs later as Zafar and Nisha, another activist, debate the uses of the law. As the initial momentum of the judge's decision is compromised, Nisha asks, "And when the government that is supposed to protect us manipulates the law against us, of what use then is the law?"[76] What use indeed. From Nisha's complaints we can extrapolate an imaginary of the state produced from its broken promises. The pathos of her complaint arises precisely from long-held expectations of protection and rule of law that are finally wearing thin. Nisha knows very well what the government is supposed to do and how the law is supposed to work; it is precisely this knowledge that shapes her understanding that the law has not been used as it should. In questioning whether the courts should be discarded for other, more violent tactics against the Kampani, Nisha loses faith in the eventual fulfillment of legal justice.

Yet, no matter how disappointing it is as an institution, the court system is never dismissed or relinquished to its failures. Introduced in the novel's opening pages, *"rights, law, justice"* haunt the story, persisting as a promise that is always out of reach but that is never allowed to vanish from the narrative.[77] Kept alive by Zafar's campaign of overt investment in the courts but also in the many negative, obverse maps laid out in complaints about the law, the promise of better futures through the state's legal system persists through the unfolding of the story. For despite all its deferment, the national court system is also seen as the best way to hold the Kampani responsible for its actions. Like the original civil suit in Bhopal's district court, *Animal's People* poses state institutions as a counterbalance to the power of multinational corporations. Thus, though it seems to offer only an indirect map for better futures via characters like the Chief Minister or plot devices like the legal campaign, the narrative as a whole remains consistently invested in the possibility of corporate accountability through the state.

This investment in the Indian state is reinforced by the novel's frame narrative, which sharply critiques the possible role of international actors such as mainstream media or human rights NGOs.[78] Sinha brought insider knowledge to this critique, as he worked in humanitarian advertising before turning to fiction writing. In the summer of 1990, Sinha's London-based employer Collett Dickenson Pearce, an advertising agency most well known for producing ads for alcohol, tobacco, and Benson and Hedges cigarettes, signed an account with the human rights group Amnesty International. Sinha was deeply involved with Amnesty campaigns against Saddam Hussein's chemical attacks on Iraqi Kurds during the Iran-Iraq war. This work eventually led Sinha to Bhopal, and he campaigned for justice in Bhopal in the 1990s.[79] Yet Sinha also became keenly aware of the limits of international humanitarian aid, a perspective the novel offers through Animal.

As Animal narrates the novel's frame, he lambasts the way international audiences only "suck our stories from us" and describes international attention burning like "acid on my skin."[80] Animal's language situates international curiosity as a form of violence not unlike the effects of the Kampani's poisons themselves, which burned him like "red hot tongs."[81] Through such comparisons the novel draws parallels between the kind of violence enacted by the Kampani and international responses that can only fetishize and consume global South disasters like Bhopal. Rather than appealing to an international public, the frame is far more hostile to possibilities for international intervention than the remediation the state might eventually provide. In turn, the activist strategies represented within the novel remain invested in local and national responses to the ongoing effects of the gas disaster. In the body of the story, instead of only working badly, the courts and other state actors might start working well—Khaufpur might win "one day," and a change has already occurred.

But while *Animal's People* remains committed to the potential of institutions like the courts, it also imagines better futures through proposals for different and alternative kinds of states. These alternate states prioritize medical relief rather than legal accountability, and one model is proposed by Elli, a naïve but well-intentioned American doctor who moves to Khaufpur to offer free medical care. Her clinic depends on government approval to remain open, but state-run clinics do not improve during the story, and at one point Elli makes recommendations to a state doctor. The doctor is referred to synecdochally as "Government" in the narrative, and thus to "Government's" dismissal that "these people" don't know better than to live in filth, Elli shoots back, "But you do. . . . So teach them. Organise people into teams to pick up the litter. Bring in pipes, water taps, build proper latrines. . . ."[82] This hygienic version of the state is nowhere in the novel—indeed, as noted previously, the lack of clean water is an especially egregious problem. Yet in proposing such a plan Elli confronts the current state with an alternative version of itself, one that appears only in the negative, as an obverse map or absent possibility.

Rethinking medical care, however, also allows the novel to propose an even more ambitious alternative state. This version of the state is keyed to the fact of ongoing toxicity, and it is one that cannot deliver final justice. This is *not* because of inadequate state action but because ongoing redress is required if state care is to be commensurate with the morphings of toxified bodies. As Animal warns, no one knows "what horrors might yet emerge in their bodies" or when.[83] In the ever-changing physical landscapes of the explosion's aftermath, state care can in fact never be finally achieved. Thus, when Zafar asks that "simple natural justice should prevail" and elaborates that this means cleaning the factory, providing medical care, getting better compensation, and letting the case conclude, this is an "impossible wish" not only because of its extensive scope but because conclusion cannot match the continuous and unpredictable unfolding of toxicity's effects on Khaufpuri bodies and the environment.[84]

An important scene toward the end of *Animal's People* underscores this political alternative, of a state that might prioritize aleatory physical eruptions and ongoing environmental toxicity. At this point in the narrative the official legal hearing has been delayed yet again, and the Kampani's lawyers meet secretly with the Minister of Poison Relief and Chief Minister to work out a deal that would bypass a legal forum altogether. This meeting is interrupted because someone empties a stink bomb into the room's air vents. What follows is a miniature enactment of "that night"—the men in the room begin to feel burning in their noses and throats. They experience symptoms similar to those experienced by Khaufpuris after the factory explosion: coughing, breathlessness, gagging, vomiting. Though this scene is merely a mild version of what happened on "that night," it interrupts the possibility of a backroom settlement with the unexpected eruption of physical ailments. It does so to show the injustice of failing to care for survivors whose bodily symptoms are much worse than those experienced momentarily by the lawyers in the room. But ironic critique is not the novel's only point. In interrupting a process of dealmaking with unexpected bodily effects, the novel suggests that a final settlement cannot provide justice precisely because of the unruly, unpredictable, and ongoing physical consequences of toxicity. A state that provides finality cannot do justice to such unsettled bodies.

A similar alternative state that would respond to the unpredictable needs of toxified bodies is also implied in the novel's single scene of explicit confrontation, when Khaufpur's residents rebel against state police forces. In this scene human bodies are portrayed as more-than-human assemblages and as insurgent, collective forces.[85] The spark of this protest is the rumored death of Zafar, whose focus on the law has drawn on assumptions of potential future fulfillment and the desirable social goods that might be had from following state procedures. His rumored death from a hunger strike and the upsurge that immediately follows it signifies a refusal of existing political relations but also a continued and fraught engagement with the state.

In the scene in question, angry and grief-stricken Khaufpuris gather at the abandoned pesticide factory, where they clash with an antagonistic police force. But in this moment of confrontation, Animal observes:

Then a thing happens that no one could have predicted.

From nowhere a tide of ragged people surges over the police and sweeps them away.[86]

In this moment, the people are described in terms of a collective and massive force, exerting a kind of agency from below. This moment, which "no one could have predicted," is one in which the poor shift the grounds of their relationship with the state from endured neglect to active opposition. Together they rise like a "tide" to substitute the dominant approach to justice and claim-making (formal, litigious, and institutional) with another (popular, rebellious, and unplanned). Their relationship with the state is figured here not only as resistance to oppressive forms of power, but as an act of "sweeping away" these forms to stake a claim in future relations that might be different.

Much of this alternative imaginary is indexed in the novel's description of Khaufpuri bodies. Why present rebelling bodies as a collective force, a ragged tide? This question brings us to the narrative phenomenon of the voices Animal hears inside his head before the confrontation and the ways in which the novel has posed the question of toxic forces within the body. As Animal explains at the outset of the narrative, he hears the unspoken voices and thoughts of others: "Since I was small I could hear people's thoughts even when their lips were shut, plus I'd get en passant comments from all types of things, animals, birds, trees, rocks giving the time of day"; "Voices were shouting inside my head."[87]

Animal's voices might at first seem an instance of magical realism, but such a fantastic articulation can also be taken quite literally and materially, as a bodily heuristic. Seeing into the interior lives of other beings or being permeated by their thoughts and perceptions represents the breakdown of boundaries in the wake of environmental contamination.[88] Hearing voices, leaking into other points of view, or accessing the interior of other things make audible and obvious a somatic state that could otherwise be overlooked: the hybridized interior of toxic bodies, criss-crossed by other forms of life and matter. In other words, Animal's voices give voice to the teeming bodily multiplicities produced by toxic exposure. In fact, the novel confirms that Animal's voices are the result of his exposure to Kampani toxins. They "started when I was small, after I had the fever that bent my back."[89] These moments of narrative porosity presented as narrative plurality put into language the effects of toxicity on Khaufpur's hybridized, more-than-human bodies. Literary critic and environmental humanist Stacey Alaimo has made a similar argument by proposing that all bodies, but especially non-white bodies and laboring bodies, should be understood as "trans-corporeal," bodies where the environment "is always the very substance of ourselves."[90]

The novel's earlier presentation of Animal's teeming and leaky body sets up the political stakes of this later confrontation and throws into question exactly who or what that "ragged tide" of people included. These are people invaded by colonies of bacteria, microbes, organic and inorganic materials, toxins, and cancers, bodies whose multi-materiality has been facilitated by the forms of state neglect they have had to endure. Teeming bodies are preeminently political, produced out of bureaucratic deferrals, lack of medical treatment, dirty water, and continuous exposure to chemicals. The rebellion at the factory is then a moment when the state is confronted by the multiply mattered bodies it has created through its current, dominant practices of neglect. As such, the confrontational tide in *Animal's People* includes the human and more-than-human repercussions of bad state politics.

As the police are confronted with this unruly multitude, *Animal's People* casts the one instance in which residents violently confront the state as a scaled-up version of what is happening inside the individual bodies of the city's gas survivors every day. Toxic bodily effects cannot be predicted, and in scaling up what counts as the site of multiplicity, the very place and significance of such unpredictable eruptions are brought to the fore. Translating the microscalar battles waged between people and their toxified bodies into a macroscalar depiction of bodies in confrontation with the state, *Animal's People* foregrounds the question of who or what composes a complaining body and therefore the need to rethink the parameters of state response and recognition. Like the aforementioned scene with the Kampani's lawyers, this episode suggests the need for a different kind of state, one that will account for the aleatory quality of toxic effects and the teeming quality of poisoned bodies. The somatic consequences of toxicity are not always controllable, knowable, or coherent in their emergence, and in confronting the state with bodies as messy assemblages, *Animal's People* proposes a state that might engage with the unpredictable yet persistent eruptions of toxic injury.

So, too, in the novel's concluding lines Animal declares, "We are the people of the Apokalis. Tomorrow there will be more of us."[91] As noted earlier, there will be more of us in part because the long life of poison continues to reach outward to affect more and more people over time, distending slowly into the future. Both the legal campaign and sickness are ongoing: "It will take time, so we're told, to appoint a new judge in the case, the hearing's again been postponed. . . . There is still sickness all over Khaufpur, hundreds come daily to Elli doctress's clinic."[92] But as the novel couples the endless span of illness with the continuing search for legal accountability, it again suggests that fulfillment may only be one way of envisioning a better future. As important to better ecopolitical futures are state responses that exceed a final conclusion.

It might be argued that an emphasis on continuity over fulfillment threatens to justify further political inaction. But inaction is already at work in Bhopal, and the point is that *Animal's People* illuminates possibilities for state redress beyond containerized responses. In the continuing inadequacies of Bhopal's aftermath, *Animal's People* imagines concretely better futures though contrasting, plural imaginaries of the state: one keyed to the eventual fulfillment of legal justice and another attentive to the physical unpredictability of bodily harm, where the unrelenting and uncontrollable needs of poisoned bodies could guide state interventions. Both imagined states contest the dominant, existing form of the Indian state that favors global capitalism and continues to neglect Bhopal.

States beyond Borders

In the years since the Bhopal settlement, corporate accountability has become ever more elusive. But it has not disappeared as a concrete utopian vision. In August 2002 the environmental organization Greenpeace International released a report entitled *Corporate Crimes*. In it they proposed the "Bhopal Principles on Corporate Responsibility" to imagine how states could enforce corporate accountability across vast scales of space. As utopic as the antecedents to the settlement discussed at the start of the chapter, the Bhopal Principles seem fantastical in their scope and ambition. Released for the Johannesburg Earth Summit and assembled as a supplement to the Rio Declaration on Environment and Development of 1992, the principles addressed the continuing failure of states to hold transnational companies accountable for pollution, environmental degradation, and the destructive byproducts of economic development. In the opening paragraphs of the report, the writers note, "We have chosen to call them the 'Bhopal' Principles because this disaster, more than any other, highlights the current failure of governments to protect public welfare and the failure of corporations to observe basic standards."[93] But despite pointing out such general state failures and the specific Bhopal disaster that gives the principles their name, Greenpeace reaffirmed states as primary protectors of their citizens. Like the *Charan* judgment, the principles affirm that "states are ultimately responsible for public welfare."[94] In this vein they imagine an immense extension of state authority and efficacy beyond national borders.

The Bhopal Principles enact a version of utopian method by rethinking the kinds of patently negative circumstances that have allowed corporations to so often flout national protections and by turning these existing circumstances to new ends. In the Bhopal Principles, state protection has no borders. The principles envision what a borderless world would mean for corporate accountability at the hands of state power, rethinking the eroded national regulations and lax border policing that abet the movement of corporations in a global race to the bottom. These conditions are upended and proposed as a basis for extending state protections across the planet. Principle three is most striking in this regard. Titled "Ensure Corporate Liability for Damage beyond National Jurisdictions," principle three asserts that:

> states must ensure that corporations are liable for injury to persons and damage to property, biological diversity and the environment beyond the limits of national jurisdiction, and to the global commons such as atmosphere and oceans. Liability must include responsibility for environmental cleanup and restoration.[95]

The imagined state represented here is one that utilizes eroded borders to augment the protective mandate of states. If the decline of the protective state and the porousness of borders are commonly evoked to explain the slick movements of corporate capital and their disastrous externalities, Greenpeace's Bhopal Principles envision an erosion of borders that would empower states to pursue protections for their citizens with similar breadth and transnational impunity, pursuing harm to its lair. In a world where corporate-produced environmental harms cross national boundaries, the Bhopal Principles invest in the idea of state-based citizen protections that similarly span the planet, imagining states able to wield the force of national protection and corporate accountability outside national borders on the strength of a welfarist mandate.[96] They resituate an existing feature of the present, weakened border protections, "as components of a different system" in order to propose a utopic outcome.[97] Weak borders become a basis for expanded protections amidst transnational circuits of corporate malfeasance, the kind that have only become more difficult to regulate or curtail since the night of Bhopal itself.

Together, the Bhopal Principles, the Processing of Claims Act, and Bhopal's original 1986 civil suit articulate versions of the state that could match the globetrotting destruction of corporate actors. Between the settlement's ambitious antecedents and the vision of planetary corporate accountability articulated in the Bhopal Principles, *Animal's People* and *Where Do the Children Play?* call for forms of further legal redress and bodily care that matter deeply for those who remain on Bhopal's poisoned ground. These proposals depend on the potential interventions of the state, and they are examples of what Ernst Bloch called "concrete utopia[s]," ideas for improvement that are specific rather than systemic, and circumscribed rather than totally transformative.[98] They lie at the "point of contact between dreams and life" and pursue forms of "surplus . . . over and above what has been attained and thus exists."[99] In the face of the Bhopal settlement's serious limits and the economic priorities of the Indian state, the futures that survivors, activists, filmmakers, and writers imagine in Bhopal are not confined to the bad present. As they complain about state inadequacies and failures, culture-makers and gas survivors alike demand states that are otherwise, ones that might bring concrete utopian visions closer to fulfillment.

The many different imaginaries, complaints, and antecedents that have been produced around Bhopal pluralize the way the Indian state can be read. They unsettle the singular, closed future imposed by the settlement and the linear trajectories of harmful continuity that emerge from it. As they respond to conditions of ongoing toxicity and corporate impunity, complaints, promises, antecedents, and alternatives together situate the Indian state within a disjointed sense of political time that rejects the state's present forms as the limitation of the real, the imagined, or the possible. Such *"aggregate"* newness is not a transformative break but a utopic mixture of past, present, and future that challenges the obvious effects of the Bhopal explosion.[100] This utopian view does not do away with the state's violence. But it offers credence and support for the way survivors and others continue to hail the state, and it makes clear that alternative proposals for better states cannot be dismissed just because they have not come to pass. Applying a utopian method to Bhopal makes it possible to see the Indian state as a Janus-faced actor and to consider the persistence of the state's contradictory uses and imaginaries, the way bad and better versions of the state are entwined together in the history and future of the world's worst industrial disaster. These versions of the state and the futures imagined from them deeply unsettle the settlement and its containment of "that night" in Bhopal, extending instead into other spaces and times.

2
Beyond Petrostates
Oil Pollution in the Niger Delta

On April 20, 2010, the oil drilling rig *Deepwater Horizon*, operated by British Petroleum on the Macondo Prospect of the Gulf of Mexico, exploded and sank, resulting in the death of eleven workers on the rig and catastrophic leaking from the oil wellhead.[1] Over the next eighty-seven days the broken wellhead released 507 million liters of oil into the Gulf of Mexico from pipes lying 1,600 meters below the ocean surface. The wellhead was capped only on July 15 and finally sealed on September 19, 2010. Approximately 180,000 square kilometers of surface water and 2,000 kilometers of shoreline were contaminated, and over 20 million hectares of the Gulf of Mexico were closed to fishing. Spill response efforts included oil skimming, over 400 in situ burns, and the application of approximately 7 million liters of chemical dispersants at the surface and, for the first time in history, on the ocean floor.[2] Despite all these efforts, it is predicted that some areas of the Gulf of Mexico may take more than twenty years to ecologically recover. The *Deepwater Horizon* spill was the largest spill in the history of marine oil drilling. But it was not the first or last of its kind. Twenty-one years earlier, on March 24, 1989, the oil tanker *Exxon Valdez* left Port Valdez, Alaska, and ran aground on Bligh Reef in Prince William Sound on Alaska's southern coast. The vessel spilled at least 40.8 million liters of crude oil into the pristine waters of the Sound. The spill shocked the United States public, created a media frenzy, and galvanized widespread cleanup efforts by countless volunteers and organizations. By 1991, only 14 percent of the spilled oil had been recovered by cleanup operations.[3]

These enormous spills are conspicuous for the damage they did to miles of American shoreline, surface and subsurface waters, complex marine ecosystems, and local communities on the Gulf and Alaskan coasts. They are also conspicuous for the way they were spotlighted in national and international media and followed by massive, multi-year cleanup campaigns, which succeeded in remediating some but not all of the oil damage. These efforts, undertaken by civilian groups and scientific experts and funded by huge sums of money from the United States government, are unusual for spills. Outside North America, in the global South, where neither the manpower nor the resources for such cleanup efforts are available, spills go unreported, underinvestigated, and largely unremediated.

In the world's richest country, arsenals of expertise and funding could not completely contain the effects of large oil spills or address the local environments and peoples affected. What possibilities are there for oil remediation efforts elsewhere, then? In the Niger Delta, where multinational oil corporations like Shell have drilled for oil since the 1960s, it is difficult to know just how much oil has been spilled. But it is clear that the devastation is extensive. An Amnesty International investigation, using hundreds of crowdsourced data points, found that since 2011 Shell has reported 1,010 spills that have resulted in at least 17.5 million liters of oil lost into the Delta. That's enough to fill seven Olympic swimming pools. Since 2014, the Italian company Eni reported 820 spills and 4.1 million liters of oil spilled in the Delta.[4] These numbers are likely conservative, and they account for the spills of only two companies over a handful of recent years. Considering how many companies have drilled in the Niger Delta for decades, the scale of its oil contamination is truly staggering. In the global South, the polluting externalities of the oil industry are magnified and concentrated many times over. In the Niger Delta, considered one of the most polluted places on earth, the deadly material costs of oil sink into the soil and coat the waterways, while profits stream away to global markets and the pockets of corporate executives. And unlike their counterparts in the global North, these spills prompt little outrage or attention, and cleanup efforts are meager, at best.

Locals in the Niger Delta have attempted to contain the spills that threaten their lands and livelihoods. But such large and frequent spills cannot be adequately addressed by the residents of spill zones, who have neither cleanup equipment, armies of volunteers, nor funding. Indeed, the *Deepwater Horizon* and *Exxon Valdez* spills suggest that even massive amounts of manpower and state resources are not always enough. Yet such state-supported cleanup efforts after spills in the global North dramatize that this *is* the scale of intervention needed to counteract the petroviolence of global oil corporations. If anyone or anything could respond to and contest the immensity of oil pollution, it is states, with their own powerful arsenals of expertise, media access, money, and personnel.

Indeed, even in Nigeria, one of the world's most concentrated spill zones, the history of oil pollution reveals that the state at times fought oil corporations and mobilized its own powers to counteract the environmental devastation of corporate drilling. On the eve of national independence and at the start of the burgeoning oil industry that would come to dominate its economy, the Nigerian state foresaw the need to regulate oil companies and hold them accountable for oil spills, pipeline breaks, and other environmental costs of drilling. The Nigerian state once imagined oil pipelines in particular as sites of corporate responsibility, which oil majors should maintain in good order, repair, and upkeep. It imagined the pipelines that crisscross the Delta and connect to cities in the hinterland as liable to breakage and spillage, and it empowered local communities to pursue compensation. In imagining the possibilities of the oil industry, the Nigerian state sought to hold corporations accountable for pipeline spills. In short, the Nigerian state once thought seriously about the dangers of oil and anticipated the material costs of its extraction.

This version of a protective state that views oil as a pollutant has come to seem nigh unthinkable in Nigeria's present, where petrodollars reign. This is because, despite its earlier attempts at corporate regulation and local protections, the Niger Delta has become so polluted in part because of the privileged partnerships that have developed between oil corporations and the Nigerian state. One regime after another has worked hand in glove with the oil companies that spearhead petroleum extraction in the mangrove deltas of the country's southeast. In 2000, the World Bank coined the term "state capture" to describe such partnerships.[5] In captured states, private actors like corporations or elite individuals take control of the levers of state policy, laws, and contracts for themselves while simultaneously weakening or impeding public accountability and civic access to state power. Such captured states work well for the private actors who control them and badly for ordinary citizens who are shut out of influencing or shaping the state. Indeed, communities in the Niger Delta have, time and again, been ignored, marginalized, or outright repressed by state forces working to protect oil profits.

Yet even so, the Nigerian state has clearly not always been captured by corporate oil interests. In addition to its own early environmental awareness of oil, the Nigerian state has at times affirmed a large range of goals and aspirational interventions that aimed to harness the good of oil for the nation's citizens rather than for corporate profits. Oil revenue has been thought of as the basis of material provisions and equal political treatment for all. Moreover, in recent years the state has weakly affirmed civilian rights to a clean environment against the claims of corporations. The Nigerian state's role in the oil industry and in the lives of Delta residents is not simply one of state capture or corporate collusion. Looking at how the state has been imagined and addressed by Delta residents who suffer from pollution and poverty, the state's own early regulation of the oil industry, and recent, if tenuous, attempts at corporate accountability all suggest a more complex place for the state. In the Niger Delta, as in other sites of environmental harm, the state has been a bad actor, but it has also been a site of appeal. In the decades since the development of the oil industry, Nigerian writers and communities across the Delta have turned to the state to demand concrete utopias or specific and emplaced forms of betterment. These include environmental protections, material provisions, and greater forms of political inclusion. Like the Janus-faced view of oil inaugurated by the state itself, communities at the sites of oil's derivation have imagined both reckonings for oil corporations and access to the goods of oil through the state.

Black Gold Genocide

These kinds of complexities have been obscured by the petroviolence that is so obviously at work in the Niger Delta. Petroviolence is a shorthand for the way environmental destruction from petroleum extraction goes hand in hand with state collusion, corporate profiteering, and competition for petrodollars. In the oil-slicked waterways and blackened fields of Ogoniland in the Delta's southeast, farmers harvest rotted crops, once-plentiful fish float belly up in the creeks, and children read not under the light of electric bulbs but the endless flame of gas flare towers. Petroleum companies and a variety of Nigerian regimes, both military and civilian, have colluded to impose poverty and pollution on Delta peoples like the Ogoni while securing wealth for themselves, and this first section lays out petroviolence's mutually entwined forces. The entrenchment of petroviolence's negative feedbacks means they cannot be overlooked, and before we can consider the ways the Nigerian state has erratically pursued environmental protections or been imagined as a potentially beneficial actor by writers and citizens, we must attend to oil's detrimental effects in the Delta. The discourses of petroviolence rightly dominate how postcolonialists and environmental humanists write about the Niger Delta, even as they have also made other imaginaries of the state in Nigeria difficult to see.

In Nigeria, as in other oil-producing states, oil is described as "black gold," and it is a national resource par excellence.[6] Like elemental yellow gold, black gold produces fabulous wealth and fantasies of prosperity and power. Extracted from underground, seemingly there for the taking and with minimal requirements for labor or infrastructure, oil's relatively low production costs and its high monetary value make it seem "magically" profitable.[7] Since commercial quantities of oil were discovered in January 1956 at Oloibiri, a small creek community ninety kilometers west of the city of Port Harcourt, oil has been the mainstay of the Nigerian economy. In fact, since independence in 1960 Nigeria has become the eleventh-largest producer and eighth-largest exporter of crude oil and natural gas in the world, and in 2007 oil still made up over 87 percent of government revenues. It is no exaggeration to say that in Nigeria "oil is king!" or that the economy runs on black gold.[8]

Oil's centrality in the Nigerian economy has in turn made it a site of competing claims and exclusionary practices between the state's federal center, other levels of government, and citizens across the country. The perception of oil as a national resource means that it is not only seen as a resource for the state, but one to which everyone in Nigeria has a right. As political geographer Michael Watts puts it, even ordinary people "in virtue of its national character, plausibly claim their share of this national cake as a citizenship right."[9] This perception of nationwide ownership has created competitive senses of entitlement among Nigeria's many political participants, rather than a sense of common plenty. Political scientist Peter Ekeh observes, "*Government is conceived as sharing the fruits of power. The hero in Nigerian politics is one who brings such fruits from the Centre to his own people.*"[10] And anthropologist Andrew Apter notes similarly that "public resources flowed back into private hands. These flows took many forms . . . the diversion of public resources and funds was at the core of the Nigerian career trajectory, which required powerful patrons, loyal clients, and a 'long leg.'"[11]

This view of oil as a divisible national resource has justified maximizing its profits, as all sectors of the Nigerian economy, from individual households to small businesses and government agencies, compete for shares of the national "oil cake." In turn this reliance on petrodollars naturalizes oil's material costs, which appear as massive environmental pollution in the Niger Delta, where oil is actually extracted, and Delta claims to a share of oil benefits are rendered a challenge to the prosperity of everyone else. The mobius of oil's profit and pollution has underpinned its violent effects in the Niger Delta, where oil's contamination is concentrated and extended over time even as local residents are continuously marginalized and excluded from the benefits oil is supposed to bring to Nigeria as a whole.

In October 1990 the Ogoni, one of the Delta's many small resident ethnic groups, sent the Ogoni Bill of Rights to Nigeria's military leader Ibrahim Babangida to complain about these twinned burdens of pollution and poverty. During the 1990s, Ogoniland's plight gained worldwide attention through the efforts of Ken Saro-Wiwa, an Ogoni activist, poet, and novelist who campaigned widely for his people on both environmental and human rights grounds. A prolific writer, Saro-Wiwa published the chillingly titled *Genocide in Nigeria* only a few years before his own death at the hands of the Sani Abacha regime on November 10, 1995. In *Genocide*, Saro-Wiwa argued that the Ogoni "have been gradually ground to dust by the combined effort of the multi-national oil company, Shell Petroleum Development Company, the murderous ethnic majority in Nigeria and the country's military dictatorships."[12] In the Ogoni Bill, Garrick B. Leton, fellow activist and then-president of the Movement for the Survival of the Ogoni People (MOSOP), echoed Saro-Wiwa by bluntly summing up the Ogoni experience in a statement prefacing the bill: "Ogoni is being killed so that Nigeria can live."[13] Leton went on to describe how "the Ogoni case is of genocide being committed in the dying years of the twentieth century by multi-national oil companies under the supervision of the Government of the Federal Republic of Nigeria."[14] Though they do not use the term "state capture," Saro-Wiwa and Leton both astutely diagnosed the rampant pollution of the Niger Delta as the effect of corporations working hand in hand with the state. In Ogoniland, "all one sees and feels around is death. Death is everywhere in Ogoni."[15] Grassroots documents by other minority groups living elsewhere in the Delta, like the Kaiama Declaration of the Ijaw people or the Ikwerre Rescue Charter, testify to the way the entire Delta, and not just Ogoniland, has been similarly polluted and marginalized by the pursuit of oil.

Over decades of drilling and spilling in the Niger Delta, writers taking up the cause of local residents have recorded the extensive environmental destruction of oil and the politics of scarcity that arise from both state-corporate partnerships and national competition over oil money. These kinds of conflicts are central to Isidore Okpewho's novel *Tides* (1993), a petronovel that tracks the unequal distribution of harms that have made up Delta experience under the regime of petrodollars. Okpewho, who was both a novelist and a scholar, wrote extensively about African oral culture and folklore and taught at the University of Ibadan before moving to SUNY Binghamton. *Tides*, which won the Commonwealth Writers Prize for Africa in 1993, is his only work of petrofiction, a genre that probes the place of petroleum in society.[16]

Published only a few years after the Ogoni Bill but set during the 1970s boom years of Nigeria's oil economy, *Tides*' diegesis unfolds during a high-water mark of Nigerian affluence, which only underscores its representations of the plight of the Niger Delta.[17] As an epistolary novel, the letters that compose the body of *Tides* move between accounts of oil pollution in the Delta and political machinations and agitations around oil in the city of Lagos, Nigeria's financial capital. From almost the first page, a competitive economy is set up between the needs of Delta communities and the rest of the nation. As one fisherman notes, "Oil is money.... Money for the government. Money for many people. But not our people. And they do not mind what they do to us so long as they protect this money."[18]

At times, the fictionalized Nigerian state in Okpewho's novel appears willing to listen to vulnerable Delta communities adversely affected by oil drilling. Tonwe, as one half of the novel's epistolary team, reports that a committee is set up to "investigate the environmental and developmental problems of the oil-producing areas, and make concrete recommendations."[19] Its premise is soon undermined, though, as the committee ends up further entrenching Delta marginalization:

> [The minister] however reminded everyone that the Federal Government was committed to petroleum as the mainstay of the nation's economy, its chief source of wealth. He appealed for the cooperation of everyone concerned, both the oil companies and the communities in which they worked, toward the achievement of the government's development goals, of which petroleum was seen as the principle key.[20]

A competitive resource logic that subordinates the particularity of Delta's needs to the good of the national whole is apparent in the minister's address. Even though Delta communities are part of the "everyone" whose cooperation is needed, the minister does not actually appeal for a range of needs that might include Delta concerns. Instead, he appeals only for the government's "commitment to petroleum." Though this meeting is initially presented as a dialogue among varied groups with different priorities, that the state favors the oil money is quickly revealed. The novel here reflects the way Delta concerns are sacrificed to the commitments "everyone" should support in ways that naturalize and justify the localized environmental costs of oil.

It could be said that to some extent, *Tides'* epistolary form contradicts its pessimistic content. By offering a plurality of perspectives, the letters through which the narrative unfolds are a means for Tonwe and his narrative partner, Piriye, to debate such questions as "ethnic chauvinism" and whether Delta oil should be for the benefit of Delta ethnic groups or the nation as a whole.[21] Indeed, such debate is an affordance of epistolary novels more generally, as they privilege "sequence over closure" and are "unlikely to suggest inexorable progress towards a significant and predetermined end."[22] The epistolary novel's attention to continuity over resolution allows *Tides* to formally convey the open-ended status of these national questions in Tonwe and Piriye's exchanges. Unlike the minister's address, Piriye and Tonwe's letters suggest a flexible quality to these debates, suggesting too that the role of oil has remained undecided from the novel's temporal setting in the 1970s through its publication in the 1990s.

But such indeterminacy is closed down at the end of the novel as the state's petro-priorities become more entrenched. *Tides* ends in the middle of things, its closing epistle cut off mid-word, without being finished. This is not a hopeful irresolution, which extends the way the novel's larger epistolary form worked to unsettle the certainty of state oil hierarchies through discussion. Rather, it reads like the closure of discussions about oil. In Tonwe's last letter, readers learn that the Delta has been swamped with oil after a refinery explosion. He despairs to Piriye that "you cannot imagine how much oil is floating about now in these creeks. It is better seen than described."[23] This oil, which exceeds narrative description, also exceeds the Delta's earlier oil pollution many times over; it is the last missive readers receive about the Delta, and this condition of heightened pollution is presented as extending beyond the book's formal end. The end of Tonwe's narrative and the end of the novel's epistolary debate are reinforced materially in this total contamination of the Delta.[24] Piriye writes a few more letters from Lagos, but these are never answered, and the back and forth between Lagos and the Delta, through which the ambiguous status of claims to oil could be kept open, likewise fades. *Tides* ends with the expansion and entrenchment of the Delta's pollution and an end to debates over how to divide the benefits of oil.

The environmental violence of oil in the Niger Delta traverses many aspects of life: gas flaring changes the quality of the air, making it heavy to breathe and hot to live around. Flaring contributes to acid rain that eats through local roofing materials and damages trees. Oil spills in the rivers have devastated fish, crabs, and other local nonhuman populations. For the Ogoni, who depend on the rivers for food and who traditionally made their livelihoods from fishing, oil in the rivers has threatened communal practices and basic needs. Oil in the soil spoils traditionally cultivated root crops, and oil has gotten into water used for drinking and irrigation. Before his narrative disappearance at the end of *Tides*, Towne notes that even in the 1970s, fish catches were dwindling. Being surrounded by oil residues in the air, water, soil, and food has led to extensive bodily illnesses for Delta residents. Human life expectancy in the Niger Delta has declined to under fifty, and cancers are common, likely the result of constant exposure to the heavy metals and carcinogens in unrefined crude oil.[25] In the face of ongoing contestations over oil revenue's national cake, texts like *Tides* record the devastating effects of decades of oil drilling and spilling on Delta bodies and the environment.

Oil's material effects are laid out in even more excruciating detail in Imbolo Mbue's more recent petronovel, *How Beautiful We Were*, published in

2021. With the publication of her first novel, *Behold the Dreamers*, in 2016, which garnered a million-dollar contract from Random House and won the PEN/Faulkner award for fiction, Mbue became a breakout star in the world of African letters. *Behold the Dreamers* addressed the struggles of an African immigrant family affected by the U.S. banking crisis of 2008, but Mbue's second novel goes back to the African continent. *How Beautiful We Were* is set in a fictional African village called Kosawa that hews closely to Ogoni experiences: like Ogoniland, Kosawa is drowning in oil and locked in a David-and-Goliath fight against Pexton, a fictional oil company that resembles Shell. One of its protagonists, Thula, studies abroad and mobilizes international support for Kosawa's fight, but most of the novel is concerned with those who stay behind in Kosawa's deadly oil fields, struggling to preserve their environment and way of life with few resources and in the face of constant danger.

How Beautiful We Were opens with the contamination of the environment and the sickness of bodies: "When the sky began to pour acid and rivers began to turn green, we should have known our land would soon be dead . . . we began to wobble and stagger, tumbling and snapping like feeble little branches."[26] Bringing together the poisoning of air, earth, river, and bodies in its opening paragraph and rendering humans and nonhumans comparable through the simile of bodies and branches, Mbue's novel tracks the many deaths, across species and materials, that oil brings. Like Garrick Leton's statement in the Ogoni Bill, death is everywhere in Mbue's novel. But it registers first as the deaths of children, and it is often narrated in a collective voice that emphasizes the accumulation of deaths over time: "Within five months of Wambi's death, two of us would be dead. Those of us who survived feared our death was close; we were certain we'd be the next, though sometimes we feared we'd be the last."[27] The future conditional tense here registers the unconditional certainty of death: "Some of us cried for fear that death would arrive the next day, others for the illness that might lead to death the next month. We all knew the truth: death was at hand."[28] Rather than subjunctive possibility or open-endedness, "would" designates determinism. Mbue's novel also describes oil deaths in individual, embodied detail: the effects of breathing and drinking petroleum, the taste of kerosene in water, the way some children develop fevers, others only have coughs, some have edema, and others display few symptoms before dying. Yet the pace and variety of bodily tolls only underscore the pervasiveness of oil's devastating effects. While most Delta oil novels complain about death, Mbue's collective narrator brings the felt experience of being killed over time and cumulatively into focus.

These deaths are not, however, only a product of the effects of oil contamination on the environment. They must also be considered in relation to corporate profiteering and state capture; indeed, these go hand in hand. Outside the novel, in Nigeria, the corporations that benefit from the state's "commitment to petroleum" have overwhelmingly been multinational giants like Shell and BP as they partner in joint ventures with Nigeria's own national oil company, the Nigerian National Petroleum Corporation (NNPC). The NNPC prioritizes corporate profits and oil-drilling activity over other things that could be prioritized, like the promotion of local agriculture and fishing industries, environmental clean-up, the development of social infrastructures, or local jobs with the oil companies. These have all been proposed in Delta grassroots documents and petrofiction as alternatives to the state's myopic focus on oil revenue.

In *How Beautiful We Were*, these corporate-state partnerships are sharply critiqued. The novel's fictional oil company, Pexton, makes no attempt to hide or ameliorate its harmful activities because this is neither encouraged nor required by Mbue's fictional petrostate. The company's lawyers "wouldn't try to dispute that the waste on the big river was from their oil field."[29] Instead, "all they would need to show was evidence that our government had relieved them of any responsibility to the land and people in exchange for splitting the oil profits."[30] The corporation can ignore the village of Kosawa largely because the state allows it to. Pexton's profit is facilitated by a foundation of state-sanctioned neglect, a material effect of the way corporate priorities have captured the state. Environmental pollution is abetted by the way the state in Mbue's novel deprioritizes the villages and environments of oil country, as does the Nigerian petrostate outside the novel's pages.[31] Through this it becomes extremely clear how the Nigerian petrostate, so called because it prioritizes oil monies rather than its people, is an exemplary kind of captured state.[32]

These collusions between corporations and the Nigerian state have made the Niger Delta a notorious case of environmental injustice and an equally notorious example of state capture and corruption. This is the bad present to which oil writers and Delta activists respond and through which they imagine the state. Given the way the Nigerian state has systemically underdeveloped and impoverished the Niger Delta as well as the way it has facilitated corporate profiteering and rampant oil pollution, could it ever be viewed as more than a bad actor in the Delta? Could the state do more than enable corporate profit-making? As unlikely as it seems, the answer is yes. Even in the Niger Delta, where pollution and poverty are the underside of black gold and where environmental humanists working on the Nigerian state have focused almost exclusively on its collusive violence, the state has contradicted itself. In its early years, and again in the years after the Ogoni Bill, the state attempted to regulate the oil industry and hold companies accountable for making Ogoniland and the Niger Delta as a whole a place of death.

Pipeline Profits and Protections

As it turns out, the materiality of oil is foundational to the Nigerian state. Long before Okpewho and Mbue's novels or the Ogoni Bill's complaints about oil pollution, the Nigerian state sought to regulate corporate oil spills and minimize the possibility of pipeline ruptures. In 1956, on the eve of Nigerian independence and at the birth of the Nigerian oil industry, Nigerian leaders passed the Oil Pipelines Act, an ur-text of Nigerian oil legislation that pluralizes the Nigerian petrostate from its origins. Passed during the period of intensified self-rule that preceded formal independence from Britain in 1960, the Oil Pipelines Act also preceded the boom of Nigeria's oil industry and the environmental devastation that was produced in its wake.[33] It is especially striking as an anticipatory act of governance. The OPA both speculated that the oil industry would succeed and foresaw that local compensation and protection would be a necessary byproduct of pursuing this form of revenue. While other Nigerian laws like the Petroleum Act of 1969 pursue oil only as profit, the Oil Pipelines Act of 1956 took up the twinning of oil's profit and pollution as early matters of governance, and it shows that regulating oil companies was one of the Nigerian state's first acts. From this vantage, corporate accountability and environmental protection are not new demands found in 1990s activist literature or petrofiction, but long-standing and already-existent concrete utopias that challenge the state's own commitments to oil money. The Oil Pipelines Act contests the state's petro-present from within its own past, giving form to the plurality, surplus, and contradiction of the state itself over time.

The Oil Pipelines Act offers an example of oil governance attuned to competing needs and competing claims without the zero-sum structure of winners and losers that dominates Nigeria's more recent oil revenue practices ("Ogoni is being killed so Nigeria can live"). In its opening statement, the OPA declares itself "an Act to make provision for licenses to be granted for the establishment and maintenance of pipelines incidental and supplementary to oil fields and oil mining, and for purposes ancillary to such pipelines."[34] In other words, it set out guidelines that facilitated the business of oil companies and the national profits to be made from extracting and transporting oil. As noted in a recent court case, *The Bodo Community and Others v. The Shell Petroleum Development Company of Nigeria Limited* (2014), the OPA was meant to "provide a statutory framework for the creation of an oil industry."[35] This case cites Muhammadu Ribadu, the Minister of Land, Mines and

Power, who explicated such aims to the House of Representatives on August 2, 1956:

> I point out that mineral resources are a national asset in the hands of the Federation. . . . Mr. Speaker, Sir, I must make it clear to hon. Members that facilities must be given to these people who spend millions of pounds in order to find oil in our country, which in turn will go a long way to assist the economy of our country.[36]

The OPA was put in place before the expansion of the industry, and it assumed that the Nigerian state would want to facilitate oil extraction for the national benefit. However, the OPA simultaneously imposed nationally mandated burdens upon companies to maintain their pipelines in good order and held them liable for land damaged by oil spills if they did not. It was in violation of these premises that *Bodo v. Shell* was settled out of court for £55 million in 2014, one of the largest payouts for oil damages to date.[37] Thus, though the OPA's commitment to oil extraction may seem to naturalize the environmental costs of oil drilling and transportation, it also instituted safety measures and standards intended to minimize harm and granted agency to local communities to respond to oil spills when they arose.

The Oil Pipeline Act's basis for citizen claims to oil damage is focused in part 4, section 11, which concerns the "rights and obligations of the holder of a license."[38] Section 11(5) specifies when "the holder of a license shall pay compensation" and goes on to recognize damage to land as a basis for compensation both under a general mandate in 11(5)(a) and then more specifically for cases of land damaged by equipment neglect, leakage, or breakage in 11(5)(b) and (c). *Bodo v. Shell* assessed these specific and general provisions for claim-making as "much more generous overall for the victims than the common law in many respects. In this context, it is of course correspondingly more restrictive and onerous on the licence holder than under the common law."[39] Section 11 of the OPA articulated national safeguards and regulations for the oil industry while also offering nationally sanctioned grounds for citizens to pursue compensation when oil spills did occur. The 1956 Oil Pipelines Act enshrined these rights for local residents and the expectation that corporations would take care of their own infrastructures alongside its other guidelines for facilitating oil extraction.

How should we understand this early regulation? An ineffective counter within the state's own archive, aside from the 2014 *Bodo* case, the Oil Pipelines Act has not been applied with any stringency. Are such protective state antecedents merely farce? Do they only reinforce the triumph of the petrostate's commitment to oil money, no matter the environmental cost? A utopian reading of the Nigerian state resists such a narrative. People living under duress cannot produce the concrete utopias they want, and corporations never will. The only possible actor with the capacity to bring concrete utopias of environmental protection and corporate accountability to pass, to make them more real at scale and in a particular place, is the state. If it does so in ways that are partial and inadequate, as the Nigerian state has with the OPA, these efforts cannot simply be ignored. They are no less real than the state's failures and its violence. Utopian method refuses to treat inadequacy as a repetitive hall of endless mirrors and instead insists that plurality shadows the state at every turn.

In fact, the Oil Pipelines Act is not only important for its corporate regulations. The OPA's legislative imaginary also crucially disputes the dematerialized view of oil as "magical" profit and the competitive, zero-sum ethos that has characterized Nigeria's stance toward oil benefits. This is because the OPA legislates for oil as a material pollutant whose threat is distributed by the infrastructures of its production. In other words, it begins from an understanding of pipelines' physical exposure and fragility, in anticipation of their corrosion from oil within or from wear without. Unlike the proverbial Heideggerian hammer whose materiality becomes known by its breakdown, the Oil Pipelines Act anticipates material failure. This contrasts with more common visions of rarified pipeline production. Political theorist Timothy Mitchell has shown, for instance, that the relative lack of human labor power needed to pump and transport petroleum has made it amenable to profit monopoly by oil companies and states in ways that other forms of energy are not.[40] From this perspective, oil pipelines are seen as enclosed and separated from their surroundings. They offer "a rural landscape emptied of rural labour and of labourers . . . from which the facts of production had been banished." This description of British landscaping, originally from Marxist cultural critic Raymond Williams, applies just as well to the closed pipeline view of oil.[41] However, by contrast the Oil Pipelines Act re-embeds oil in the landscapes through which pipelines travel and repopulates the surroundings of oil production—not with those who labor on pipelines—but with those who suffer harm from oil spills.

The OPA's treatment of oil infrastructures also suggests that local vulnerabilities are generalizable to national scale. Insofar as pipelines actually cross the landscape, moving from the Delta to refineries in the southern cities of Warri and Port Harcourt to Kaduna in the north, they distribute the possibility of leakage or breakage nationwide. Re-materializing oil as distributed pollution rather than de-materializing it as revenue situates oil within the auspices of a potential shared threat, where local investments in environmental protection may end up being shared by those far from the oil fields. In this way the OPA's anticipation of oil's infrastructural risk can serve a connective purpose within Nigeria's fractured national imaginary. Environmental humanist

Ursula K. Heise has argued similarly that risk connects global and local scales. As Heise puts it, "Risk awareness has also come to reshape the imagination of the global in its environmentalist as well as other dimensions. To some extent, one could argue that . . . an awareness of ecological and cultural connectedness implies a knowledge of the kinds of risk that are generated by such connectivity."[42] Despite being written at a time when Nigeria had only three regions, the OPA's imaginative dispersal of oil's polluting risk can serve a similar connective purpose within the competitive national view of oil. It might be objected that this characterization of the threatening material properties of oil and oil pipelines seems to replace political inclusion with a kind of blunt infrastructural determinism. But inclusion continues to be elusive in the Delta, and material inclusion is better than none.

With the Oil Pipelines Act, Nigeria gave itself a multifaceted model of resource governance, one that aimed to facilitate both oil monies and protection from oil spills. Before the full-fledged development of the oil industry, the revenue narrative that oil facilitated, and the environmental wreckage that was its byproduct, the OPA institutionalized a nuanced and entangled view of oil. Its anticipatory and protective stance toward the environment can be seen as a contrary precursor to Nigeria's destructive extractivism and the petrostate that has come to support it. The OPA's conception of oil as pollutant testifies to another kind of state, a parallel state thrown forward and running alongside the current Nigerian state with its de-materialized revenue narratives and polluted sacrifice zones. It reveals that even the most entrenched state practices are never absolute and that the state is not coterminous with its dominant versions but full of plurality and contradiction over time.

This has also been borne out more recently, for the state has not only regulated oil corporations in the distant past. In 1999, nine years after the publication of the Ogoni Bill and well into its commitment to petroleum, Nigeria passed a new constitution in which the environment as a whole appeared for the first time as an object of national protection: "The State shall protect and improve the environment and safeguard the water, air and land, forest and wild life of Nigeria."[43] The 1999 Constitution was the first Nigerian constitution to mention environmental protection; other major national legislation aimed at the environment, like the Land Use Act of 1978, was primarily aimed at exploiting the land's oil and natural gas potential.[44] And in November 2005, the Federal High Court of Benin City, the capital of Edo state in the western part of the Delta, passed the kind of ruling the writers of the Ogoni Bill could only dream of: a ruling in favor of a clean environment and against the activities of oil multinationals. This case, *Mr. Jonah Gbemre v. Shell Petroleum Development Company Nigeria Limited and Others*, differed from the majority of Delta declarations and other Delta cases brought against multinational corporations, including the 2014 *Bodo* case. Other cases have focused on seeking financial compensation for oil pollution.[45] In contrast, *Gbemre* "[addressed] the relegation or outright neglect of environmental protection through the development of a robust regulatory framework."[46] The *Gbemre* case arose primarily in response to gas flaring in the Delta community of Iwherekan and argued that such flaring violated articles 33(1) and 34(1) of the new constitution. These articles fall within the "Fundamental Rights" guaranteed by the constitution and name the right to life and the right to the dignity of the human person, respectively. *Gbemre v. Shell* made a number of interrelated claims for relief against Shell's gas flaring activities in Iwherekan based on these rights, including requests that the court declare "that the Constitutionally guaranteed fundamental rights to life and dignity of human person . . . inevitably includes the right to a clean poison-free, pollution-free and healthy environment" and that gas flaring constituted a "violation of their fundamental rights to life (including healthy environment)."[47]

In a stunning reversal of petro-priorities, the High Court in Benin City agreed. It declared that the constitutional right to life did indeed include the right to a clean environment, that continued gas flaring was a gross violation of the community's rights, and it ordered that Shell stop flaring immediately.[48] The court ignored counterarguments made by Shell and granted all the forms of relief requested in the suit. This kind of order never happened during Saro-Wiwa's campaigning or in the larger movement of Delta declarations that followed the Ogoni Bill's example in the 1990s. The *Gbemre* case's ruling was, however, immediately contested. Shell appealed the ruling, and the court's order to cease gas flaring has been summarily ignored by both Shell and its partners elsewhere in the Nigerian government. As of 2019, "no cogent action has been undertaken by either the executive or legislative arm of the government to actualise its spirit" or its letter, despite the ruling or the constitutional protections that undergird it.[49] Like the Oil Pipelines Act, the *Gbemre* case has quickly become an occluded testament to a better state. And at the same time, with the OPA and the new constitution's environmental clause, the *Gbemre* case complicates the Nigerian petrostate, interrupting and exceeding its captured form.

Hailing the State: Provision and Inclusion in the Ogoni Bill

The 1956 Oil Pipelines Act and the 2005 *Gbemre* ruling were state attempts to hold oil corporations accountable for the environmental harms they produced. At the beginning of the Nigerian oil industry and again in recent years, despite the lure of petrodollars, the Nigerian state has occasionally contradicted its own revenue views of oil. What would Ogoniland be like if the OPA had been regularly enforced instead of regularly ignored? Or if the Ogoni Bill had been written after the adoption of the 1999 Constitution, with its institutionalization of environmental protection and the right to life? Perhaps Ogoniland would still be green. Nevertheless, even when it failed to protect the environment or hold corporations accountable, Delta residents and oil writers have never imagined the state exclusively as a petrostate devoted to corporate interests.

When MOSOP, the Movement for the Survival of the Ogoni People, sent the Ogoni Bill of Rights to Ibrahim Babangida in 1990, they appealed to a version of the Nigerian state very different from the one that imposed petroviolence on the Delta. The Ogoni Bill certainly responded to the logics of political marginalization and concentrated pollution that brought death to the Delta. But it also complained about the failure of material provisions and forms of political inclusion found in yet another version of the constitution, promulgated in 1979. The 1979 Constitution was instituted after the Nigerian Civil War (1967–70). It did not include environmental protections, but it did affirm goals of social provision as well as a "federal character principle" that sought to protect minority groups and facilitate fair political representation within the republic. The Ogoni Bill took up these premises in its own complaints. Like many of the Delta grassroots documents that followed it during the later 1990s, the Ogoni Bill envisioned its own future through the state, and it complained to make claims upon the state. In the wake of the OPA, when corporate responsibility and local compensation remained pipedreams and before the *Gbemre* case and the new Constitution of 1999, Delta residents like the Ogoni turned to the state to imagine their own better futures. Even as the OPA was ignored, the state was not totally captured by oil, but weakly affirmed goals like material provision and greater political inclusion for Delta residents. These concrete utopias were as urgently desired in the Delta as environmental protections. While the state failed to hold corporations accountable for spills, Ogoni complaints reveal how concrete utopias of material support and greater political inclusion offered other terms through which the Ogoni could make themselves visible in Nigeria's uneven political landscape and contest the hold of state capture.

The Ogoni Bill did this by complaining about the destitution of Ogoniland's people. It drew on affirmations of widespread material provision articulated in the 1979 Constitution's "Fundamental Directives and Objectives of State Policy," which laid out the state's economic and social goals. They included a huge range of goods the state should provide, from ensuring adequate shelter and food (article 16, section 2d), "opportunities for suitable employment" (article 17, section 3a), and "just and humane" work conditions (article 17, section 3b), to "adequate medical and health facilities for all persons" (article 17, section 3d), and free education (article 18, section 3a–d). Fundamental directives are not strictly enforceable, but they tend to lay out important aspirational principles that states want to promote.[50] These goals of widespread social provision and intervention were initially promulgated while Nigeria was under a military regime, and they may be read suspiciously as legitimating the extension of state power and control into many aspects of civilian life. But they also institutionalized state provision as an expectation Nigerians could and should have of the state regardless of the regime at the helm, much like their right to a slice of the national "oil cake."

The 1979 Constitution as a whole restructured the political economy of power in Nigeria, consolidating power in the federal center. The initial independence Constitution of 1960 had instituted a weak federal center and delegated many powers, such as controlling natural resource revenues, and duties, such as providing electricity, to the federation's regional states. But by 1979 Nigeria had emerged from the devastation of the civil war, and this constitution was written with the goal of transitioning back to civilian rule. It therefore concentrated powers for service provision and revenue distribution in the center, in what political scientist Eghosa Osaghae has described as a sort of "Father Christmas" model.[51] In their appeals to Babangida's administration, the Ogoni replicated the language of particular directives but also hailed the more general distributive role the Nigerian state had set up for itself.

For example, the Ogoni Bill posed many of the Fundamental Directives as promises the state had made but not fulfilled in Ogoniland. "In return" for the millions in oil revenue they provided to the rest of Nigeria, the bill argued that "the Ogoni people have received NOTHING."[52] This nothing included things like:

(i) No representation whatsoever in ALL institutions of the Federal Government of Nigeria;
(ii) No pipe-borne water;
(iii) No electricity;
(iv) No job opportunities for the citizens in Federal, State, public sector or private sector companies;
(v) No social or economic project of the Federal Government[53]

The complaints in this section, which range from concrete infrastructures to political representation, replicate many of the actual goals found in the Fundamental Directives. Elsewhere, complaints that focused on food scarcity or a lack of educational facilities likewise accused the state of failing to provide the goods its own directives laid out. Complaints like these are simultaneously catalogues of negativity and demands upon state power. Through the use of heightened rhetoric and capitalization ("NOTHING," "ALL") the Ogoni Bill mobilized and stressed the state's own discourses of provision in its complaints.

It is true that the constitution's provisionary frame came to seem hollow in the years after 1979. Power switched hands again between civilian and military regimes, and the constitution was for a time actually suspended. In these unstable years it is little surprise that centralized power did not result in equal provision but rather in unequal and privatized distribution, or what anthropologist Daniel Jordan Smith has called a "culture of corruption."[54] As noted earlier, *"The hero in Nigerian politics is one who brings such fruits from the Centre to his own people,"* and such practices extended throughout the many levels of state administration.[55] But in such a landscape, the state's provisionary directives and role still provided the Ogoni with an alternative and contrary locus of claim-making. Strategically and formally, the bill used the state's own provisionary parameters to demand "what ought to be, but is not" and to frame Ogoni's own imagined futures.[56] While the bill was by no means a straightforward representation of Ogoni desires, it proffered a version of Ogoni futurity that was keyed to the kinds of inclusion and provision the state had once affirmed and theoretically tasked itself with providing to all. However mediated and however negative on their surface, utopian method here means attending to the way the bill's complaints imagined different futures through, rather than apart from, the state.

And while material support was sorely needed, given Ogoniland's poverty and lack of basic amenities, the Ogoni Bill also situated its demands for provision as the rights due to "*equal* members of the Nigerian Federation who contribute and have contributed to the growth of the Federation and have a right to expect full returns."[57] This language of equality was not misplaced. The 1979 Constitution did attempt to "assure every group, state and region access to power in the federation."[58] This was a major concern of small ethnic groups, who worried that larger ethnic majorities would, on the basis of numbers, crowd them out of power, representation, and resources. In the winddown from the Nigerian Civil War, which was in part driven by ethnic separatism, the 1979 Constitution explicitly attempted to protect ethnic minorities from exploitation and to address their fears of political marginalization through mechanisms of regional state creation and a new federal character principle. Formalized in section 14(3) of the 1979 Constitution, the federal character principle specified:

The composition of the Government of the Federation or any of its agencies and the conduct of its affairs shall be carried out in such manner as to reflect the federal character of Nigeria and the need to promote national unity, and also to command national loyalty thereby ensuring that there shall be no predominance of persons from a few States or from a few ethnic or other sectional groups in that government or in any of its agencies.[59]

Like the shift to centrally disbursed revenue, the federal character principle was meant to address the many needs and players within Nigeria's federation. However polemical in tone, the Ogoni Bill echoed the federal character principle's own assertions when it stated, "In a true federation, each ethnic group no matter how small, is entitled to the same treatment as any other ethnic group, no matter how large."[60] Demands for provision were only one facet of larger Ogoni demands for equal political treatment from the state.

Ultimately, the Ogoni Bill expanded upon the state's premises of centralized distribution and ethnic power-sharing to assert "that the Ogoni people be granted POLITICAL AUTONOMY to participate in the affairs of the Republic as a distinct and separate unit by whatever name called."[61] The bill's calls for local autonomy rejected the existing configuration of Nigeria's federation, which at the time of the bill's writing had proliferated into thirty separate ethnically based regional states, each financially dependent on oil revenue extracted from the Delta. Within this distribution of ethnic states, the Ogoni did not have their own state but were included in Rivers, which "consists of several ethnic nationalities with different cultures, languages and aspirations."[62] Thanks to the 1979 Constitution's consolidation of power, the Nigerian federal center tended to distribute representation and resources from the center to these ethnically based regional states, making "the effective elements of the federation . . . neither territorial units called states nor ethnic groups, but ethnic groups with their own states."[63] By demanding autonomy within their own representative unit, the Ogoni Bill took up the state's own practices of revenue distribution and ethnic state creation to propose a place for themselves within Nigeria's federal structure.

The Ogoni did not explicitly call this distinct and separate unit an ethnically based state, but later Delta declarations inspired by the Ogoni Bill, like the Kaiama Declaration of the Ijaw peoples, did call for their own states. Such propositions may seem to embrace ethnic chauvinism and could be critiqued for perpetuating the kind of antagonistic separatism that Nigeria inherited from colonial rule and that was at work during the civil war.[64] But more than twenty years after the bill was published, the Ogoni still do not have their own state, nor do the Delta's other small minority groups. Not without their own shortcomings, Ogoni's demands for local autonomy and representative statehood take up and expand upon Nigeria's already-existing practices of ethnic federalism to imagine a polity that might work better for them.

It could easily be argued that playing by these state rules severely limited what the Ogoni could demand. Yet these state parameters also provided a particular kind of scaffolding for Ogoni visions of futurity. When state provisions and inclusions fail, as they have in Ogoniland, complaints record their popular purchase. As provisionary directives and inclusionary principles circulated between the Ogoni and the ruling regime, they indexed a specific kind of imagined state, one viewed through the potential of its absent or unfulfilled interventions. In the Niger Delta, complaints have tended to centralize around access to oil money, but they also flow out into many other demands on the state, like equal treatment for all ethnic groups. Complaining about how the state has failed them is one way in which disempowered groups like the Ogoni produce themselves as rights-bearing citizens and attempt to more fully inhabit the political goods they are entitled to but have not enjoyed.

Ogoni complaints were eventually rerouted to the international community as Saro-Wiwa stepped up campaigning to international human rights groups and environmental organizations in 1992. But before this shift, the Ogoni used state provisions as tools in hand, proposing a vision of the future that initially worked by mobilizing terms the state provided rather than turning from the state. As angry and impoverished Delta residents evoked the state outside their actual experience, they situated the state within a range of possible versions, of which the petrostate was only one. In the spill zones of Nigeria's oil wealth, where pollution and poverty stretch far into the future, for a time Ogoni activists and others utilized the state's provisionary languages and role to pursue their own goals, including concrete utopias of material support and greater political inclusion that "ought to be, but are not" in Ogoniland.[65]

Divesting from Resource Logics in *Anthills of the Savannah*

Like the Ogoni Bill, many Nigerian novels have been centrally concerned with the relationship between national resources, state governance, and political inclusion. Chimamanda Ngozi Adichie's *Half of a Yellow Sun* (2006) and Ken Saro-Wiwa's *Sozaboy* (1985), for instance, probe the material bases of sectarianism during the Nigerian civil war. But though much Nigerian fiction is committed to interrogating the political economy of oil and its violence, some novels also propose alternative kinds of states that move beyond petroleum's resource logics. One such work is Chinua Achebe's *Anthills of the Savannah*

(1987). Achebe is considered the founding father of African fiction, and during his life he was Africa's best-known novelist; indeed, there are few more towering figures in the world of postcolonial letters as a whole. With the publication of his first novel, *Things Fall Apart*, in 1958, Achebe wrote back to colonial portrayals of Africa but also rethought the role and form of the novel on the continent. Achebe famously championed the use of English in the postcolonial writer's arsenal, claiming that "I feel that the English language will be able to carry the weight of my African experience. But it will have to be a new English, still in full communion with its ancestral home but altered to suit its new African surroundings."[66] His novels are often characterized by a self-conscious and canny narrative voice that reflects his long-standing concern with the role of writers in shaping the nation and society, as well as a hybrid style that brings elements of African orature and traditional knowledge into the novel's written form. Achebe's influence has loomed, as both inspiration and constraint, over other novelists in Nigeria and well across the African continent.

Anthills of the Savannah was the last novel published in Achebe's lifetime, more than twenty years after the tetralogy of *Things Fall Apart* (1958), *No Longer at Ease* (1960), *Arrow of God* (1964), and *A Man of the People* (1966), which cover the history of Nigeria from pre-colonization to the first post-independence military coup. The intervening years included further military coups and the Nigerian civil war. It is little surprise, then, that while *Anthills of the Savannah* continued many of the aesthetic and political concerns of Achebe's previous books, it is especially focused on the challenges of post-independence unity and political leadership. *Anthills* is narrated by three elite protagonists: Commissioner for Information Christopher Oriko, newspaper editor Ikem Osodi, and Finance Ministry employee Beatrice Okoh, all of whom are metaphorically "on trial" for the plight of the country alongside its dictator, Sam. Because of this, Africanist literary scholars have tended to read *Anthills* as a fictional response to the problem of Nigerian leadership Achebe posed in the short book *The Trouble with Nigeria*: "The trouble with Nigeria is simply and squarely a failure of leadership."[67] Neil ten Kortenaar and Ali Erroutouni have argued that this book is principally concerned with critiquing the distance and alienation between Nigerian political leaders and ordinary citizens. They argue that Achebe's last novel explores the strategies and challenges of creating connection between political elites and everyday people, between the state and the nation, and between the traditional and the modern. Jennifer Wenzel takes up the opposite position to make a similar point about political distance, arguing that Achebe's interest in the problem of leadership leads him to exclude the perspective of the masses from his narrative.[68] Yet the novel's concerns about governance go beyond bridging political divides. *Anthills of the Savan-*

nah is equally cognizant of the way resources mediate political relationships, especially the relationships between ordinary citizens and the state. To this end, the novel mobilizes a resource heuristic to critique authoritarian governance's violent monopoly over resources and its repression of the subsistence needs of ordinary people. And it calls, in turn, for a state that divests from the kind of competitive, zero-sum resource logics that have been central to the Nigerian oil economy and petrostate.

This alternative state emerges largely through the subplot of Abazon, which figures doubly in *Anthills'* narrative. Abazon offers a myth of violent resource appropriation "long, long ago in legend" and simultaneously the correction and displacement of that model through a "peaceful and loyal and goodwill delegation" in the diegetic present of the story.[69] In the diegesis, Abazon is a drought-stricken region in the north of Kangan, the fictional African country where the novel is set. Its origins are related in a prose-poem, "Hymn to the Sun," which employs stylistic elements of oral narrative, most prominently apostrophe.[70] Premised by an address to the sun or "Single Eye of God," the poem opens with a meditation on violent force, both climatic and political: "Wide-eyed, insomniac, you go out at cock-crow spitting malediction at a beaten, recumbent world.... Relent then for your own sake; for that bulging eye of madness that may be blinded by soaring motes of an incinerated world."[71] This invocation to the sun seems at first an account of Kangan's climate, as the poem is introduced shortly after a radio transmission detailing the unrelenting heat and drought Abazon is experiencing. It also, however, gestures to Sam, Kangan's dictator, whom the first chapter compares to a burning sun: "And he is almost friendly and conciliatory, the amazing man. In that instant the day changes. The fiery sun retires temporarily behind a cloud."[72]

The poem's opening call to incendiary power hovers ambivalently between a metaphorical reference to unrestrained political clout and the desiccating force of the sun's heat, both of which oppress Abazon in the present. But "Hymn to the Sun" also posits a causal link between these forces, between power and drought, in its account of Abazon's history. Of Abazon's origins readers are told:

> The earth broke the hoes of the grave-diggers and bent the iron tip of their spears. Then the people knew the time had come to desert their land.... Such was the man and such his remnant fellows who one night set upon the sleeping inhabitants of the tiny village of Ose and wiped them out and drank the brown water in their wells and took their land and renamed it Abazon.[73]

It turns out that Abazon was founded explicitly out of genocidal violence, conquest, and resource appropriation. In the Abazon of legend, political power is equated with securing water, and questions of countervailing obligations or limits on appropriation are obviated by the overwhelming mandate of securing bodily survival. Unlike the control of oil in Nigeria, Abazon's control over water is presumably a matter of communal survival rather than one of economic convenience. But the same resource lessons persist: control over and access to resources is a competitive enterprise. Whether water or oil, resources cannot be shared and must be unilaterally taken.

Abazon's origins in legendary time may lend militant resource control a dubious credence. Its legitimacy becomes altogether questionable, however, in the practices of the modern Kanganian state. For in the present time of Kangan, Abazon reappears as a modern political constituency victimized by state-produced resource scarcity and political marginalization:

> Because you said no to the Big Chief he is very angry and has ordered all the water bore-holes they are digging in your area to be closed so that you will know what it means to offend the sun. You will suffer so much that in your next reincarnation you will need no one to tell you to say yes whether the matter is clear to you or not.[74]

Construed as noncompliant political troublemakers, those who invaded Ose and created Abazon for the sake of resource security have in turn become a population defined by and governed through state-induced resource scarcity. Now as then, political and environmental violence are mutually reinforcing.

Abazon's cyclic shift from resource beneficiary to resource victim and its corresponding temporal shift from mythic founding to the novel's historical present illustrate how resource control perpetuates its own violent logic over time. And yet, in *Anthills*, Abazon's victimization in the present does not generate a search for a new Ose. Rather than repeating its foundational violence, a new form of political behavior emerges. Once again faced with life-threatening drought, the people of Abazon in the diegesis, as opposed to the Abazon of extradiegetic legend, acknowledge the national government to which they are subject and to whom they must turn for redress. Zero-sum resource control and violent usurpation are no longer possible for Abazonians: "Today no one can rise and march south by starlight abandoning crippled kindred in the wild savannah and arrive stealthily at a tiny village and fall upon its inhabitants and slay them and take their land."[75] The residents of Abazon "send instead a deputation of elders to the government who hold the yam today, and hold the knife, to seek help of them."[76] Abazon's new political dispensation, of supplication and requests of aid from the state, places it within a line of historical change. Its new political strategy can be seen to mark the development of an interventionist government as well as the nation-state, whose boundaries now circumscribe the possibility of free movement across land and the genocidal violence needed to secure it. Such a shift from violence to peace and from usurpation to supplication tracks a historical shift to a world structured by bordered states, which nullifies certain earlier political possibilities of resource seizure. The political model of appropriation and conquest has, between Abazon's founding and its present, been replaced by new modes of political order and claim-making.

This shift, though, also suggests that the violent model of Abazon's founding has become anachronistic. Abazon's movement from an atemporal "legend" to a political actor within the modern time of Kangan suggests that the role of political power is now provisionary rather than appropriative. Indeed, an Abazonian delegation has gone to Bassa, Kangan's capital, "personally to invite [Sam] to pay them a visit and see their problems."[77] Sam refuses, but like the Ogoni Bill, this civilian request hails the state's ability to promote bodily survival and provide desired resources. In the time of legend, the need to survive justified resource violence, and Abazon's delegation in the present presents their subsistence needs as no less of a mandate. It is, however, one they approach through expectations of provision and mutual obligation rather than force. The delegation leader notes, "It is proper that a beggar should visit a king," the assumption being that the king recognizes the beggar and his needs, that power recognizes the terms by which it is supplicated and responds to address them.[78] Abazon's delegation assumes that its requests for state provision will not be refused or result in the kind of annihilation that happened at Ose. In the governing model to which Abazon now adheres, something like a welfarist social contract is apparent, where needs and obligations structure the political behaviors of civilians and rulers.

Abazon's delegation members further underscore this expectation by positioning themselves as novices within a modern order of reciprocal political duties and recognition whose rules must be learned: "We do not fully understand the ways of today yet but we are learning. . . . So we are ready to learn new things and mend our old, useless ways."[79] A new role for the state plays out in the temporal shift of Abazon's signification. While Kangan is still dominated by a resource-appropriative and authoritarian state, Abazon's counterpoint of peaceful appeal and temporal development asserts the untimeliness and "uselessness" of violent rule in "the ways of today," if not its actual end. In figuring state provision within a temporal trajectory, Achebe promotes more welfarist political responses while eroding the seeming unchangeableness of practices like resource hoarding and authoritarian violence. Postcolonial scholar Neil ten Kortenaar has noted that the meaning of Abazon in *Anthills* is ambivalent, since it shifts in scale spatially between a single village and an arid region in Kangan's north.[80] Kortenaar reads such spatial slippages for the way Abazon addresses different levels of national fragmentation. But Abazon can equally be understood through its temporal slipperiness. Its modern iteration asserts the anachronism of authoritarian violence in the time of interventionist states and thus the untimeliness of states that continue to rule by force.

In addition to providing a temporal critique of authoritarianism, the modernized version of Abazon also allows Achebe to critique states that withdraw from their people. *Anthills of the Savannah* in fact opens with a discussion of Abazon in the present, where it functions less like a temporal rebuke and more like a call for an alternative kind of state that is politically accessible and responsive. *Anthills* opens in a closed cabinet meeting where readers are given privileged access to a cloistered realm of shut windows, air conditioning, and unilateral decisions. Sam, Kangan's dictatorial leader, has just declared, "YOU'RE WASTING everybody's time, Mr. Commissioner for Information. I will not go to Abazon. Finish! *Kabisa!*"[81] This refusal comes in response to Commissioner for Information Chris Oriko's suggestion that Sam visit Abazon to assess the drought.

As dictatorial fiat, *"Kabisa"* should do things in the world. *Kabisa* as authoritarian speech act should mold external circumstances to Sam's will. And yet, the whole first chapter enacts a questioning of this kind of unilateral decision-making and refusal of citizen address. Chris begins by mentally satirizing Sam's cabinet meetings, where decisions of state are enacted through "ceremonial capitulation" by the cabinet.[82] When Sam exits the meeting, he is forced back into the room moments later by the sounds of a "chanting multitude" that turns out to be the goodwill delegation of Abazonian elders as well as "Abazon indigenes in Bassa: motor mechanics, retail traders, tailors, vulanizers, taxi- and bus-drivers . . . and others doing all kinds of odd jobs or nothing at all in the city. A truly motley crowd!"[83] Abazon has come to the capital, and its "chanting multitude" answers the regime's silence and failure to acknowledge its requests for aid with an insurgent demand for recognition. As Sam puts it, "They want personally to invite me to pay them a visit and see their problems."[84] This invitation and the need for environmental redress within it continue to reverberate against the finality of Sam's refusal. Things are not finished, and *Kabisa* as a failed speech act highlights the illegitimacy and instability of dictatorship.

Over the course of the story, all three of Achebe's elite narrators forge bonds and relationships with ordinary citizens, and at the end of the novel Sam has been killed. But so too have newspaper editor Ikem Osodi and Commissioner for Information Christopher Oriko. The only narrator left alive is Beatrice Okoh, who works in the Finance Ministry. Notable for being the only female narrator and a woman in a rare position of power, she brings together another "motley crowd" of diverse citizens under her own responsive leadership at novel's end. Beatrice is, readers are told, "a captain whose leadership was sharpened more and more by sensitivity to the peculiar needs of her company."[85] Beatrice's sensitivity and responsiveness to the people pose her as a foil to Sam's monolithic will, and the community she facilitates is itself represented as a hybrid household, made up of members from different classes, genders, professions, ethnicities, and religions.[86]

Though it is tempting to read this household as a feminized alternative that posits chosen kin or private community in lieu of the public nation, Beatrice's household can equally be read as an allegory *for* an ideal nation, because it depicts just the kind of integrated community that neither Kangan nor Nigeria has been able to fully achieve.[87] In *Reading Chinua Achebe*, postcolonial literary critic Simon Gikandi noted that throughout his career Achebe was invested in the nation-state as the future of African political life and in the novel's role in facilitating a common sense of national identity. Achebe's closing household in *Anthills of the Savannah* once again affirms this message by proposing a symbolic model for an inclusive nation-state and showing how it might function. Achebe thus ends *Anthills of the Savannah* with a microcosm of his ideal polity, adding to the novel's critique of violent governance an allegorical polity that contains diverse members and unifies their conflicting interests under good state leadership.

Achebe's closing community also underscores the importance of shared participation and equal membership because it coheres around the birth of a child, paradigmatic symbol of the future.[88] Amaechina is the daughter of Elewa, a market woman, and newspaper editor Ikem Osodi, one of the elite narrators. Amaechina embodies the harmonious mingling of elites and commoners that is also modeled more widely in Beatrice's hybrid household. Together the household names Amaechina and assumes collective parental duties over her. By embracing Amaechina outside traditional bounds of filiation and eschewing a priori social roles or categorical group affiliations, the household offers a model of democratic inclusion and collective life. These values are also enacted by the polyvocal exchange that closes the novel:

> "What brings us here is the child [God] sent us. May her path be straight . . ."
>
> "*Isé!*" replied all the company.
>
> "May she have life and may her mother have life."
>
> "*Isé!*"
>
> "What happened to her father, may it not happen again."

"Isé!"

"When I asked who named her they told me All of Us. May this child be the daughter of all of us."

"Isé!"

"May all of us have life!"

"Isé!"

. . . .

"Everybody's life!"

"Isé!"

"The life of Bassa!"

"Isé!"

"The life of Kangan."

"Isé!"[89]

This call and response sequence recreates the participatory style of African oral culture and appears as a communal catharsis to the violence and loss that preceded it under Sam's rule.[90] As the exchange goes on, it becomes progressively more expansive: it moves from calling for the futurity and well-being of Amaechina and Elewa as individuals to a more general call for the well-being of All of Us, a proper noun that at first seems to denote the members of the household and the political alternative they represent. But "all of us" is also repeated without capitalization, shifting to an improper noun that no longer designates a specific recipient or beneficiary of "life" and instead might invite and encompass all the citizens of Kangan, which the exchange goes on to do in its hailing of "The life of Bassa" and "The life of Kangan." This sequence thus moves from addressing specific members to embracing the national whole within a dialogic community that shares in a common "life."

Yet at the same time, Achebe's inclusive vision of political change is incomplete. For he proposes only a political solution to what was an ecopolitical problem, leaving aside the environmental privation that motivated his earlier critique of authoritarianism. While Abazon moves in an arc from violent conquest to peaceful claim-making, from legendary atemporality to the modern time of the nation-state, the resource scarcity that prompted both its founding and its turn to state supplication drops out of the novel's democratic conclusion. Abazon's delegation aligns with the goals of a politically inclusive future, but there is little indication that Achebe's ideal polity addresses, or even acknowledges, either Abazon's contribution to governmental reform or the environmental hardship it continues to endure. Indeed, the novel's closing community is heavily associated with the life of Bassa, Kangan's urban center.[91] Democracy might have metaphorically replaced authoritarianism, but it never reaches the "heart of the disaster" in rural, desiccated Abazon.[92] Abazon's drought remains an unresolved and unaddressed disaster outside the novel's vista of reformed state leadership and national community. The problem of resources is thus an environmental remainder in *Anthills'* political imaginary of a better state.

Recursion and Alternatives in *How Beautiful We Were*

Imbolo Mbue's petronovel *How Beautiful We Were* also thinks seriously about alternative states. Rather than divesting from authoritarian violence and resource logics, however, this novel turns to political plurality and nonlinear time to rethink the possibilities of the state. In Mbue's novel, as noted earlier, the state colludes with corporations. It is largely metonymized through His Excellency, an allegorical dictator who views the country as his personal "property" and who "harvests whatever pleases him and destroys whoever displeases him."[93] Yet the novel nonetheless at times separates His Excellency from other state officials and state institutions, and it complicates its own dominant portrayal of state capture and corruption with a plethora of other engagements with the state.

Like Achebe's novel, *How Beautiful We Were* is narrated by a rotating cast of characters. Rather than political elites, Mbue focuses her story through different members of the village of Kosawa, each of whom sheds light on particular aspects of its collective experience, its history, and its long fight against oil pollution. This narrative multiplicity allows the novel to assess many diverse responses to Pexton's oil drilling. These include the suggestion of Konga, the village madman, that Kosawa must save itself by asserting sovereignty over its land; the many other villagers who ridicule Konga and argue that this is both dangerous and impossible; Thula, who earns a scholarship to study abroad and partners with lawyers and NGO groups to bring suits against Pexton in American courts; and the Five, a group of young men from the village who begin assassinating Pexton workers to vent their rage. But the narrative also includes those who turn to the state for help.

Arguing about the people in the capital city of Bézam, Lusaka, who lost his two sons to Pexton's poisons, insists that "we know Bézam is where evil has built its house and where it raises its children. But we also know that good men live there."[94] So too Malabo, Thula's father, goes to Bézam to petition the government after his son Juba dies and is brought back to life by the local medicine man: "And what did he die from? From something the government can put an end to."[95] Malabo vows not to return until he has received "a guarantee from the government and Pexton that our land would be restored to what it was before Pexton arrived."[96] Malabo and Lusaka do not see the state as an impenetrably corrupt bureaucracy or coextensive with His Excellency, but rather suggest, "Is the government not humans like us—people who have children, mothers and fathers who know what it's like to have a sick child?"[97] Indeed, when they arrive in Bézam, Malabo and his companions are aided by Gono, a Pexton worker but also the son of their local chief, or *woja*, who takes them to two health ministry employees. After meeting with the employees, Malabo and his companions disappear, and their fate can only be surmised by their families and the readers. Malabo's end reinforces the monolithic and violent perception Kosawa has of the state as a whole, yet his meeting with the health ministry suggests that things could have ended differently. Such possibilities are raised and extinguished time and again, yet their prevalence in the novel challenges Kosawa's primary experience of the state as an institution that "cared nothing for the welfare of its people."[98]

Likewise, when Malabo's brother Bongo is arrested after the villagers take Pexton workers hostage some years later, a trial date is eventually set. Upon hearing this, the villagers

> rejoiced. We prayed the Four would get sagacious judges before whom they would prove their innocence. . . . We would accept any sentence. We would ask only that it be fair, that the crimes of those who had pushed us into our transgressions be considered first if those who judged us were to call themselves just.[99]

The possibility of a fair trial, where Bongo and Kosawa's actions would be assessed alongside the violence Pexton has imposed on them, initially frames the villagers' hopes for the trial. They assume they have a chance at justice and a fair hearing, where the crimes of both parties will be considered.

This possibility, too, is raised only to be foreclosed. Instead, the village delegation that travels to Bézam learns that Bongo and his companions (collectively called the Four) were executed even before they arrived for the trial. The letter they receive from the government makes a mockery of the national court system and Bongo's actual death: "We wish to inform you that the four accused were hanged to death earlier this week. . . . Our fair and balanced team of judges, representing the people of our country, deliberated for hours after listening to all witnesses, including the kidnap victims and the accused, before finding the accused guilty."[100] The bureaucratic, impersonal language ("we wish to inform you") and passive voice ("were hanged") underscores the deadly irony of the letter, highlighting the distance between the fair trial it describes and what actually happened—a closed sentencing. While the delegation from Kosawa arrived expecting to witness the trial of their kinsmen under the deliberation of "sagacious judges," what they receive is a fait accompli of the state's unilateral sentencing. Indeed, Mbue's kangaroo court replicates in many ways the closed trial and trumped-up charges under which Saro-Wiwa and eight other Ogoni activists were falsely accused and sentenced to death under the Abacha regime in 1995.[101]

These pursuits of state petitioning and state justice seem on their surface to only reinforce the state as a bad actor, to reinstall the perception that Mbue's fictional state is only a petrostate that "cared nothing for the welfare of its people."[102] Yet from the perspective of utopian method, such disappointing, patently negative elements can also be read against the grain for the potentials they reveal. As the novel details all the ways the state has failed, it also maps its opposite, providing a vision of what better, alternative states could be like. A state that could have responded to citizen appeals to clean the environment, worked to counteract Pexton's pollution, and offered a fair trial that accounted for both sides appears in the text, but only in the negative. Indeed, though it contains other possibilities that may seem more appealing, like international pressure, local sovereignty, or armed resistance, the novel's many and varied engagements with the state cannot be overlooked. Through all these experiments the novel itself adopts something like utopian method, refusing to accept the singularity or inevitability of the state's existing practices and forms.

In fact, despite the disappointments it records, *How Beautiful We Were* also proposes large-scale alternatives to His Excellency's dictatorial regime and thinks seriously through possibilities for changing the state. Like the other possibilities that fill the novel, these explicit alternatives appear and are shut down; nevertheless, they attest to what Ernst Bloch has called the pursuit of a "surplus . . . over and above what has been attained," a process of *"contradicting the badly existing"* that saturates the novel.[103] Both Thula, who comes closest to being the novel's protagonist, and her brother Juba, who died and was brought back to life, work to change the state from within. Having gained political consciousness about resisting injustice while living abroad, Thula returns home to advocate for Kosawa. Her foreign credentials land her a position in the top ranks of government educators, and Thula uses her position to rally students and friends against the authoritarianism of His Excellency: "Our voices will be the fire that will burn down every system of injustice, and from the ashes will we build a new nation."[104] Her incendiary rhetoric is, however, coupled with peaceful means. Thula does not advocate assassination, violent resistance, or a coup but instead works to facilitate the country's first democratic elections. Citing experiences of unjust violence happening elsewhere in the country, Thula hopes that people might realize "they have choices, they can do something about their government."[105] Democratic change is stymied both because His Excellency rigs the election results, returning a favorable ruling for himself, and because some of Thula's associates, known as the Five, do turn to violence, including the murder and kidnapping of oil workers. At the end of the novel, Thula and the Five have been killed and discredited, and news outlets outside the country present them all as dangerous radicals. Picking up only on Thula's incendiary rhetoric, her utopian vision of democratic change is buried.

In contrast, Thula's brother Juba seeks to "climb to the top of the government."[106] Admitted to the government leadership school, he proposes an equally ambitious alternative to His Excellency's autocratic state:

> I told her about all the ways my being in government could help villages like Kosawa. What the country needed was a government made of people like us, those who had suffered the consequences of bad policies and knew how things ought to be.... We would use our abundant wealth for healthcare, for education, jobs creation.... Wasn't it evident, I asked her, that good government was the solution to the ills of our nation? I told her I believed we could do it, our generation. We could be the ones to uplift and equalize, no citizen greater or lesser than another. We could create a beautiful country. But first we had to wait our turn.[107]

Juba essentially envisions a welfare state, one committed to providing social goods like healthcare, education, and jobs to all citizens. He evokes state resources turned to good distribution, but he also believes that change cannot be forced; in contrast to Thula's active campaign, he believes those who want to change the state must "wait their turn." Eventually, though, Juba yields to the existing system rather than following through on his alternative plan. He climbs to the head of the state's distributive apparatus, the national taxation office, but "abscond[s]" with riches for himself and his family rather than redistributing resources outward.[108] So Juba's vision for a distributive welfare state is co-opted into the existing system, while Thula's democratic project is cut short by her death. Yet the novel refuses to fully close down either alternative. *How Beautiful We Were* instead returns to both these possibilities, enacting in its narrative structure an idea proposed earlier in the story: "How can we know that a strategy won't prove itself worthwhile generations after being deemed a failure?"[109] It turns, in short, to recursion, a utopic way of reading history where the past repeats with a difference to unsettle both the present and the future. These repetitions, as Stoler pointed out, *"fold back on themselves* and, in that refolding, reveal new surfaces, and new planes. Recursions open to novel contingent possibilities."[110] In the face of persistent corruption and the ongoing rule of His Excellency, Juba and Thula's alternative states might appear as extinguished possibilities; but utopian method suggests such potentials and past proposals cannot be dismissed just because they were not achieved in a given moment.

In fact, the novel's entire narrative architecture reveals a utopic commitment to recursion and the ongoing salience of past possibilities. This is particularly visible in the perspective of the novel's collective narrator, The Children. While individual characters like Juba and Thula narrate interim sections, the novel opens and closes with The Children. The Children offer a communal perspective but more crucially a perspective that spans long eras of time. Earlier I considered how this collective narrator voiced the cumulative toll of oil deaths in Kosawa. But The Children also narrate the last chapter of the novel, where, instead of offering a kind of "final coherence," they resurrect past possibilities that were once cut short.[111] They end the novel with a cyclical return, not to simple repetition but precisely to the kinds of alternatives that make up the novel's imaginary about oil resistance and about the state, alternatives with which the novel undoes The Children's formal position of ending the narrative:

> Often, while visiting our children in Bézam, or America, or Europe, we sit on the couch, looking at the television but not seeing it. We're there, but we're not there. We're somewhere else, thinking of Kosawa, thinking of Thula. We're wondering if Thula would still be fighting if she were alive. It's at such moments that the children of our children come to us and say, please, Yaya, please, Big Papa, tell us a story.[112]

Thula's unfinished story of political change reappears at the end of the novel. Its end was not an end, but instead a future alternative that was cut short and might return. This evocation of Thula as the novel's closing story works like what queer theorist José Esteban Muñoz, speaking in a different context, has called a utopian "backward glance that enacts a future vision" and is "propelled by a desire for futurity."[113] Thula's vision, and by extension Juba's, are generative antecedents or recursive possibilities that contest ongoing forms of state violence. These alternatives are condensed in this reference to Thula's unfinished fight, and neither are invalidated because they did not come to pass the first time. Such an orientation toward political change echoes the novel's more general formal commitments to scrambling linear time and contesting the finality of endings. In this way, Mbue's narrative structure shares with utopian method a commitment to the positive potentials within patently negative circumstances and an understanding that "past, present, and future" are not "discrete time frames" but tangle together to create contingency.[114] The slow violent present of oil pollution and political authoritarianism is constantly contested by the novel's enactments of political alternatives that may "prove [themselves] worthwhile" in the future. Imbolo Mbue's novel thus foregrounds the affordances of utopian method for political change and refuses both authoritarianism and a petrostate by foregrounding political plurality across time.

Mbue's fictional alternatives, raised but not achieved, share much in common with the possibilities of corporate regulation, material provision, and political inclusion that were once proposed but have not come to pass in Nigeria. Between the corporate accountability envisioned in the 1956 Oil Pipelines Act and efforts to protect the environment and curtail corporations after 1999, the Nigerian state institutionalized aspirations to a wide range of social services, affirming centralized provisions and ethnic protections that it never really fulfilled. Nonetheless, these alternatives to the petrostate persist in the Nigerian state's own archive, in petrofiction, and in the complaints of Delta residents who imagine the Nigerian state beyond its capture by oil money. In these archives, concrete utopias of provision, inclusion, and environmental protection appear as testaments to other states that have not disappeared but might "ignite" again in the future.[115] As they continue to accumulate in the decades since oil was struck at Oloibiri, these possibilities insert plurality into the Nigerian state's ongoing petroviolence, making the state visible as an imagined form whose better versions are not yet achieved but also not erased by the state capture still at work today.

3
Undoing Apartheid
Water Pasts and Futures in Cape Town

Water is the basis of life on earth. It makes up 60 percent of the human body on average and covers 71 percent of the earth's surface. But only about 3 percent of the planet's water is fresh. And of that, a precious *half percent* can be accessed and used.[1] As fossil-fueled climate change heats the world's atmosphere, freshwater is dwindling. Winters are becoming milder, producing less snowfall. Evaporation is speeding up, and rainfall patterns are changing. In some places this means torrential and unseasonable floods. In others, it means drought. Desertification is in fact one of the most alarming effects of human-induced climate change, as the edges of deserts creep outward into savannahs and drylands. Countless plant and animal species are facing shifting habitats and waning supplies of drinkable water. And so, too, are the planet's most vulnerable humans. It is estimated that two billion people already do not have reliable access to clean freshwater for drinking, and roughly half the world's population experiences serious water stress for parts of the year.[2] When water is life, a desiccated planet is a dying one.

Corporations are at both ends of this drying of the earth. Fossil fuel companies continue to greenwash their own activities to keep up consumption and gaslight the world's consumers into thinking there is no alternative to fossil fuels, an idea as false from the mouth of petroleum executives as it was when Margaret Thatcher argued there was no alternative to the free market. And while their partners in the fossil fuel industry drive the carbon emissions that are turning the world to desert, a handful of corporations such as Saur International and Thames Water are stepping in to make the worst of a precarious situation by privatizing water.[3] Initiatives to privatize public water have skyrocketed since the 1990s as earlier arguments against market control of water have been replaced with arguments about state failure. These often hinge on the state's lack of "efficiency" and its inability to maximize water's "highest market value."[4] This shift is symptomatic of a more pernicious underlying change, one where water is increasingly viewed as a commodity rather than a public good. Could anything be more collectively suicidal? The very idea of turning public water into a tradable object should send a shiver down the spine, a visceral clench in the gut, because no amount of PR or market logic can change the basic fact that water is life.

The influence of biopolitical theories has by now made it commonplace to think about how life is regulated to unequally impose death on some populations. But the scaled-up potential of such practices is nowhere balder than in the turn to privatizing water. Water privatization turns capitalism's commodifying modus operandi into the rule that if you can pay for your life, you will, and the poor cannot. Corporations, motored by the bottom line, do not subsidize water for marginalized groups, try to ensure it is equitably distributed, or lay water pipes in slums and shantytowns. Indeed, in 2002 J. F. Talbot, chief executive of Saur International, the fourth-largest water company in the world, stated that water could not be delivered to poor areas because "the scale of the need far out reaches the financial and risk taking capacities of the private sector."[5] Here as elsewhere, corporations ignore the consequences and externalities—that is, the massive forms of privation and suffering—that result from capitalism's profit myopia. Water privatization erodes collective rights and threatens physical needs because corporations view everything, including water, as a source of profit and not as a human right, a global commons, or the basis of life. Of all the things that could be done with freshwater on a drying planet, what could be worse?

But the triumph of water privatization is not entrenched everywhere. In Italy, Ireland, and elsewhere in Europe, assemblages of water activists have fought to preserve water as a public good.[6] Water privatization efforts in the Indian cities of Bangalore and Delhi collapsed after vehement public opposition, and in Mumbai, anthropologist Nikhil Anand has shown that slum residents exerted "pressure" on state officials to keep the city's water public.[7] In South Africa, too, distributing water has remained a state prerogative, foundational to the African National Congress's platform before it took power in 1994, and a goal the state has progressively worked toward ever since the apartheid transition. But if putting conditions on water access is a rising global trend, in South Africa it is also old. In South Africa, extending water infrastructure has been a major cornerstone of the post-apartheid state precisely because it was once racially segregated. Under apartheid, the South African state divided access to water by race, laying pipes in white areas and not in Black townships, dividing and engineering society as much through infrastructure as through its more infamous pass books.

This history of racial inequality is only being exacerbated by climate change's water scarcity, in what I call an "Anthropocene conjuncture." Anthropocene conjunctures name the way new challenges from human-induced climate change meet with and intensify older, pre-existing forms of inequality. In South Africa, this kind of conjuncture was dramatized during Day Zero, when the city of Cape Town was predicted to run out of water after three years of drought in 2015–18. As a climate event, Day Zero suggested multiple ends at once. African studies scholar Nick Shephard has described it as the "idea of a countdown, the scene of a disaster (ground zero) and an apocalyptic end-time (the end of days)" that brought together "anxieties about the future" with "conditions on the ground."[8] Day Zero was in many ways an unprecedented experience of urban water scarcity produced by climate change. But it also brought together future and past by exacerbating apartheid's historic water inequalities. As an Anthropocene conjuncture, Day Zero signaled the collision of multiple histories in struggles over urban water.[9]

Water struggles predate Day Zero in part because transition away from apartheid has been highly compromised. The triumphalist narrative of a democratic "new South Africa" has come to be marred by perceptions of incompletion or suspension as Black and Coloured South Africans continue to be excluded from economic opportunities and material access to basic infrastructures like piped water. In this view of the present, the liberatory potential of just and inclusive rule after South Africa's transition to democracy has fizzled, leaving behind ongoing injustices still largely shaped by apartheid's racist segregations. In this disappointing present, exclusion from political participation and economic agency is indexed in the continuing material inequalities that characterize South African life, especially regarding services like housing and water. These legacies in turn have made encroaching climate change effects like water scarcity even more burdensome for poor and Black South Africans. The continuities between apartheid and its transition exacerbate the racialized burdens of climate change and contribute to narratives of failed political change.

And yet, the new South African state has pursued countless forms of social improvement and material provision since taking power, especially with regard to the very water infrastructures that also mark its limits.[10] In the post-transition, the state has enacted a constellation of extensive policy reforms, legislative initiatives, and infrastructure projects that extend greater social inclusion, political recognition, and material equality to all citizens, with a special focus in this chapter on housing and water. The state's goals of undoing apartheid and producing a more democratic and inclusive South Africa are incomplete, but many of its actions reveal how it has pursued concrete utopias or specific forms of betterment that have had profound effects on the lives of the nation's Black citizens. Undoing apartheid is necessarily a gradual process; systemic injustice can by no means be transformed overnight or even in a few decades. And yet, the fact is that concrete utopias of better access to water and greater political inclusion are progressively coming to pass. Achieved for some, still unfulfilled for many, like toxicity and oil pollution in the earlier parts of this book, water scarcity in Cape Town "carries and surfaces state-citizen relations" as demands for water mediate relations with the state before and after the end of apartheid.[11]

This longer history of state intervention throws the Anthropocene conjuncture of Day Zero into a new light. Day Zero was predicted to herald an apocalyptic future of dry taps and social conflict. But faced with the threat of running out of water, Cape Town's government did not turn to privatization, and it did not impose further restrictions on poor residents in the townships. In the face of unprecedented drought, the state instead disciplined its wealthy white residents, the very groups of citizens who continue to benefit from apartheid's ongoing legacies. During Day Zero, Cape Town's leaders deployed a range of disciplinary procedures to curb the water consumption of affluent water users. While the state could have responded to water scarcity by blaming the city's Black residents or by turning to corporate solutions, it instead attempted to continue providing water for all by focusing on those who used the most. From this vantage, Day Zero was not only an Anthropocene conjuncture in which climate change–induced drought exacerbated existing water scarcity. Nor was it only the prediction of an apocalyptic end times, the kind of times the planet as a whole is moving toward as water becomes scarcer. It was also another opportunity to chip away at the apartheid past, to intervene once again in the infrastructural and material inequalities that still obtain between whites and Blacks in South Africa. In Cape Town, state intervention ensured more just water futures, but this was only the latest move within a gradual, concretely utopian endeavor of undoing apartheid's legacies.

Apartheid Continuities and Anthropocene Conjunctures

Before we can consider how the South African state has worked to undermine the apartheid system it inherited, both during and before Day Zero, we must consider the legacies of apartheid that continue to constrain South Africa's present. Apartheid is well known as a racist state project, a system of race-based segregation and white minority rule that divided nearly all aspects of South African life. Since the mid-twentieth century, the apartheid regime sought to engineer a racially divided society that benefitted the white minority, racializing everything from political rights to infrastructural access to the occupation of space.[12] Citizenship under apartheid was explicitly racialized, and indigenous Black Africans were even deemed "foreigners" in white areas; many policies such as pass books and the Group Areas Act of 1950 sought to control the movement of Black bodies in space for the sake of white industry.[13] Black Africans were relocated to remote and inhospitable rural "homelands" without viable agriculture or industry or confined to equally inhospitable townships in urban centers. Townships were not spaces for community life but intended as temporary lodgings for transient Black labor. Filled with dormitories and laid out according to military-style grids, townships generally lacked infrastructural amenities like water taps; services like electricity were provided not in residences but first for public streetlights to facilitate surveillance at night.[14] If apartheid is perhaps first thought of as a racist form of governmentality where white supremacist rule and white wealth were systematically built on Black oppression, it also operated materially, through the production of certain kinds of infrastructures, by policing access to basic amenities like water and housing, and through the regulation of Black African bodies in space.[15]

Racial exclusions continue to plague the new South Africa, manifesting in ongoing inequalities in rights, wealth, and employment but most importantly here, in unequal access to basic needs like housing and piped water. Such continuities challenge and undermine narratives of the "miracle" of South Africa's transition from apartheid to its first democratically elected and Black-led government under Nelson Mandela in 1994. When Mandela and the African National Congress (ANC) came to power, they set out to address and rectify apartheid's sprawling system of racial inequity and inequality. But even from the outset many of these attempts were compromised. Of the numerous indications that the post-apartheid state would not in fact break cleanly from its predecessor, commentators have often focused on the Growth, Employment, and Redistribution (GEAR) Act passed only two years into Mandala's presidential term. Despite the last word in its title, the GEAR Act followed a neoliberal blueprint. Positioning social redistribution as a trickle-down effect of economic development rather than integrating the two, it stressed the creation of jobs, a competitive economy, and restructuring the public sector for "efficiency" rather than redistribution.[16]

As such, the GEAR Act sharply departs from earlier positions articulated by the ANC in its Reconstruction and Development Programme (RDP), which focused explicitly on redistributing resources and reckoning with the racialized nature of South African society. This chapter will turn to the RDP later. For now, we should note that for many the GEAR Act symbolized continuity with the apartheid regime or what sociologist Patrick Bond has criticized as an "elite transition" worked out between the ANC and global capitalist actors like the World Bank that curtailed the imperatives of social and economic redistribution that once made up the ANC's platform.[17] This elite transition left wealth still concentrated in white hands, and to this day South Africa remains economically stratified. Especially in Cape Town, often dubbed South Africa's most unequal city, "race and class coincide."[18] Wealthy whites and poor Blacks coexist in close proximity in the post-apartheid city in ways that replicate apartheid disparities.

Policies like GEAR and the hierarchical racial inequalities it left intact contribute to what has been called the "suspended" transition or "incomplete liberation" of South Africa's post-apartheid society.[19] For though the political transition from white rule is rightly lauded as a decisive accomplishment, economic and material change for the Black majority has been much more incomplete. Anthropologists like Jean and John Comaroff describe this dynamic as the twinning of "liberation and liberalization" in South Africa.[20] Apartheid continuity manifests in many different ways, including slum clearances reminiscent of apartheid relocation campaigns.[21] But significantly for this chapter, since 2004 widespread protests over state infrastructural services like water, housing, and sanitation have erupted across the country and occurred in Cape Town perhaps most spectacularly in July 2013. Dubbed the "poo wars" in local newspapers, angry protesters emptied buckets of sewage at central locations to protest the lack of sanitation in the city's townships.[22] These Cape Town protests were one part of a larger trend of South African service delivery protests. The protests are commonly understood to manifest "disappointment with the fruits of democracy" and feelings of abandonment by the state, even though formal political rights have been extended to all.[23]

In the context of a post-apartheid present deemed too much like the apartheid past, service delivery protests mark the continuity of apartheid's material inequities and the place of state-based infrastructures in them. In South Africa, as geographer Charlotte Lemanski and others have noted, "the provision and maintenance of infrastructure is intrinsically connected to citizenship identities and practices."[24] This is because, given apartheid's history of segregation, government services in South Africa are not mundane. Rather, they are deeply desired and symbolic: "In South Africa the definition [of service delivery] certainly is more encompassing and includes not only the ability to provide users with services needed or demanded, but also a sense of redress; that the services should raise the standard of living of the majority and confirm their citizenship in the new South Africa."[25] Once denied to the Black majority, infrastructural services like urban water supply have, in the post-apartheid present, become one way to track the expansion of state recognition and social inclusion—or their failures and limitations. The protests that have erupted since 2004 are symptomatic of widespread perceptions among Black citizens that they are still excluded from full political belonging and state recognition. Perceptions of the post-transition present are thus mediated by infrastructures and experienced through service disparities. When viewed through unequal access to water, the postcolonial, post-apartheid state has not only failed to change apartheid's legacies but has in fact perpetuated them in ways that continue to disempower the Black majority. Policing access to water or failing to provide water was once a hallmark of apartheid repression. In the post-apartheid present, the continuing inadequacy of water access and water infrastructure is one way the limitations of democratic transition appear in everyday life.

While activists and ordinary citizens have taken to the streets to demonstrate outrage over the limits of the "new South Africa," South African writers have been concerned with the way the triumphalist narrative of apartheid's overcoming has faded into a disappointing present where "endings and inaugurations compete simultaneously for recognitions."[26] African literature scholar David Attwell and postcolonial critic Barbara Harlow note that this "discomfort of compromise" makes up South Africa's "larger predicament" and preoccupies post-apartheid literature as a whole.[27] The compromises and limits of South Africa's transition are widespread in post-apartheid literature and feature prominently in two novels published about a decade apart: Henrietta Rose-Innes's *Nineveh* (2011) and K. Sello Duiker's *Thirteen Cents* (2000). In *Nineveh* and *Thirteen Cents*, the limits of South Africa's transition and the continuing racial and class exclusions of Cape Town, in particular, appear in relation to state-based services like housing and water. But unlike service delivery protests, these novels also register Anthropocene conjunctures: the way ongoing apartheid inequalities collide with and exacerbate the burdens of climate change for Cape Town's Black urban communities.

Rose-Innes is an established name in South African literature, and her work has garnered steady attention from postcolonial environmental humanities scholars. Her short story "Poison" won the 2008 Caine Prize for African Writing, and her novels consistently contend with social and environmental issues around Cape Town as well as human-nonhuman relationships. In her second novel, *Nineveh*, the unredressed racial and economic legacies of apartheid appear through two allegorical houses as well as the swarming "goggas" or invasive beetles that are central to the plot. Gender studies and African literature scholar Deirdre Byrne notes that swarming insects have long been a metaphor for "die swart gevaar ('the black danger')" within the white South African imaginary.[28] White anxieties about being "overwhelm[ed]" or "invad[ed]" by Black Africans were often expressed by representations of insects, whose numbers and physical difference from humans made them apt metaphors for racist white anxiety.[29] In Rose-Innes's novel, these familiar tropes of Black invasion into white spaces are replicated in the dark swarm of insects that threaten a white housing complex called Nineveh, which gives the book its title.

Nineveh is both literally and metaphorically white. Built of white stone, it is owned by white developer Martin Brand and marketed as a luxury housing estate that will cater to largely white residents. Mr. Brand hires Katya Grubbs, a white pest control expert, to get rid of the invasive goggas. But this proves impossible, and the beetles end up filling the premises after a heavy rain. At the novel's close, the beetles have not been destroyed but have instead overwhelmed Mr. Brand and the security guards who work in the complex; the guards flee, and Mr. Brand falls through a hole in the floor through which the bugs have entered. This metaphoric Black invasion of a wealthy white space allegorizes the unredressed racial and wealth inequalities of apartheid, as white property owners like Mr. Brand and his erstwhile customers continue to try cordoning off their space from the Black majority. That the insects eventually enter Nineveh proves that such separations are impossible, but the struggle over keeping the insects, like the Black poor, out of such spaces speaks to the persistence of these apartheid legacies.

These racial dynamics, symbolically displaced onto Nineveh's beetles, replicate the raced divisions of apartheid and South Africa's earlier colonial invasions by the Dutch and British in only thinly veiled ways. Indeed, though the insects are certainly ecological beings in their own right, they are better understood as stand-ins for Cape Town's indigenous Black population. This symbolic work is reinforced by their Latin name, *"Promeces palustris."*[30] History of science scholar Daniel Williams has pointed out that "palustris" means "marsh," and Nineveh is built on the edges of a wetland.[31] Far from being invaders, these insects, like Black South Africans, are in fact indigenous to the region and the environment. It is Mr. Brand and whites like him who have invaded the marshlands in pursuit of white space and, as Brand's name suggests, white capital.

Katya Grubbs is also a highly symbolic figure. She may be seen as a stand-in for the new South African state, tasked with "policing borders" and keeping everyone "in their proper place."[32] That Katya figures the state is confirmed by the fact that her business is one of pest "relocation," a word that cannot be used without evoking the specter of the apartheid state and its forced relocation of Blacks to arbitrary homelands. Having inherited the business from her father, Len, Katya is interested in "painless" relocations in contrast to her father's brutal use of "exterminator" tactics to control pests.³³ In the transition between father and daughter, Katya's version of the business seems to offer an allegory of South Africa's transition to a post-apartheid state that employs less force against its Black populace but still regulates it in ways complicit with white interests.

Because Katya can be seen as a stand-in for the post-apartheid state, it is also appropriate that the novel's second allegorical house is hers, a "Victorian" affair with shaky foundations.³⁴ The Victorian or colonial character of her house and the fact that it is riven with cracks makes it an apt metaphor for South Africa's fragmented society.³⁵ It should be noted that the cracks have been caused by a recent development project, as the park in her neighborhood is destroyed to make way for housing—not affordable housing for the urban poor, but a new and expensive apartment complex. As it is cracked in the process of destroying a public park that provided shelter to homeless citizens, Katya's shaky Victorian house symbolizes the cracked status of the nation as it invests in elite economic development over public spaces.

However, *Nineveh*'s two allegorical houses do more than point to the fragile national community or ongoing tensions over space and wealth in the new South Africa. They also occasion Katya's—and implicitly the state's—acknowledgment of how climate change is unevenly affecting the city's residents. Katya becomes concerned about the shack dwellers who live around the Nineveh complex and Derek, a homeless man who used to live in her neighborhood park, when it rains. Observing the deluge that eventually brings the beetles out of hiding and into Nineveh:

> She thinks of her neighbors, not too far away, in their small shacks with the rain hammering on tin roofs. And what about Derek and his companions? She wonders what they'll do in the rain, now that they only have the alley for shelter. She pictures Derek getting wet, his saturated bandages growing heavier, pulling him to the ground and plastering him there like soggy toilet paper. When she gets home, she'll give Derek some cash, or an old jersey or two. Promise.³⁶

This passage exemplifies the disappointing minimalism of the post-apartheid state. Though aware of the needs of Nineveh's shack dwellers and the park's homeless residents, Katya's imaginary, and through her the state's, can only encompass a small promise of "cash or an old jersey or two," and even these promises of provision remain unfulfilled. Likewise, Derek is compared to "soggy toilet paper" or used-up waste, highlighting the abject status of the city's poor. But even so, as Katya thinks about the small shacks and Derek's sodden clothing, the scene gestures to the way increasingly severe flooding endangers

Black bodies outside the novel. For one major challenge of township living is the annual winter rains. The Cape Flats, where Cape Town's biggest township Khayelitsha is located, are sandy and low-lying. Like the shacks around marshy Nineveh, shacks in the Cape Flats are vulnerable to floods and are often washed away during the winter rains. Rain in this novel surfaces the racial and wealth divisions of apartheid but also the increasing challenge that flooding poses to township dwellers.

Precarious urban living in the post-apartheid present is equally central to K. Sello Duiker's work. Duiker focused on marginal urban figures, from sex workers and street children to immigrants. Deemed one of the most exciting and provocative voices of his generation, Duiker's literary career was brief and ended when he committed suicide in 2005, at the age of thirty. Yet the three novels he wrote during his lifetime had a profound impact on South Africa's post-transition literature.[37] His work was characterized by a dark intensity and explored themes "that had up to that point not been dealt with by black writers."[38] These qualities are immediately apparent in Duiker's debut novel *Thirteen Cents*, which dwells on Cape Town's "shadow-side."

The protagonist of *Thirteen Cents* is a homeless orphaned boy named Azure, who scratches out a miserable existence in the Cape Flats and around the edges of Cape Town's central business district. Subjected to extensive forms of brutality including starvation, imprisonment, physical beatings, and psychological deception by the adults around him, Azure wanders through the city and survives largely by prostituting himself to wealthy gay men. Though they pay for his services and indeed provide his only income, these men exploit him as much as the more physically violent criminals and street gangsters Azure interacts with. Azure's orphaned status, extreme poverty, vulnerability, and exploitation exemplify the failures of post-apartheid inclusion. This critique is reinforced by the novel's single reference to Nelson Mandela, when Azure goes to a grimy and ill-functioning block of flats that "stinks of piss and shit" and where "*Mandela se poes*" is written on the wall.[39] Being taken to this run-down building is part of Azure's initiation into the brutalities of street gangs. With neither parents nor the state to protect him, Azure is left to the whims of crime lords and anyone else to use as they please.

Azure's life encapsulates urban Black hardship in post-transition South Africa. To this end he also embodies the failure of a post-racial future. Azure, born with "blue eyes and a dark skin," at first seems to manifest South Africa's aspiration to be a deracinated rainbow nation where the once rigid categorization of citizens into white, Black, or Coloured has given way.[40] But in fact, Azure is constantly subjected to racialization. One of the first things he narrates is the reifying looks he has received all his life: "I'm used to people staring at me, mostly grown-ups . . . grown-ups, they pierce you with their stare."⁴¹ Postcolonial critic Meg Samuelson has noted that this description is akin to Fanon's narration of the racially objectifying gaze in *Black Skin, White Masks*, and Azure's objectified status is further reinforced by the way he is a sexually exploited "trick" through much of the narrative.⁴² Simultaneously and conversely, Azure tends to enrage those around him precisely because he cannot be cleanly fixed into a racial category. Bringing together blue eyes and dark skin, he is an object of racial animus in a society still saturated with hierarchical racial prejudice against Black people. "He thinks he's white because he's got straight hair and a light skin. . . . He'd love to have your blue eyes," Azure's friend Vincent tells him after he is nearly beaten to death by Gerald, a white-passing crime boss.⁴³ Azure's eyes contradict and threaten the racial hierarchies still at work in post-apartheid Cape Town, where those with lighter skin continue to assert their dominance. Rather than heralding a postracial rainbow future, Azure's blue eyes reveal the entrenchment of apartheid-era hierarchies of race.

In addition to these racial prejudices, Azure's blue eyes suggest a "blue view" attuned to the presence of water and continuing inequalities over its access.⁴⁴ We will return to the more positive elements of Azure's blue view later. For now we may note that Azure, who "love[s] water," is systemically barred from its public use; in particular, while he sleeps near the public swimming pool on Cape Town's beach, he cannot afford to access it.⁴⁵ Later on, after climbing Table Mountain to escape the clutches of Gerald and his gang, he is told about a reservoir and dreams of swimming in it. But a state worker tells him, "You're not allowed to be here. Regulations."⁴⁶ Following Indian ecofeminist Vandana Shiva, Samuelson notes that these might be thought of as "captive waters" or waters that are not considered a common good but are instead privatized or used in ways that privilege the rich.⁴⁷ Azure cannot pay the fee for the pool, and he is not allowed to swim in the reservoir; instead, its water is used to provide piped water to individual homes, the kind of homes where Azure must often commit sexual tricks. Brought to these homes by wealthy white men, Azure briefly enjoys the "heaven with warm water" in their houses and thus the privatized, individual, and classed uses to which reservoir water is restricted or captured.⁴⁸

At the same time, like Rose-Innes's novel *Nineveh*, *Thirteen Cents* illustrates how these raced inequalities are compounded by climate change. The conclusion of Duiker's novel brings European colonialism, apartheid's racial legacies, and the climate changes of the Anthropocene together in spectacular fashion. *Thirteen Cents* was published in 2000, the same year atmospheric chemist Paul Crutzen and limnologist Eugene Stoermer popularized the idea of the Anthropocene, the current age in which humans as a species have become a planet-altering, geological force.[49] Through the massive production of fossil fuels, humans have disrupted the geophysical cycles of the planet in ways previously unimaginable. The huge levels of carbon dioxide pumped into the atmosphere from cars and the production of petroleum products like plastic have contributed to warming and acidifying oceans, sealevel rise, melting polar ice caps, and disrupted oceanic and atmospheric patterns, producing both unprecedented drought and flooding. And while these effects are felt globally, they are also highly uneven, falling with especially destructive force on global South communities that have relatively few resources and have historically contributed little to climate change.

In *Thirteen Cents* this unequal planetary history appears in the novel's denouement as a huge, tsunami-like wave rushes toward Cape Town and destroys the entire city. Humans and nonhumans are swept up, but the narrative nevertheless notes the cars and "white bodies" in the water as Cape Town is laid to waste.[50] In describing total destruction while singling out Cape Town's cars and white populace, the novel attends to both shared calamity and the forces of white capital and petroleum that have brought about the destructive wave. So too, moments before the wave arrives, Azure says, "You can't really tell that it's water. It just looks like a blue plastic thing that reflects the sun and moves gently like a conveyor belt."[51] Such phrasing literally describes the material of the world's oceans, which are full of plastic debris. And since plastic is a petroleum product, his statement also directly links the tsunami to fossil fuels. On top of this, Azure's comment points to the way the oceans have been destructive pathways or "conveyors" bringing white colonists and settlers to South Africa's shores. The wave, rushing toward Cape Town from across the ocean, replicates how the sea has brought destruction to South Africa since its earliest histories of European contact in the seventeenth century, when the Dutch East India Company settled by Table Mountain. Beginning in 1652, the Dutch went to war with indigenous San and Khoekhoen populations, driving them from their lands and the natural springs that arise from the rocks of Table Mountain to establish Cape Town as a refreshment station for the company's trade ships.[52] Thus, Duiker's ending scene brings together a cataclysmic and unrecognizable ocean produced by plastic, anthropogenic fossil fuels, and climate change, but also suggests these forces are only the latest wave of destruction to be conveyed to South Africa's shores.

Duiker's novel ends with an Anthropocene conjuncture, a moment where the impending effects of climate change met pre-existing inequalities. But this kind of conjuncture also appeared outside fiction, during Day Zero. As the water in the six dams that provide water to Cape Town fell dangerously low after three years of drought, the city at times prioritized global capital and racial interests at the expense of public resources. Companies like Coca Cola and South African Breweries were accused of using huge amounts of water to produce commercial beverages for global sale while local individuals and households faced increasingly tight water restrictions. Numerous activist groups, like the Water Crisis Coalition, emerged around Day Zero to protest what they saw as the state's turn to water privatization.[53] This dynamic can also be seen in the fate of the public spring in Newlands, an affluent suburb at the foot of Table Mountain. Newlands spring was one of the oldest springs in the city and is one of many Table Mountain springs that provided clean, sweet-tasting water since before Dutch colonization. During restrictions implemented to avoid Day Zero, hundreds of people of every race and economic strata queued daily to collect quotas of free water from the spring. However, once Day Zero was officially called off in March 2018 and then pushed even further away with the arrival of winter rains that year, Newlands spring was paved over. Its water was redirected a kilometer away to a new collection point by the Newlands swimming pool.

Though Newlands spring water was still technically available, the original site, which had been a public space for centuries, was now inaccessible. The official justification was a need for security, since altercations had happened around the spring. But it must also be understood as an example of the state's prioritization of private property and white wealth. Many of the white, affluent residents of the surrounding Newlands suburb complained about the crowds, trash, noise, and general "nightmare" the spring had become as a result of the influx of strangers from across the city.[54] Like the characters in *Nineveh*, during Day Zero, Newlands residents drew on long-standing discourses of invaded space to express class anxiety and the desire to maintain their property against the proximity of racial and economic others. Day Zero, like Rose-Innes's and Duiker's novels, revealed how ongoing histories of past inequality overlapped with anthropogenic climate change during Cape Town's Anthropocene conjuncture.

Post-Apartheid Fulfillment / Housing Concrete Utopias

From service delivery protests, post-transition novels, and the tensions around Day Zero, it is clear that the South African state has not fully rectified the legacies of apartheid, much less the encroaching effects of climate change. At times the state even reinforced the primacy of racial hierarchies and global capitalism that are making the effects of both worse for the urban poor. But these failures are only one aspect of the South African state. The post-apartheid state must be understood, too, as a site of appeal and desirable intervention, one that despite its limits has actually facilitated many concrete utopias or specific forms of betterment for the Black majority. In previous chapters, the state was often hailed through a language of unfulfilled promises and called upon to better achieve what it had left unaccomplished. In Bhopal and the Niger Delta, reading the state through what Seyla Benhabib termed a "politics of fulfillment" illuminated the continuing purchase of state promises despite their deeply unfulfilled quality. In this chapter, some promises have been fulfilled. The South African state *has* partially achieved forms of post-apartheid inclusion and it *has* been committed to rectifying the historical injustices of apartheid. Despite its "incomplete transition," the state has an extensive record of taking action to bring about the concrete utopia of a more equal future.

Since Nelson Mandela became South Africa's first majority-rule president and the African National Congress (ANC) came into power in 1994, the South African government has pursued a huge array of policies, legislation, and infrastructure projects to rectify the racist society it inherited. This mission was explicitly laid out in the Reconstruction and Development Programme (RDP), a policy framework drawn up in the years before the ANC came to power. Unlike the later GEAR Act, which largely voided the language of inequality, the RDP was saturated with awareness of South Africa's racialized hierarchies and divisions. It defined itself as a framework seeking to "mobilise all our people and our country's resources toward the final eradication of apartheid and the building of a democratic, non-racial and non-sexist future."[55] This equal future had to be pursued precisely because apartheid produced a society in which "our income distribution is racially distorted," and indeed, so was "every sphere of our society."[56] The ANC's task was enormous, yet the RDP centered racial justice in its policy framework and elaborated a number of interlocking points and goals in its pursuit of a more just future. Central to this program was "meeting basic needs" because "poverty is the single greatest burden of South Africa's people, and is the direct result of the apartheid system."[57] Poverty here meant not merely a lack of income for Black South Africans but also a lack of basic needs to support life, including food, housing, land, and access to water.

As a whole, the ANC's Reconstruction and Development Programme laid out a policy framework in which reconstructing South Africa as a society was the post-apartheid state's raison d'être. Such a society, one that enfranchises all its citizens equally and can provide basic needs to all, not only the white minority, would require a massive outlay of resources. The RDP stressed that "attacking poverty and deprivation must therefore be the first priority" of the democratic government and that it would pursue this goal through redistribution, sustainable development, and the extension of basic services.[58]

The RDP stipulated plans for land redistribution for rural residents and in urban centers focused on remedying the lack of adequate housing, sanitation, and water. As noted earlier, densely packed townships were never intended to support Black communities, businesses, or social life but were built as security-oriented zones of Black labor control. The RDP proposed huge expansions of housing and services to rectify apartheid's infrastructures of temporary urban habitation. It proposed that the state build one million low-cost houses in its first five years and endorsed a general right to housing that was not simply a right to be sheltered from the elements but "a right to a secure place in which to live in peace and dignity."[59] It further laid out housing standards, such as "all housing must provide protection from weather, a durable structure, and reasonable living space and privacy."[60] Houses had to include amenities like sanitary facilities and convenient access to clean water. In the short-term the RDP aimed to provide every household per capita with a clean, safe supply of 20–30 liters of water per day; in the medium term it proposed providing better sanitation and larger quantities of clean water.[61] Expanded access to piped water has thus gone hand in hand with ANC efforts to expand housing. The provision of water has been treated in tandem with and sometimes as part of the right to housing within the ANC's platform of redressing apartheid's entrenched poverty and infrastructural divisions.

The 1996 GEAR Act departed from the RDP's vision by prioritizing capital development and posing racial restitution as an aftereffect of a robust economy, minimizing spending, and creating jobs. This disappointing turn has not, however, obliterated the RDP's program or the goals of social and racial justice that informed the ANC's platform. Indeed, the South African Constitution, ratified in December 1996 and lauded as one of the most socially progressive in the world, enshrined many of the same rights and proposals first laid out in the RDP. Its preamble notes the need to "heal the divisions of the past and establish a society based on democratic values, social justice, and fundamental human rights."[62] Its founding provisions are wide-ranging and, like the RDP, explicitly institutionalize non-racism and non-sexism as foundational to the new state, along with the principle of equality for all citizens. Its lengthy Bill of Rights incorporates a huge range of rights, including rights to what the RDP called "basic needs." These include the right to housing and rights of access to food and water.[63] The constitution thus carries over much of the reconstructive and socially just vision of the Reconstruction and Development Programme.

Unsurprisingly, the ambitions of the RDP and the Constitution's enshrinement of rights have not been universally or immediately achieved. In fact, both the RDP and the Constitution can be said to acknowledge a politics of fulfillment—the eventual realization of a more socially just future—as the working conditions of South Africa's transition. The RDP originally proposed one million new houses and that more houses would be built over time; similarly that a smaller quantity of clean water in the "short-term" would be replaced with larger quantities "in the medium term."[64] In the Constitution, the right to housing is framed as at once universal—"everyone has the right to have access to adequate housing" and gradual—"the state must take reasonable legislative and other measures, within its available resources, to achieve the *progressive realisation* of this right."[65] In the same way, rights to water are acknowledged as both universal rights and ones that could in practice only be progressively or gradually realized.[66] Even as the post-apartheid transition and the 1996 Constitution inaugurated newness, a more equal society would take time. The idea that transition would be a gradual process and thus partially unfulfilled at any given moment is built into these founding political documents and their vision of a new South Africa.

The Constitution and the RDP offer a political vision in the grammar of the present progressive, acknowledging ongoing action and the continuing expansion of state services over time.[67] As it inherited apartheid's divisions, the South African state both set out a hugely ambitious scope for social change and acknowledged that such changes would take place slowly: that is, incompletion would necessarily characterize the transition toward social reconstruction at any given moment. Yet such unfulfillment is not simply a cause for critique, disappointment, or censure, but a characteristic of how transition works. No revolutionary catharsis can immediately undo centuries of racialized discrimination and decades of formal apartheid. The ANC's future vision incorporated a temporal span that cannily acknowledged present unfulfillment or imperfection. Rather than seeing such unfulfillment as stalling or stasis, the sign of apartheid continuity or incomplete liberation, unfulfillment can be seen as a symptom of and part of making progress.

The partial but continuing fulfillment of concrete utopias in South Africa's post-transition present should be seen against the backdrop of inherited apartheid; they should also be seen through the complex hopes and expectations for better futures that many South Africans continue to experience through the state. Unfulfilled promises do not tend to be situated within an empty trajectory that will never change but are seen as concrete utopias or specific and desired forms of improvement that have already been fulfilled for some. Housing, water, and more political recognition may well be realized, even if it is not clear when. Benhabib's politics of fulfillment, in which "the society of the future attains more adequately what present society has left unaccomplished," captures precisely the uneven, fraught, ongoing process of pursuing more just futures in South Africa, where the structures of the past cannot be instantly obliterated but only slowly and painstakingly replaced over time.[68]

These temporalities of transition also appear in South African fiction. In Rose-Innes's *Nineveh*, the politics of fulfillment and present progression are, like its critique of apartheid legacies, centered through housing and water. The earlier section considered how Martin Brand's housing complex and Katya Grubb's old Victorian residence respectively allegorize apartheid's ongoing racial exclusions and fractures within the nation's imagined community. Yet these houses also eventually become sites of greater material inclusion for Cape Town's marginalized populace. They capture both apartheid continuity and the partial fulfillment of post-apartheid change. To this end, the Nineveh estate becomes home to those it once excluded. Not only do the indigenous beetles Katya was hired to relocate eventually swarm the property, but the impoverished shack dwellers who always lived in the marshy fringes around the complex take up residence inside.

In her excursions around Nineveh, Katya interacts with the shack dwellers and observes their settlements, nestled under the trees and exposed to rain. But it turns out that like the beetles, they have also been moving in and out of Nineveh the whole time: the shack dwellers have accessed many of Nineveh's materials for their own small trading through the same broken floorboards that allowed the beetles to enter. The porousness of Nineveh to both nonhuman and human life underscores the novel's criticism of segregationist thinking and its eventual undermining of dreams of "policing borders." Through this access point the shack dwellers have redistributed Nineveh's hoarded resources; they strip Nineveh's tiles, copper, statues, and other materials to support their own precarious lives, thus demonstrating the permeability of raced and classed boundaries. Rather than serving as status symbols or decor, bathroom tiles exchanged by the side of the road become money to buy food and other necessities.

After Mr. Brand leaves Nineveh, the shack dwellers no longer pilfer secretly but move in directly. Nineveh's earlier pretensions to exclusion were always flimsy, and at novel's end it becomes a place of explicitly mixed race and mixed use. The once "ice white" walls are "smudged black and brown," reflecting the change in the racial composition of the estate's occupants.[69] Once confined to wretched accommodations where "the water seems to lap right up against the outer shacks and infiltrate the muddy alleys between them. It must be hellish when it's cold," the former shack dwellers come to benefit from the "luxurious" and "high-quality" stone of Nineveh.[70] For Nineveh's shack dwellers, the estate provides shelter from cold, flooding, and torrential rain. In turn, the shack dwellers make Nineveh livable in a way it never was when Katya and Mr. Brand tried to retain it as an exclusively white space. When Katya arrived, she noted that Nineveh had an "unfinished feel" and that the ground was "a raw field of mud."[71] The shack dwellers make it homey: "There's colored cloth up in the windows" and "The place is not as muddy now: here and there, people have sunk half-bricks and pieces of wood into the muck, to step on."[72] Thus, though Nineveh is still technically incomplete at novel's close, it offers a desirable and appreciated home for the shack dwellers.

So too Derek, the Black homeless man in Katya's neighborhood whom Katya once promised to provide for, takes up residence in the garage of her newly spruced-up Victorian house. Katya's cracked and imperfect Victorian home eventually becomes shelter for Derek and other homeless residents who were displaced from the park. These shelters are not totally finished or perfectly sound, yet they are better than the alternatives they replaced. As the city's poor come to dwell in and benefit from these imperfect spaces, *Nineveh* adds a nuanced view of the uses of unfinished structures to its critique of apartheid-era legacies. They do not fulfill a dream of perfect housing, but the Nineveh complex and Katya's old Victorian nonetheless offer solid shelter, respite, access to water, and other amenities to those who previously lacked them. Like South Africa's pursuit of housing and basic services more generally, the incomplete quality of these improvements must be acknowledged, along with their positive impact on the lives of the urban poor.

In writing about the experience of waiting for housing in South Africa, many social scientists have similarly stressed the way incompletion does not lead simply to pessimism. Rather, state promises of housing, even when unfulfilled or only partly fulfilled, sustain visions of better futures. Geographers Sophie Oldfield and Saskia Greyling note that waiting for state-provided homes is "normal, a taken-for-granted, everyday, intergenerational condition."[73] Though it can take decades to receive a state-built home, many Black South Africans continue "to wait, to hope for, and to expect a formal house" from the state in part because there is no other way for them to obtain an individual home.[74] The constitutional right to housing and RDP-era promises of addressing poverty tend to appear in everyday experience as "waiting for the state" to provide what it has promised.[75] For many families formal housing remains deeply desired, a concrete utopia that is "spoken of as a dream."[76] It includes not only the building itself but a sense of security, privacy, political recognition, and inclusion in South Africa's post-apartheid society. Those waiting on houses visit local offices to see where they are on the list, to make sure all their documents are accounted for, and to keep their neighborhoods on the city's agenda, "trying to ensure that the promised housing materialises."[77] Some register the hardships of waiting: "It's pain[ful], like you feel you are in pain of waiting for this house."[78] How to live before one receives a house is also a challenge, and houses have been criticized for their low quality, given the costs required to provide so many. Yet with few other options, given the country's continuing disparities in income and employment, thousands of Black South Africans remain attached to concrete utopias of state-provided housing and the social validation it offers.

In such a context, applying for and waiting on housing is legitimate and agentive. As one woman told Oldfield and Greyling, "I'm urging, I'm praying, I'm crying already, I just need a safe place to live. . . . I personally don't know when we're going to get houses. Yes, I know it's in the pipeline."[79] Urging, crying, and praying highlight this woman's investment in state promises of housing and the everyday activities through which she attempts to bring the promised house closer to fulfillment. The profoundly affective language she uses to characterize her period of waiting on the state speaks to the burden and uncertainty of unfulfilled promises, yet equally to the way her hopes for the future depend on them. Such investments are not cruel optimism, for it is important to note that these are not empty promises.[80] Since 1994 the postapartheid state has built over four million homes through the National Housing Subsidy Programme, which was introduced by the ANC-led government. Most government expenditure on housing has in fact been on RDP or state-built homes targeting the poor; these homes are aimed at the 54 percent of South African households that fall below a R3,500 income threshold.[81] Waiting on these houses is "a state-driven legal and administrative procedure which citizens consciously sign up to in their application for housing."[82] The state's commitment to provide recognition and inclusion through housing and other basic amenities like water "is precisely why citizens wait, conscious that the state is arbitrary despite its procedures, yet knowing that this process is one of the few ways to access a formal home."[83] It is unclear when a house will arrive; yet citizens continue to wait on the state and to hope for the kind of better future the state has already provided to some, including their near neighbors.

In their work on RDP or state-built housing in Johannesburg and Durban, urban studies scholars Sarah Charlton and Paula Meth note that residents living in RDP housing "were near-unanimous in their joy over the improvement in their everyday quality of life."[84] As one interviewee, Florence, told them, "[The RDP house] means everything. . . . Yes. Because now . . . when it's raining, I'm sleeping comfortably. It's not like when I was in the shack."[85] Housing has improved the life of this woman in ways that parallel the shack dwellers in *Nineveh*. Compared to informal housing, state housing is more weatherproof and has water and toilet facilities. Others note that receiving state housing has given them a greater sense of security and maturity: "My family didn't want to visit me in the shack because [they] were so shocked to see where I lived . . . they are fearful to come again to visit. They started now after I got the new house and I feel like I'm a real parent because of the house and I'm owning. My family and relatives visit me without any fear now."[86] For many residents, accessing formal housing constitutes a concrete utopia, a specific and desired way to improve their lives.

These better circumstances are of course not perfect. As noted, the process of waiting can be painful. The amenities provided through housing can also be expensive; once they receive a house, water and electricity above a free basic amount must be paid for, and many residents feel they are unfairly billed or are worried about going into debt. The responsibilities that accompany becoming homeowners compete with the benefits of having a home and reinforce the "conflicting roles and rationalities" through which state provision is experienced, its complex and Janus-faced quality.[87] Nonetheless, to receive a state-provided house is to receive a tangible improvement, one described as "like heaven," hoped and prayed for, but uncertain in its arrival.[88] The fulfillment of South Africa's promises of housing and basic needs are riven with problems and limits, yet they are also clearly concrete utopias for many.

State Water

State-provided homes include water pipes directly inside them or in close proximity, and they have been one important way for the state to expand water access to urban Black communities. But policy analyst Lucy Rodina and resource governance scholar Leila M. Harris have also shown how water services themselves mediate citizens' experiences of formal rights and social inclusion in South African cities. Their interviews in Khayelitsha, Cape Town's largest township, reveal that contestations over water trace "evolving senses of the municipal government, or state."[89] Despite the imperfect condition of taps and water access, some Khayelitsha residents understand that the state has taken pains to provide water to the township. Most of those Rodina and Harris interviewed were migrants from the drier Eastern Cape, where access to piped water inside dwellings is the lowest in the country. There, water is seen as a natural resource or commons, a "gift from God" that should not be paid for.[90] Some residents have evoked the idea of water as a commons or a divine gift to question paying for it in the city; yet others mention that city water is not the same as water in the countryside because it is mediated by state infrastructures. As one woman put it, "Water cannot be free in a city—unlike in the Eastern

Cape, because there we were getting water from the rivers. . . . We have to pay because the water that is provided by the City is different from the one in the Eastern Cape. Here in the city the water is treated and pumped."[91] Here the work the state does to provide water—piping, treating, and pumping it—is recognized as part of its cost, and so access to water in the city is not natural but an infrastructurally mediated state service. Because of these state interventions, residents tend to have a sense that the state plays a paramount role in ensuring their access to water. These mediations are part of producing "notions of what the state is, or should be."[92]

For those receiving water in Khayelitsha, the state emerges as an important provider of water infrastructure and water services. Like Oldfield and Greyling's work, Rodina and Harris note that residents who have received newly built homes tend to valorize and legitimate the state and its role as a service provider, while those who have not yet received homes tend to feel excluded and see the state as neglectful. Both these responses highlight the centrality of state provision in the imaginaries of ordinary citizens and the political recognition signaled by state services. A man living in the shacks complained,

> We do not have the same rights, because some people are staying in good houses . . . and in beautiful houses, which have been built with good conditions! But other people are still staying in the shacks! How can we (shack dwellers) pay for water? [.] We are not going to pay water (because) we are still staying in shacks![93]

This man's refusal to pay for water is part of the wider trend of service delivery protests and nonpayment practices that have rocked Cape Town and South Africa as a whole. But since the extension of services has been foundational to political recognition and social inclusion after democracy's inception in South Africa, protests over service delivery are more than expressions of disappointment with the post-apartheid present. They are also easily readable as demands for the better fulfillment of state promises and equal citizenship. These contests over the meaning of water payments and water services offer another manifestation of what partial fulfillment looks and feels like in any given moment, as a gradual and sometimes unsatisfying process in which people are deeply invested.[94]

In her work on South African community activism in Cape Town, anthropologist Kerry Ryan Chance observed similar dynamics as demands for water facilitate political visibility and contact with the state. Water is a "political conductor" because it "obliges residents to interact with state states [sic], be it by paying a household water bill to a local government council, or drinking from an outdoor communal water tap managed by state agents."[95] When Cape Town's poor access water, they engage with the state, whether through state-provided infrastructures or face-to-face contact with state personnel. Residents of QR, a shack settlement that is endangered by winter floods and lacks drinking water, did just this when they protested at the Provincial Parliament in Cape Town's city center, the legislative seat of Western Cape province. Chance reports that during this march QR's protestors demanded that a member of the provincial cabinet appear in person to receive a memorandum that listed the resident's collective demands. These included complaints about the local lack of infrastructure, scarcity of drinking water, and the winter flooding that regularly washed shacks away. Such memoranda are not simply pro forma gestures but, like many of the complaints in this book, are part of an "open-ended negotiation. The ritual mirrors a contract signing, where residents and state agents play the part of mutual partners in a process of transforming existing infrastructure."[96] Such acts kept QR's residents in touch with the state. They did not automatically produce new results, but they reveal the way promises of intervention mediate interactions with the state and are actively mobilized by urban residents for their own ends. This protest drew on the language of basic needs and basic services that have been central to South Africa's democratic transition. Through such language and actions, state-based concrete utopias become visible in the process of being fulfilled, neither foreclosed nor yet fully achieved. A utopian method of reading here highlights the actual plurality that shapes how communities relate to the South African state. Those waiting on the state testify to both the disappointments of transition and the partial improvements and in-process concrete utopias around them.

The significance of these state pluralities is captured in South African novels like *Nineveh*, as discussed previously, and even in works that seem unequivocally bleak, like *Thirteen Cents*. As noted, Duiker's novel searingly chronicles the failures of post-apartheid transition. Yet surprisingly, it is also attentive to state provision, which lies in the background and supports marginal life in the city in mundane ways. Attending to water is imperative here. As discussed earlier, Azure's "blue view" tracks the failure of a post-racial future and ongoing inequalities in water access. Yet following the novel's attention to water also reveals how public, state-provided water resources support Azure's movement through the city. Azure's blue view of Cape Town is also a view saturated with the provision of public water, and it supports a utopian reading of the state even amidst the novel's more obvious depictions of state violence and failure.

Sprinkled throughout *Thirteen Cents* are numerous moments when Azure interacts with state-provided taps and public toilets: he rinses at the tap every morning, drinks to quench his thirst, and avoids a hangover by hydrating before sleep. "Always thirsty," the public taps are Azure's most consistent source of drinking water.[97] Some are located "right outside the Men's toilet."[98] Putting clean drinking water close to dirty toilets may seem to suggest the second-tier status of those forced to use these facilities. Yet the proximity of toilets and taps also highlights the necessary bodily functions of marginalized inhabitants—to drink water, wash, urinate, and defecate. Having reliable access to taps and toilets is an important component of Azure's movement through the city and his ability to survive in Cape Town. Like QR's residents, when Azure accesses public water, he engages with the state. The novel's pairing of toilets and taps thus highlights how only the state provides for the bodily needs of the Black poor, an attention to physical necessities that echoes the ANC's central platform of "basic needs."[99]

These state infrastructures often crop up during unremarkable moments, when Azure is walking around the city or is otherwise unmolested. Compared to the unrelenting brutality that takes up much of his narrative, these quiet moments of infrastructural use are easy to miss. Yet they reveal how state infrastructures support Azure's body and offer some of the few moments of respite in the novel: "I feel thirsty and go to a public toilet on Bree street. . . . At the basin I pour water over my face as it is boiling hot and drink till my stomach swells and I burp. I sigh and feel my high returning."[100] Here Azure enjoys the warm temperature of the water and is able to quench his thirst. Reading the proximity of toilets and taps against the grain, the state can be read through utopian method for the way its infrastructures support Azure's basic needs and offer brief moments of pleasure away from the violence of the streets.

So, too, even though an official forbids Azure from using the city reservoir, he "wake[s] up early and swim[s] at the reservoir before that man comes to work. [He has] great swims and learn[s] to play with water alone."[101] State water is again a source of rare pleasure; and in turning the reservoir to his own use, Azure's swimming pushes against the way reservoir water otherwise appears as paid-for tap water in wealthy white houses. Using the reservoir outdoors underscores its public character, the way such reservoirs are actually the ultimate source of water for everyone in Cape Town, feeding private and public taps alike.[102] Before the catastrophic final wave, *Thirteen Cents*' attention to water highlights state-supported inequalities that reinforce raced and classed water access, but also the public quality of state water infrastructures that support the basic needs of Black urban dwellers.

Day Zero: Disciplining Water Citizens, Preventing Apocalypse

Expanding housing and public water have been part of the South African state's efforts to fulfill promises of post-apartheid democracy. But public water changed valences dramatically during Day Zero, when it became a threat rather than a promise. After three years of drought from 2015 to 2018, the six dams that provide water to Cape Town were running out of water altogether. Day Zero named the day water reserves would run so low that private taps would be turned off and public water would become the norm for everyone. Scratching the surface of Day Zero media coverage reveals a storm of apocalyptic predictions and dire warnings about this shift: queueing at public collection points for rationed water would bring Cape Town into "Mad Max territory," a shorthand for social anarchy and fights over dwindling water supplies.[103] Yet Day Zero never fully arrived, nor did the predictions that were made about it. What is most interesting about Day Zero is, therefore, not the sensationalism of its news headlines but the way the state intervened to prevent Day Zero's actual occurrence. In the lead-up to Day Zero, Cape Town's government worked to prevent the arrival of a dry future. They did this by deploying an extensive campaign of state discipline, focusing on wealthy upper- and middle-class white residents who, as the privileged inheritors of apartheid, also used most of the city's water. But as we will see later, they also projected an apocalyptic "worst-case scenario" to induce action in the present. This turn to apocalyptic prevention blurred the boundaries between fiction and policy during Day Zero as Cape Town's government replicated the generic tenets of apocalypse that have been developed not in policy, but in climate fictions. To face down Day Zero, the state responded to both climate novelty and apartheid history, and it drew on a wide arsenal of moves, from discipline to the kind of preventive projections that are more often thought to be part of fiction.

During the lead-up to Day Zero, Cape Town's leaders worked to produce certain kinds of water citizens: ones who would be responsible or wise about their water use, citizens who were aware of how much water they used, how they used it, and who would be careful not to go above restrictions. Frequent water updates on the level of Cape Town's dams and public pronouncements on the state of Cape Town's water disseminated on government websites, in public statements by officials like Cape Town's executive mayor Patricia de Lille, educational flyers and tips, frightening warnings, and punitive measures alongside news coverage and social media campaigns, all worked to discipline Cape Town's high water users into more "water-wise" citizens.[104] Following the implementation of Day Zero rhetoric by the state, residents responded by adjusting their behavior toward water, policing their own water use, coming up with creative strategies to reuse or minimize water use, and often discussing water-saving tactics with each other.[105] Anthropologist Steven Robins chronicles how ordinary residents engaged in specialized forms of "water talk," becoming knowledgeable about dam levels, desalinization, groundwater, water pressure levels, city by-laws, and other aspects of urban water delivery that had previously been invisible.[106] Such water talk helped produce public consciousness and awareness of how water was being used, and these individual practices were in turn reinforced and bolstered by the many water updates and educational materials disseminated by Cape Town's leaders.

Educational materials included the flyer "Top Ten Ways to Use Water Wisely This Summer," posted online. It advised residents to "find and fix leaks," "take short, stop-start showers" or "turn off taps when not using the flow." Likewise, the flyer "Your Guide to 50L or Less per Day" was laid out like a water wheel or pie chart and broke common household activities down in terms of their water use while offering recommendations on how to minimize water. Household cleaning for instance could be done "every second day" using 5 liters or, even better, with waterless products for 0 liters. Flushing the toilet could be done with graywater, the water collected from other uses like showering, and "if it's yellow, let it mellow" became widespread behavior. Residents like Sittara Stodel attest to the way these tips and awareness came to pervade even the unconscious minds of Capetonians: "I'm constantly thinking about running out of water and worrying about 'Day Zero.' . . . I'm even having nightmares about wasting water. The other day I had a dream that I took a long shower by mistake!"[107] Such state disciplining incorporated elements usually considered negative extensions of state policing and surveillance. The bottom of the "Top Ten Ways to Use Water Wisely" flyer listed a WhatsApp and telephone number where residents could "report water wastage." The state also installed water meters that would monitor and automatically cut off households using excess water. And it published a water map through which neighbors could police each other's water use. On the map, each household was represented by a green or red dot; those in compliance were green, and red households could be reported on by their neighbors. Such surveillance and monitoring tactics are invasive and can easily be considered an overreach or abuse of state power.

Yet these disciplinary measures can also be read through utopian method, against the grain. First, they were largely successful. Cape Town's water consumption drastically decreased, and Day Zero was never fully implemented. Over the course of the 2015–18 drought, Capetonians cut their water use by 50 percent, from 1.2 billion liters per day in 2015 to 516 million liters per day in March 2018.[108] This dramatic fall in water use is striking, especially when compared to other affluent cities facing drought; it took Melbourne over a decade to cut its water use by 40 percent during the Millennium Drought of 2000–2010.[109] This reveals how much Capetonians were galvanized by the threatening rhetoric and disciplinary restrictions of Day Zero. In acting before even more extreme water restrictions would have to be implemented, Capetonians effectively produced a different and better water future for the city.

Importantly, state restrictions did not target everyone equally. They were primarily aimed at middle- and upper-income households. These households were most affected by restrictions and targeted by disciplinary measures because approximately 70 percent of Cape Town's water is used for residential or domestic purposes, and within that, townships use only about 5 percent.[110] The vast majority of water use in Cape Town was, in fact, by middle- and upper-class residents for activities like showering, washing dishes and cars, watering gardens, and filling swimming pools. It was these uses that Day Zero water restrictions and the state's educational campaigns, water updates, water map, and other disciplinary measures sought to curtail, and it was these city dwellers in particular who needed to be disciplined into more water-wise citizens.

Many Capetonians did take it upon themselves to find creative ways to use less water. But not all did. In a statement released on December 3, 2017, mayor Patricia de Lille called out and criticized high-water-use households. While thanking the "water-saving heroes" of the city, she noted that Cape Town's Water and Sanitation department was in an "ongoing" struggle to "restrict households who, despite warnings and appeals to reduce water usage, are still using excessive amounts of water."[111] De Lille's statement went on to publicize how water meters had recently been installed forcibly on properties in the affluent neighborhoods of Pinelands and Thornton, where water usage over the preceding six months ranged from 19,000 to 48,000 liters per month.[112] De Lille singled out these high water users as "stubborn" and "delinquent" in contrast to the "heroes" who had abided by Day Zero water restrictions and were doing their part to curb water use.[113]

This moralizing rhetoric of struggle, where high water users became not only criminals but implicit villains or threats to the city in contrast to its "water heroes," is surprising because it was applied to privileged residents. In de Lille's statement it is wealthy users who are castigated as the city's delinquents, and since wealth correlates closely with race in Cape Town, these were almost certainly white households. The state's punitive measures and exclusionary language are cause for concern, but de Lille correctly identified the city's middle and upper classes as special targets in need of being disciplined into water-wise practices. Rather than blaming the poor or Cape Town's Black residents, here the Cape Town government recognized that it was in fact affluent white suburbanites who threatened the city's water as a whole and were bringing Day Zero closer to Cape Town's only possible future.

Middle-class writer, editor, and activist Helen Moffett echoed de Lille's diagnosis of privileged water use. In a blog entry "1001 ways to save water: a start" posted after de Lille's statements, Moffett insisted, "But this is on us, the middle classes. . . . Because WE are the problem."[114] Moffett criticized the general excess of Capetonian middle-class life and called out the way white racism underpins assumptions about water waste. "Racism," she said, will lead other middle-class residents to "whine about 'running standpipes' and 'taxi-washing' in the townships." But township residents were not to blame. Instead, she drew a damning contrast with the waste of her fellow white suburbanites: "Do you have water piped into your home? A flush toilet? Indoor bathrooms? A pool? A lawn? . . . STFU."[115]

Likewise, in addition to disciplining and rhetorically criminalizing affluent water users, it has to be noted that the Cape Town government remained explicitly committed to providing "drinking water through normal channels" to townships even as it imposed Day Zero water restrictions across the city.[116] Cape Town's government never implemented further restrictions on townships, and in fact it reiterated its provision of the free basic water amount and introduced cross-subsidizing taxes on the rich.[117] Townships use little water, since they still have limited access to it. But it is all too easy to imagine a regime that would have unequivocally protected wealthy users' access to water or cut water from poor Black areas first. Cape Town's government did neither of these things. Instead, it astutely diagnosed and regulated affluent white water users.

Cape Town's disciplinary measures certainly had their downsides: the water map encouraged neighbors to surveil each other, and some lower-income residents, especially those with large families, were burdened by water meter cutoffs or fines for exceeding the quota of 50 liters of water per person per day. Conversely, the state was not able to discipline ultra-wealthy residents who refused state regulations altogether by hoarding water or digging their own backyard boreholes. These residents tended to pursue their own individualized and privatized water uses at the expense of the rest of the city. Examples can be seen in the short documentary *Cape Town: Life without Water*, directed by Juliet Riddel. Toward the end of the film, a white family successfully digs a backyard borehole, and the female homeowner immediately says, "We can have a swimming pool, we can have a garden, and we don't have to worry."[118] Yet despite the limits of its actions and the negative light in which state punishment and surveillance are usually viewed, Day Zero was successful largely because state disciplinary practices were imposed on and taken up by a large number of middle- and upper-class households. State discipline during Day Zero can be read not only for its negative effects but also for the positive outcome it produced. The state's educational guides, awareness campaigns, and punitive policies were all instrumental in producing more water-wise citizens and ultimately a better ecopolitical future for the city, one where Day Zero never fully arrived.

Yet this was not all Cape Town did to discipline its citizens and turn the city away from a dry future. It also projected an apocalyptic "worst-case scenario" of what might happen if water-consuming behavior did not change. This preventative tactic, of projecting a bad future in order to induce change in the present, is striking for the way it echoes the generic hallmarks of apocalyptic climate fiction. Such fictions traffic in what SF scholar Gerry Canavan has described as "the true fantasy of apocalypse," which is "not so much that we will be destroyed but that *something might intervene in time to force us to change*."[119] Apocalyptic climate fictions consistently seek to prevent the worst-case futures they depict from coming to pass, in turn posing the present as a time when change is still possible.[120] While they also diagnose the forces that lead to bad futures, an aesthetic commitment to prevention is one of the most recognizable hallmarks of the apocalyptic climate fiction genre. This preventative impulse features in speculative global blockbusters like Paolo Bacigalupi's *The Water Knife* and Margaret Atwood's *The Year of the Flood*. But during Day Zero, such apocalyptic prevention burst the boundaries of fiction and bled into Capetonian policy.

In the lead-up to Day Zero, the formal structure of prevention that literary critics typically associate with apocalyptic climate fiction could be seen in Cape Town's climate adaptations, as the government raised the specter of what it called a "worst-case scenario" in order to prevent its actual occurrence.[121] Helen Zille, premier of the Western Cape province, which includes Cape Town, compared Day Zero to a calamity like "the Second World War or 9/11" and worried how the city would "prevent anarchy."[122] To avoid a future in which the city's taps would actually be shut off, Cape Town's leaders deployed alarmist, end-times rhetoric and restrictive policies. In tandem with its disciplinary measures, these efforts galvanized widespread social action and succeeded in maintaining the city's water reserves at usable levels, as just discussed. It is certainly easy to critique the state's scaremongering. But these actions should be read as more than instances of state oppression, for they also allowed the city to pluralize its future from within the pre-Day Zero present. Rather than continuing on the path of rampant water consumption that would have brought Cape Town *inevitably* to Day Zero, Cape Town's leaders intervened to produce a less dire water future.

There were several turning points in the rhetoric of water restrictions and Capetonians' responses. One of the most pivotal was the release of the city's "Critical Water Shortages Disaster Plan" in late 2017. When the plan was released, Cape Town was already in a phase of voluntary restrictions known as Phase One. Phase Two would have culminated in Day Zero, when millions of households and non-emergency businesses would no longer be able to access water privately but would have to wait at 200 collective municipal taps for just 25 liters of water per person per day. This phase was set to take effect if water storage in the city's six dams dropped below 13.5 percent. Another turning point was on January 18, 2018, when Cape Town's mayor, Patricia de Lille, announced that the city had "reached a point of no return" in its water supplies, and Day Zero was inevitable.[123] This statement was followed by new, steeper water restrictions, which limited people to 50 liters of water per day and more punitive tariffs for those households that exceeded this allowance.

What often goes unremarked in assessments of the city's apocalyptic projections and increasingly tight water restrictions is that Day Zero itself was not in fact the most severe water scenario. Beyond Day Zero and Phase Two, the city had planned for Phase Three, when even collection point water would not be available. Phase Three's "full-scale disaster implementation" would occur when all surface water was exhausted and only non-surface water, like aquifers, remained.[124] In this possible future, water would only be available for drinking (not for showers or household chores as was still possible under Phase Two), and water would be cut off even from emergency services and the crowded townships. By publicizing the possibility of Day Zero, the Cape Town government avoided actually implementing both city-wide water cutoffs and the even worse scenario of Phase Three.[125]

In the lead-up to Day Zero, apocalyptic climate fiction's aesthetic structure of prevention, or depicting an unwanted future in order to induce preventative action in the present, became municipal policy. It appeared in the political behavior of the local state and the water-saving measures taken by individual households. Reading negativity against the grain here reveals how the city of Cape Town's strict tactics and its projection of a frightening future succeeded in warding off a worst-case scenario. At this time state officials did not, of course, cite theories of climate fiction or the preventative fantasy of apocalypse. But their actions bear out the capacities and effects of anticipatory prevention that scholars in the environmental humanities have theorized through apocalyptic climate fiction. In Cape Town, the threat of a dry city was an impetus to force change within conditions of unprecedented water scarcity. State officials took up the narrative of Day Zero's bad possible future to challenge the givenness of high water-consumption practices, to change action in the present and thus avoid a future where Cape Town's taps ran dry. These water-saving efforts were eventually supplemented by winter rains in 2018, and by early 2019 Day Zero was officially dismissed as an immediate threat to Cape Town's water. But in the blurry boundary between new climate futures and existing political systems, Cape Town's preventative techniques can be understood through insights first developed through literary approaches to speculative climate apocalypse.

Indeed, how closely Capetonian policies followed the pattern of apocalyptic prevention can be seen through a comparison with Alistair Mackay's debut climate novel, *It Doesn't Have to Be This Way* (2022). Best known for writing an LGBTQ+ lifestyle column and queer short fiction, Mackay released *It Doesn't Have to Be This Way* a few years after Day Zero ended. Focused on the perspective of three queer characters, the novel "counts down" from a recognizably realist present where native South African trees and forms of representative government still exist to a more speculative future given over to corporate rule and endless consumption on the one hand and abject poverty on the other. The novel tracks the slide from some time like the contemporary reader's present toward an apocalyptic, desiccated, drought-stricken climate future where climate refugees and the poor live on Kapelitsha Island and the affluent are enclosed in the climate-controlled Citadel behind a security dome. In the Citadel, material comfort and new technology abound while outside the Citadel, the poor exchange human waste for protein powder made of dried maggots and cannot move during the hottest parts of the day without risking death from overheating. This climate future is ravaged by the kind of intensified drought, scorching heat, and strong winds scientists have predicted for Cape Town as global temperatures increase.[126]

Mackay has stated that dystopian elements of the present, including Cape Town's existing economic inequalities and apathy to climate change, motivated the writing of his novel; parts of the novel thus bear strong similarities with the present.[127] These include the future slum Kapelitsha, whose name is only two letters away from Khayelitsha, and the fact that those living in the area have to get water from public collection points. The latter detail, in particular, recreates the dire predictions made in the lead-up to Day Zero. Day Zero itself appears as an episode in the childhood of one of the narrators: "Luthando remembers the great drought that brought Cape Town to its knees. . . . he remembers Day Zero."[128] But despite these similarities, *It Doesn't Have to Be This Way* draws primarily on the preventative impulse found in speculative climate apocalypses. In presenting a worst-case future, such fictions seek to induce preventative action in the present. They traffic, again, in that "fantasy of apocalypse" that is "that *something might intervene in time to force us to change*."[129] The similarities between the present and future in the novel are thus largely overshadowed by how much worse that future is. If Khayelitsha's residents must today collect water at taps, Mackay strategically deploys other details, such as the maggot farms, to evoke revulsion and recoil. The novel's scenes of intensified poverty and climate hardship are thus presented as a future that can and should be avoided. In fact, each section of the novel works to produce a sense of preventative urgency by counting down toward this impending future: "Fifteen years to go."[130] The need to prevent the novel's apocalyptic climate future is moreover summed up as an instruction for readers in the novel's title (it doesn't have to be this way), and it recurs throughout the narrative as a refrain Malcolm and Luthando, two climate activists, deploy as they spearhead a global media campaign to avoid the kind of climate future that arrives in the latter part of the novel.

It Doesn't Have to Be This Way's demand for preventative change is aimed at the kinds of collective behaviors that have produced climate catastrophe, such as rampant resource consumption. But it also envisions a utopic alternative to the existing South African state and calls for the creation of a state with more environmentally just priorities. The state appears only in the novel's early sections, in the first years of the "countdown," which coincide more or less with a twenty-first-century climate present. States are later replaced with corporate rule. But during this early window, Luthando organizes a climate march to the capital, mobilizing slogans similar to those used by climate activists today: "'What do we want?' . . . 'Climate action!' 'When do we want it?' 'Now!'"[131] Their demands to the state name a huge list of possible actions:

> Ban fossil fuels. Ban plastics. Extend the nature reserves. Convert at least fifty per cent of all commercial timber plantations back into indigenous forest. Enforce stricter building codes for insulation and energy use. Build water treatment and recycling facilities. Increase the carbon tax and tax on meat by five hundred percent.[132]

This range of demands replicates the many interlinked calls being made for climate change action today, such as divesting from fossil fuels, petroleum, and carbon energy, reinforcing or restoring ecosystems, and reforming human relationships to food and other resources.

During the march, anti-climate reactionaries clash violently with Luthando's activists and police drones destroy their signs. In this moment Mackay's fictional state attacks and silences those clamoring for a better climate future. It defends the status quo of fossil fuels, meat eating, and water waste. Yet such a scene also lays out the huge scope of possible state actions that could be taken. Just as the novel lays out a miserable climate future that "doesn't have to be this way," it also represents a repressive state committed to capitalist interests that likewise "doesn't have to be this way." While the novel seeks to induce preventative action in the present by depicting horrifying scenes of poverty and climate exposure in future Kapelitsha, it also deploys something like utopian method by sketching an obverse map for a better state, using negative circumstances to name positive potentials.

The novel further emphasizes this need for political change and its call for an alternative, better state when it aligns Luthando's most radical act of climate activism with apartheid-era infrastructure protests. After the climate march is routed, Luthando finds a small group of militant and radical activists who are willing to attack the Mepudi power station, a large coal-fired power plant that is part of South Africa's national electricity company Eskom. This bombing by climate subversives harkens back to infrastructural attacks carried out by the ANC's militant wing uMkhonto weSizwe during apartheid rule, such as the bombings of the Sasol oil refinery in 1980 and Koeberg nuclear power station in 1982.[133] Luthando's infrastructural attacks in the name of a more just climate future unrecognized by the current regime offer a parallel to South Africa's earlier history of struggle against apartheid; similarly, Luthando's imprisonment and torture after the bombing replicate the kinds of repressive measures the apartheid state once took against anti-apartheid actors. Mackay thus critiques state repression of climate activism but more generally can be seen to call for a transformation of the current South African state on par with the scale of change envisioned during the anti-apartheid struggle. To this end he lays out an extensive proposal for how the state could be and the kinds of actions it could support to bring about a "new" new South Africa. While the novel's countdown might suggest an inevitable trajectory, the preventative impulse of its speculative apocalyptic form, combined with the parallels it draws between the transition away from fossil fuels and an earlier transition away from apartheid, suggest a larger vision. Mackay's title *It Doesn't Have to Be This Way* gestures to both a preventative impulse common to apocalyptic climate fiction and a historical precedent. It suggests that the South African state has undergone one radical transformation before—from apartheid—and could do so again—to combat climate change. A utopian method can be seen in these alternatives and antecedents. For reading patently negative circumstances against the grain for their positive potentials is, if nothing else, a way of seeing the world that assumes things do not have to be the way they are.

Day Zero as History

Mackay's incorporation of an alternative state vision also returns us to the historical precedents that underpinned Day Zero. For the classed and raced quality of Day Zero's water scarcity led some to point out that township residents have lived in Day Zero all along. Day Zero from this vantage was a new and frightening possibility only for Cape Town's upper and middle classes. For township residents, the experience of water scarcity, water cut-offs, and waiting in line to collect water from communal taps was not new at all.[134] Unless township residents have received a state-built RDP house, they experience Day Zero on a daily basis: they access water through shared taps, and many use only a few liters of water a day. Pointing out this disparity, though, is not simply to point out the inadequacies and failures of post-apartheid state delivery to townships. Instead, it gives Day Zero a radically new meaning.

From the perspective of water deprivation in the townships, Day Zero is history. It is not a new climate event but an old apartheid-era legacy. For it was the apartheid system that laid water pipes in white areas and not in townships, that relegated townships to extreme water scarcity, and that bequeathed to the post-apartheid state a vastly inadequate water infrastructure. To consider Day Zero conditions as history must also be to assess how the post-apartheid state has addressed this legacy—its many efforts to expand water access to those systemically denied piped urban water since taking power only a few decades ago. Since then, the state has sought to ensure water to the poorest through various programs and initiatives, and however imperfect, these efforts have also been specific and concretely utopian efforts to rectify the inequalities of apartheid. This is not to say that the state has heroically rescued poor residents from a long experience of Day Zero but that it has continuously attempted to make the conditions of Day Zero it inherited from apartheid more livable and less dire, more hopeful and less painful. The novelty of Day Zero for middle- and upper-class residents might threaten to overshadow the historic reality of Day Zero in the townships. But the complex way township residents themselves relate to the state highlights the concrete utopias of housing, water, and political inclusion that depend on the state. The kind of water scarcity Day Zero heralded could not be prevented for township residents, and it did not plunge townships or the city into social anarchy. Instead, Day Zero as history requires ongoing redress from the state, like apartheid's other legacies.

4
Making Time
Pacific Futurity and Rising Seas

In 2016 the residents of Isle de Jean Charles left their homes to the rising waters of the Gulf of Mexico. Since 1955, Isle de Jean Charles, a narrow sliver of land off the Louisiana coast eighty miles southwest of New Orleans, has shrunk by 98 percent as a result of flooding, erosion, and subsidence.[1] Most of its residents belong to the Isle de Jean Charles Band of Biloxi-Chitimacha-Choctaw tribe, who were relocated from Louisiana's mainland in the 1830s after the Indian Removal Act forced Indigenous nations to migrate west of the Mississippi River. And now, land erosion and sea level rise fueled by climate change and the fossil fuel industry are forcing them to move once again.

Sea levels have been rising slowly for over a century. But their recent acceleration is the product of fossil-fueled climate change.[2] To this day energy corporations fight tooth and nail to hold on to profits, propagating feel-good campaigns about their embrace of zero emission goals and carbon alternatives like solar and wind power even as they lobby governments and climate forums like the UN for their own interests. This was nowhere more glaring than at the 28th Conference of the Parties to the United Nations Framework Convention on Climate Change (COP28) in Dubai. COP28 was presided over by Sultan al-Jaber, who was both chairman of the United Arab Emirates' state-backed renewable energy company Masdar and chief executive of its state-owned oil company, ADNOC. Like al-Jaber's dueling roles, COP28 yielded mixed results. It was a major milestone in some ways—there was progress on commitments to reducing coal and methane, a heat-trapping greenhouse gas more potent than carbon dioxide; more than 120 countries pledged to triple renewable energy use; and $700 million was pledged to developing countries suffering "loss and damage" from climate change.[3] But even before talks began, leaked documents revealed that the UAE had planned to discuss fossil fuel deals with over fifteen countries, including France, Egypt, China, and Brazil, during the climate talks.[4] OPEC itself had a prominent pavilion at the conference, and it remains committed to expanding investments in oil and natural gas. Indeed, as a member of OPEC, the United Arab Emirates is working to increase its oil production capacity to a million barrels a day by 2027. Though there has been some movement on addressing climate change, climate diplomacy has been uneven and slow—sometimes because states continue to prioritize fossil-fuel-based economic growth over mitigating greenhouse gas emissions, and sometimes because corporate lobbyists have inertia, deep pockets, and the now-dominant logic of the free market on their side.

Yet these drags and obfuscations do not change the fact that seas are rising. Greenhouse gases produced from burning fossil fuels are warming the atmosphere more every year, causing seawater to thermally expand and melting huge quantities of polar ice. In 2016 the residents of Isle de Jean Charles were relocated after Louisiana was awarded a $48.3 million grant to resettle the tribe in the first federally funded effort in the United States to move an entire community due to climate change. The plan was to relocate and reunite the tribe forty miles north of Isle de Jean Charles in the higher, drier planned community of New Isle.[5] But climate scientists predict that much more than coastal islands like Jean Charles will be lost and much larger populations will have to be relocated. In Bangladesh, 20 million people are predicted to be at risk from sea level rise by 2050.[6] Much of the country is less than twelve meters above sea level, and a one-meter rise will inundate over 17 percent of the country's land mass.[7] Worldwide, hundreds of millions of people, mostly subsistence fishers and farmers, could be displaced because of climate change by 2050.[8] Some of these millions of people will be able to move to higher ground. But many will not be able to escape a flooding landscape.

In the Pacific regions of Micronesia and Polynesia, land is dwarfed by water, and there is nowhere to move to. The island nations central to this chapter—Tuvalu, Kiribati, and the Marshall Islands—rise barely above sea level.[9] Rising waters are predicted to swallow these island nations—not only portions of them, but in whole. What can be done when the sea is coming and all land disappears, when inundation is an imminent threat? As global temperatures rise and sea levels with them, mainstream media outlets, climate scientists, and NGOs outside the Pacific have increasingly touted climate refugeeism—the mass displacement of Pacific peoples from their islands due to sea level rise—as the inevitable future of low-lying Pacific states.[10] And though "climate refugeeism" is more figurative than formal, since international refugee conventions do not include climate displacement, the term highlights the involuntary, forced displacements that will accompany rising oceans.[11]

Yet just as chapter 3 considered Anthropocene conjunctures in Cape Town, where new climate threats of water scarcity and drought converged with the ongoing history of apartheid's water inequalities, so too in the Pacific the impending catastrophe of sea level rise must be understood in relation to past histories of violence. While conjunctures characterized the meeting of climate futures and apartheid pasts in chapter 3, here colonial history takes on a palimpsestic quality: sea level rise as impending destruction is layered on top of histories of colonial genocide and disease, economic exploitation, and militarism of the ordinary and nuclear kind. Sea level rise is from this vantage only the latest iteration of a history of futurelessness that has been imposed on Pacific islanders in various guises. Sea level rise is an unprecedented physical and existential threat, endangering the very existence of Pacific islands, cultural communities, and Indigenous lifeways. But the losses and erasures it heralds cannot be separated from these previous histories of futurelessness and thus the layering of colonial, capitalist, and militarized violence in the Pacific. These previous forms of ending were predicted to be just as totally destructive and just as inescapable as sea level rise is today. And yet, they have been survived.

Thus, on the flooding shores of the Pacific's low-lying islands, state leaders, activists, and writers alike reject the inevitability of refugee narratives, which have come to define Pacific environmental destiny as one of impending victimization and communal loss. In contrast to the closure of the future naturalized by submersion and refugee predictions, Pacific peoples persistently articulate other possible futures. As with the previous chapters, recursive and nonlinear conceptions of time saturate these endeavors to imagine concrete utopian futures outside refugeeism. Pacific state leaders, writers, and activists all mobilize a fluid and plural sense of time as they imagine outlandish possibilities, call for preventative action, propose speculative alternatives to disappeared states, or suggest new uses for old practices. These efforts are ways of making time and envisioning futurity outside the teleological thrust of sea level rise and the futurelessness it is said to herald.

Climate change will raise the world's oceans. From scientific and media vantage points outside the Pacific, these climate predictions can only lead to one outcome. Teleological predictions of refugeeism draw on linear conceptions of time in which futurity is singular and, as such, is determined by the one-way thrust of cataclysmic progression in a warming world. However, the forces predicted to end Pacific futures have also generated novel forms of future-making. Despite the seeming inevitability of an inundated future,

Pacific writers and political leaders refuse refugee narratives and the temporal assumptions that undergird them. In the face of rising seas, writers and statemakers have looked to the past and the future to critique the limitations of existing political and epistemological regimes and to imagine futures beyond the limits of sea level rise. They do not contest the environmental fact of rising oceans, but they do pluralize how futures are imagined in their shadow, conceiving specific forms of futurity beyond refugee destruction and loss. Anthropogenic climate change and sea level rise, while obvious threats to existing and future Pacific worlds, have also been occasions for reimagining Pacific futurity.

Climate Inaction / Fossil Foot-Dragging

All too often, the profits of energy companies and the appetites of fossil fuel–based economies outside the Pacific have been prioritized over the needs, and now increasingly the very existence, of island states. In December 2023, at the COP28 talks, the Marshall Islands' climate envoy Tina Stege noted that even positive aspects of the negotiations, like increasing commitments to renewable energy, could not "greenwash" the fact that "countries . . . are simultaneously expanding fossil fuel production."[12] Climate action has been painfully partial and slow even as atmospheric levels of carbon dioxide and other greenhouse gases have soared. Indeed, when atmospheric CO_2 was first measured at Hawai'i's Mauna Loa Observatory in March 1958, it was 313 parts per million (ppm).[13] In 2024, the average was 422.7 ppm, higher than at any other point in human history.[14] Even the landmark Paris Agreement, adopted in 2015 as state leaders pledged to try to cut greenhouse gas emissions and prevent global temperatures from rising more than 1.5°C, has been difficult to enforce and full of loopholes.

A number of recent climate change documentaries have chronicled the dogged efforts of island leaders to influence international climate policies in the face of this stultifying climate inaction. Films in this genre include John Shenk's *The Island President* (2011), which follows Maldives' president Mohammed Nasheed during COP15 in Copenhagen, and Matthieu Rytz's documentary *Anote's Ark* (2018), which depicts Kiribati president Anote Tong's climate lobbying before he left office in 2016. Both films focus on the immediate threat sea level rise poses to these island nations, and they stress how the diplomatic efforts of leaders like Nasheed and Tong abroad are grounded in real-time losses happening at home. As Tong puts it bluntly in Rytz's film, "For those of us on the front line, it really does not matter what is agreed to in Paris, because we will continue to go under water. We would like to be able to reverse [climate change] if we could do it . . . the reality is that it will not happen."[15]

Tong and other Pacific leaders point out that small Pacific states are being wrongfully threatened by emissions: "In spite of our isolation, here we are, subjected to the global phenomenon of climate change."[16] In fact, many scholars have noted the moral component of Pacific climate complaints, for atoll nations produce negligible amounts of greenhouse gas emissions but are most severely threatened by them.[17] These emissions arise both from the fossil fuel industry and state economies. Historically, greenhouse gas–producing states were confined to Europe and North America, but they now also include large developing states like India and China, who have grown their economies by burning carbon-based fuels like coal, oil, and natural gas.

In transnational coalitions like the Alliance of Small Island States (AOSIS) as well as through individual diplomatic efforts, Pacific states have attempted to prompt other states to reduce emissions by leveraging their moral and affective positions. Toward the beginning of *Anote's Ark*, Tong asks a UN forum, "Is the global community willing to come forward? Is this Council willing to make a contribution towards getting some real action on the ground so that we can give some sense of comfort, some sense of security to our people? Who do we appeal to, and turn to, for our people's right to survive?"[18] Here Tong appeals to those countries that have the power to intervene in the fossil-fueled status quo driving sea level rise and threating Pacific futurity. Rather than simply continuing current trajectories of greater and greater carbon emissions in the coming years, large industrialized and industrializing states might bring comfort and security to Pacific peoples by taking action to turn away from fossil fuels. Such diplomatic efforts are starting to bear fruit, but not fast enough: scientists argue that limiting the atmospheric warming driving climate change will require net-zero emissions, and states would have to cut carbon dioxide emissions 48 percent from 2019 levels by 2030.[19] At present there is, to put it mildly, a "substantial 'emissions gap'" between what states are doing and what they need to do to reach this goal.[20]

Pacific states have tried to sway other states toward emissions reductions far before the current moment of heightened climate crisis. Andrea Torrice's 2000 documentary *Rising Waters: Global Warming and the Fate of the Pacific Islands* chronicles the climate struggles of a number of Pacific states, including Kiribati and the Marshall Islands, and their role in early climate negotiations during the 1990s. These efforts included lobbying during the lead-up to the 1997 Kyoto Protocol, where climate scientists recommended a staggering 60–80 percent cut in emissions to mitigate global warming. Despite island nations' urging to heed these calls, the Kyoto Protocol institutionalized only a 5 percent cut in global emissions by 2012.[21] As Samoan climatologist Penchuro Lefale put it in the documentary, "From an island perspective, that is really, really difficult to accept, because it's the security and the solvency of island nations that are at stake."[22] Subsequent climate treaties, including the Paris Agreement, have continued to fall far short of the emissions cuts necessary to stabilize, let alone reduce, climate change. The leaders of small island states have thus been working for decades against the foot-dragging of global greenhouse gas emitters.

Pacific activists have also worked to move the needle on climate inaction. They deploy slogans like, "We are fighting! We are not drowning!" to protest the naturalization of submersion and refugeeism, and they have used a range of tactics, from protesting in the streets to blocking coal ships, to bring visibility to the plight of their islands. *Anote's Ark*, which largely follows Tong, also includes scenes of climate protestors outside the 2014 UN Climate Summit in New York City. In one clip, Kathy Jetñil-Kijiner, a well-known poet and activist from the Marshall Islands, declares, "A lot of the media so far focused on where islanders will go and where we will relocate, and I want people to know that we don't want to move from our islands and we shouldn't have to move from our islands."[23] Here Jetñil-Kijiner, who also performed a protest poem at the summit, reiterates Pacific resistance to climate displacement and critiques perspectives outside the Pacific that naturalize this outcome. Despite these many efforts to secure concrete international promises that might safeguard Pacific futures, there has still been frustratingly little action on reducing the greenhouse gases produced from burning fossil fuels.

As in chapter 3's discussion of Day Zero, in the Pacific, futurity is being radically schismed between desirable and undesirable developments that depend on inducing action now in order to turn from a bad trajectory. But while Cape Town's leaders were able to mobilize their populace and avoid a dry city, Pacific states have had little success influencing the fossil fuel priorities of other states. Tong admits as much in a moment of pessimism in *Anote's Ark*: "It's not easy to try and imagine what is coming, because nobody wants to admit that maybe in the future, all of the land, which is our homeland, will no longer be there."[24] Indeed, the injustice of sea level rise and the terrible consequences of climate inaction are perhaps most starkly captured in a question once posed to Anote Tong's colleague in the Indian Ocean, Mohammed Nasheed of the Maldives: "Why is the end of the world only for us?"[25] The people of the Maldives are fighting rising seas like their Pacific counterparts, and this question captures the fears that also motor Pacific lobbying, diplomacy, protests, and other efforts to combat greenhouse emissions. It makes clear that the issue is not only that fossil-fueled climate futures are arriving first in the Pacific and Indian oceans, but that these futures are anticipated to be ones of immense cultural, epistemological, and ontological loss. Indeed, they will be ones of world-ending erasure. It is too late to prevent climate change wholesale, but refusing to at least mitigate greenhouse gas emissions and the warming, rising seas they produce is also to refuse islanders a place in the future. For low-lying island nations, climate inaction is an act: an act that will lead to futurelessness for thousands of atolls and their peoples across the world's rising oceans.

State Adaptations: Promising a Place and Repurposing the Past

Island nations have not, however, left their fates to faulty international accords or the fossil fuel inertia of other states. Rather, most Pacific states are working to bring about concrete utopias of futurity beyond refugeeism for their peoples by developing in-place adaptations at home. These national adaptations summarily reject international predictions of forced displacement. Such commitments are exemplified in Tuvalu's climate change policy *Te Kaniva*, a national climate adaptation plan that sought to draw forth lines of continuity between a familiar present and possible futures not defined by refugeeism. "Te Kaniva" refers to traditional Tuvaluan systems of weather and star-based navigation, suggesting the centrality of local practices and Indigenous knowledge to confronting the climate future. *Te Kaniva* was written after wide civilian consultation and with the participation of local leaders and dignitaries from various levels of civil society, including "church leaders, representative [sic] of primary, secondary, and tertiary schools as well as political leaders."[26] As such it is taken to "[contain] the aspirations of the people of Tuvalu on how best to address the impacts and consequences of climate change."[27] Tuvalu's *Te Kaniva*, which charted national climate policy from 2012 to 2021, focused on in-place adaptations and was committed to the continuity of Tuvaluan statehood; by extension it also sought to preserve the landed ontologies of its citizens and to resist the profound cultural and communal loss that would accompany climate migration.

Tuvalu is composed of a cluster of nine islands midway between Hawai'i and Australia, on the western edge of Polynesia. Centuries before its first European contact by Spanish explorers in the sixteenth century, Polynesian sailors had navigated the islands and used them as stepping stones to further migration westward. But despite this long history of ocean-going, in Tuvalu today some residents have proclaimed the desire to die in Tuvalu rather than leave.[28] Climate adaptation researcher Carol Farbotko, geographer Elaine Stratford, and anthropologist Heather Lazrus have identified a *"sedimentation of sedentarist feelings"* among some Tuvaluan citizens, a phrase that "[captures] an intensity of voiced commitment among some members of the population to staying rooted in place, even in the face of possible inundation of their islands."[29] As one woman told the researchers, "You know your way at home.

And then you are yourself. Your identity is there."[30] Who you are is where you are. Such inextricable entanglements of internal subjectivity and external environment are further signaled in terms like *fenua*, a Tuvaluan word that denotes an island and its community simultaneously, the mutual co-constituting of people and place.[31] Despite long-standing Tuvaluan traditions of seafaring and the important influence of Tongan and Fijian anthropologist Epeli Hau'ofa, who proposed "a sea of islands" to conceptualize the way Pacific communities are bridged and connected by the ocean, landed desires and ontologies have become more important in the face of sea level rise and they have shaped national documents like *Te Kaniva*.[32]

The section entitled "Goals" in *Te Kaniva* makes clear that it is primarily the Tuvaluan state that is charged with implementing this communal vision of staying on the islands and therefore of fulfilling a promise to remain in place that is also a concretely utopian aspiration to political and communal continuity. Of *Te Kaniva*'s seven overarching goals, six name practical measures meant to promote a future on Tuvalu, including government usage of climate data to improve disaster response programs, enhanced state access to disaster risk funds, the promotion of Tuvaluan energy security, and weather-proofing Tuvaluan infrastructures. The seventh goal then seems cumulative, providing a rationale for the aforementioned practices and a motivating logic for remaining in place: "Guaranteeing the Security of the People of Tuvalu from the Impacts of Climate Change and the Maintenance of National Sovereignty."[33]

This imperative leads to two differently envisioned futures, illustrated at the bottom of goal seven by two cannily juxtaposed photographs. Postcolonial historian Dipesh Chakrabarty has written of the parallel, mutually ongoing realities of postcolonial subjects who inhabit a capitalist-dominated modernity shot through with past perspectives and practices, thus destabilizing what may be considered "past."[34] *Te Kaniva* also meditates on heterotemporality, but these photographs do not so much comment on the entanglement of the past and present as they visualize the multiple futures emerging within Tuvalu's present moment of climate confrontation.

In both photographs (Figure 2) the eye is drawn to the background: leafy island in one, a wide blue expanse of sea in the other. These backgrounds double as horizons of potential fulfillment, organizing the citizens in each picture around, toward, or away from the different futures they represent. In the image on the left, the horizon is one of the islands of Tuvalu, still green and habitable. The foreground is dominated by a cluster of people grouped in a staggered circle. Their expressions are visible; a few appear to be in animated conversation, while those nearby incline their heads or wear furrowed looks of concentration. Trailed behind this group are small figures on white sand.

The vision we get is one of individuals who link foreground and background, a human chain where the concern visible on the faces in the foreground is presumed to extend also to those citizens whose faces we cannot see in the background. This picture poses the habitability of the island as one promised future, one it suggests will be secured through the kinds of concerted communal actions laid out in *Te Kaniva*.

Next to this image is one that presents the opposite vision. Here the immediate foreground is the edge of the beach, with the open sea and sky taking up the majority of the frame. Islanders are grouped haphazardly at the water's edge with bundles and furniture; some trail into the surf while others remain on the edge of the water. An expanse of blue sea and sky makes up the visual horizon toward which the islanders are turned, and between them is a small white boat. The line of bodies moves from the beach toward the sea and the boat; readers are presented with a scene of imminent departure. In contrast to the other image, these small figures are not identifiable or individualized; personhood is swallowed by a shared condition of departure, illustrating the perception that leaving is tantamount to the loss of Tuvaluan identity. Presented side by side at the end of Tuvalu's official climate adaptation policy, this image suggests that Tuvalu's government and its people are not merely ambivalent about the future, but that they inhabit these two possibilities simultaneously in a kind of doubled present, where the place of their future cannot be determined and thus must be presented as incommensurate and coeval. But it must be noted that both these possible futures are also alternatives to the singularity of climate refugeeism. The first photo presents an image of Tuvaluan political continuity, where Tuvalu's islands remain habitable and retain their place as the central ground of residents' communal life and identity. If the second photo belies this possibility, it is also worth noting what the

Figure 2. Two alternative futures for Tuvalu from Tuvalu's climate adaptation policy *Te Kaniva*.

image refuses. The beach and water are pristine; the people are neatly dressed and their belongings carefully packed; this is not a scene of desperation or chaotic migration after climate disaster. These closing images work to situate Tuvaluan citizens within as many futures as possible; contradiction here is less a sign of failure than it is an affirmation of state resistance to the naturalization of refugeeism. Tuvalu's two images present not only an incommensurable choice, but a moment where choice is still available. However fraught the second would be, it participates in the exercise of producing a future not determined by refugeeism.

And yet, the duality of this future is also tempered by the policy's overall emphasis on remaining in place, and examining the text that follows these images, where "strategies" and "expected outcomes" for Goal Seven are further elaborated, reveals that the migratory future and its representational image are strikingly emptied out. Rather than being an equal future, leaving Tuvalu seems to pass beyond the limit of efficacious governance and actionable political thought. Tuvalu's disavowal of its possible migratory future is revealed through the illogic of the "outcomes" and "strategies" that follow the image of migration. For example, "strategies" such as "[ensuring] that Tuvalu continued to have the capacity to remain as a nation" are paired with the "expected outcome" of "establishment of international legal framework for the resettlement and recognition of Tuvalu within another country as a sovereign state."[35] It is not at all clear how or why this kind of legal framework would be the outcome of safeguarding Tuvalu's cultural nation.[36] Not only does such a legal framework not yet exist, it bears little resemblance to other existing legal precedents and alternatives that could protect cultural nations, even without all the formal apparatuses of statehood.[37] Moreover, neither of these so-called strategies or outcomes really adhere to the categories they purportedly explain; the legal "outcome" seems more like the necessary "strategy" to ensure Tuvalu's continued national existence rather than the reverse; or, they might both be seen as desired goals, neither of which Tuvalu would be able to implement alone as part of a national strategy. There is also no elaboration about how either "ensuring the nation" or "establishing an international framework" would be pursued. Instead, these strategies and outcomes come to seem more like placeholders for a process of legislative planning between the present and a migratory future that *Te Kaniva* declines to perform.

The logical mismatch of this section indexes a limit to the political futurity imagined by the Tuvaluan state. Insofar as it resonates with citizen desires to remain on the islands and the privileged place of land for Tuvaluan peoples, this political inconceivability repudiates international pressures to migrate and the loss of statehood and place that would accompany displacement. Tuvalu's climate adaptation policy resists the naturalization of refugeeism and, along with complaints to the international community, is part of Pacific state strategies to avoid refugeeism. However problematic, in the face of sea level rise and climate change, Pacific states like Tuvalu work to promise concrete utopias of staying in place in contrast to the future ruptures and displacements that the sacrificial politics of international climate inaction threaten to bring about.

State promises here, as elsewhere, are about specific, emplaced desires and encompass the provision of a sense of desirable futurity itself. However inadequate commitments to land-based futures might seem in the face of sea level rise, these kinds of in-place strategies can be read as yet another example of utopian method, of bringing forth the positive valences within circumstances that are obviously negative. Pacific island states like Tuvalu offer their citizens frameworks to imagine concretely better futures by promising cultural, political, and social continuity at home. The gap between the articulation and the potential fulfillment of these promises is populated by all sorts of strategies: international advocacy as discussed earlier, but also in-place adaptation plans that, like their international counterparts, may or may not bring promises of a better future closer to fulfillment. In the face of sea level rise and land loss, political futurity in the Pacific becomes coextensive with a variety of promises that occupy the space between the Pacific's rapid environmental changes and the ways in which Pacific citizens and leaders are fighting to maintain and endure in their places despite those changes.

During his tenure as Kiribati's president from 2003 to 2016, Anote Tong's administration likewise pursued a number of climate adaptation initiatives. Kiribati is composed of thirty-two coral atolls and one raised coral island, Banaba, which was heavily mined for phosphorus in the early twentieth century. But this island nation in the central Pacific is mostly ocean: spreading out north and east of Tuvalu across the equator, Kiribati extends for over 1,800 miles. Of those, only 313 are land. In-place adaptations have included building seawalls, raising islands, and purchasing land in Fiji as a possible "safe haven for our people in the future."[38] But Tong also differed from other Pacific leaders by proposing that most of Kiribati's population might be relocated under the rubric of Migration with Dignity (MWD). At its most basic, Migration with Dignity was a labor migration scheme, which sought to relocate the majority of Kiribati's population outside the islands to places like New Zealand and Australia. As noted, most Pacific states have staunchly resisted the idea of any kind of relocation, and Tong's presidential successor has similarly turned away from migration, focusing on adapting in-place and even purging the language of migration from Kiribati's government website since taking office. However recent, Migration with Dignity has already become a suppressed state antecedent, and we will consider some of its drawbacks shortly. But first, we should consider how Migration with Dignity worked to promote concretely utopian futures beyond climate refugeeism by mobilizing state power and cultural precedents of voluntary labor migration. Migration with Dignity accepted the likelihood of forced migration due to sea level rise and attempted to facilitate relocation by reframing it through historic practices of labor migration rather than climate refugeeism. Under Migration with Dignity, the role of the state became "to create migrants before they become displaced peoples."[39]

I-Kiribati or Kiribati citizens have migrated for work to countries like the United States and Australia since the 1960s, and as of 2005, 2–3 percent of its population worked overseas or on oceangoing vessels.[40] If refugees are those who no longer have a national state from which they can claim rights and protections, for Tong the answer to this prospective future was not to turn to in-place adaptations alone, or to the abstraction of universal human rights, or even to an expanded definition of refugeeism that might include displacement from climate change. Instead, he and his government mobilized a suite of state-based disciplinary procedures, such as increased education and workplace training, to produce citizens with the skills to survive without the protection of a fully efficacious state. The government's migration strategy "aims to improve language, workplace skills and qualifications, in order to make i-Kiribati—Kiribati citizens—'competitive and marketable at international labour markets,' with options for labour mobility developed over time."[41] As Kiribati's Secretary of Foreign Affairs Tessie Lambourne explained, "The key element of our policy is the up-skilling of our nationals at all levels, though we are focusing on the vocational and technical levels at the moment."[42]

Tong suggested that this production of skilled migrants was part of the state's duty to care for its citizens: "People are getting quite scared now and we need immediate solutions. This is why I want to rush the solutions so there will be a sense of comfort for our people."[43] He elsewhere elaborated:

> The relocation of the 100,000 people of Kiribati cannot be done overnight. . . . It requires long-term forward planning and the sooner we act, the less stressful and the less painful it would be for all concerned. This is why my government has developed a long-term merit-based relocation strategy as an option for our people. As leaders, it is our duty to the people we serve to prepare them for the worst-case scenario.[44]

Lambourne similarly noted, "We know about the painful experience in the refugee field, both for the recipient countries and for the refugees themselves.

We do not want our people to experience this."[45] State-sponsored migration is here articulated as part of a larger self-conceived duty to protect citizen livelihoods and minimize the affective and existential toll of relocation.

In trying to produce I-Kiribati as voluntary labor migrants before they became forcibly displaced peoples, the state attempted to preserve a collective national identity by sending citizens abroad who could then provide a basis for future migrations.[46] As once articulated on Kiribati's climate change website, "opportunities must be created to enable the migration of those who wish to do so now and in the coming years. This will assist in establishing expatriate communities of I-Kiribati, who will be able to absorb and support greater numbers of migrants in the longer term."[47] Within MWD's schema, more vulnerable citizens might be accommodated and supported within the cultural communities built up by the nation's laboring avant-garde. This concrete utopian vision gestured not only to the communities of Kiribati citizens already living abroad, but also to the networks of material exchange, kinship, and remittances that already exist between overseas communities, the Kiribati state, and local villages and family networks.[48]

At its most ambitious, perhaps, Migration with Dignity sought to offer a concrete utopian future based in labor migration and diasporic community instead of confirming communal loss. Its vision of an alternate, better future was meant to enable citizens to situate migration due to sea level rise within older patterns of labor migration and therefore within alternate loci of historical experience and cultural meaning that could deflect the rupture that will come from loss of land. MWD aimed to use state discipline to produce skilled labor migrants but also delegated responsibility for preserving Kiribati futurity to the diasporic communities and informal channels of support that citizens have long provided to each other. These aspects of MWD drew on a "usable past" to provide a sense of comfort and continuity in the face of an inundated future.[49] Caught between newness and constraint, faced with unprecedented climate challenges and limited agency, Kiribati's Migration with Dignity plan drew upon past forms of labor migration to provide the outlines of an imaginable future away from the islands.

As with most state actions, Migration with Dignity was not without its own serious drawbacks. These limits are more superficially visible than its utopian potentials. For instance, in emphasizing the role of individuals in maintaining Kiribati overseas communities, MWD comes all too close to replicating the conditions of neoliberalism, which place the burden of personal responsibility upon individuals while withdrawing collective state protections.[50] And in attempting to produce relocatable citizens, MWD could have well ended up supporting the very goals of greenhouse gas–producing states and industries that see relocation as a way to defer emissions reduction. But if MWD can easily be seen to support the abstraction of labor demanded by neoliberal capital or the inertia of the fossil fuel economy, facilitating its citizens' capacities to imagine something other than a refugee future was nonetheless a concrete utopian vision. Kiribati's leaders envisioned a political community composed not only by a shared, usable past but by a common future, one oriented by the utopic possibility that its citizens might remain voluntary migrants embedded in community rather than becoming displaced individuals or climate refugees. Tong attempted to make these other futures into a "Real-Possible" from within the bind of limited present choices and an unwanted future.[51] MWD was never implemented on a large scale, but read utopically, it can be seen as an attempt to frame older forms of labor migration and the diasporic communities that have grown out of them and newer migrations in response to sea level rise as part of a shared lineage of cultural dispersal, ocean-spanning practice, and diffuse nation-building. Despite its problems, MWD pursued a concrete utopian vision.

Histories of Futurelessness

State policies like *Te Kaniva* and Migration with Dignity respond to the bad climate present of rising seas and climate inaction. But these forces are in fact only the latest in a long series of threats that have menaced futurity in the Pacific. In fact, when Mohammed Nasheed was asked, "Why is the end of the world only for us?," he was asked a question that also captures much of Pacific history. For sea level rise must be situated within a violent palimpsest of colonial encounters in the region and within a genre of what can be called Pacific extinction narratives that have long rendered the Pacific as a place and peoples with no future. Extinction narratives work by naturalizing Indigenous nonfuturity and can broadly be seen as part of the erasure of Indigenous peoples that colonialism the world over has perpetuated.[52] In the Pacific, extinction narratives have recurred historically in many different forms, and climate refugeeism, island inundation, and sea level rise are only the latest version of this genre.

An early iteration of the Pacific extinction narrative was the theory of "fatal impact." It was based on the actual decimation of islander populations as a result of encountering of European diseases in the nineteenth century.[53] Postcolonial literature scholar Michelle Keown has described the prevalence of fatal impact narratives in fin de siècle writing about the Pacific where, as islanders died of foreign contagions against which they had no immunity, a "belief that Pacific cultures were dying out as a result of contact with

Europeans gained widespread currency . . . reinforced by the application of Darwin's theory of natural selection to Indigenous societies."[54] European and American writers like Robert Louis Stevenson and Jack London perpetuated such theories and incorporated them into their fiction.[55] And while Pacific populations recovered in the twentieth century, this narrative was continuously used to justify European colonialism in the region.

Later discourses of Pacific futurelessness focused on the aftermath of Pacific independence movements in the latter half of the twentieth century and targeted Pacific political and economic viability.[56] In this view, the physical smallness and remoteness of Pacific islands from centers of continental, metropolitan capital meant that they were also isolated from the prosperity brought by the global market. International affairs scholar Greg Fry, writing of Australian representations of the Pacific in the 1990s, notes that the Pacific was regarded as facing "an approaching 'doomsday' or 'nightmare' unless Pacific Islanders remake themselves."[57] From the center-periphery model perpetuated by global capital, only a Malthusian "future nightmare of overcrowding, poverty, mass unemployment, serious environmental degradation, and a decline in health standards" seemed possible for Pacific islands.[58] Unsurprisingly, incorporating them into international networks of trade was touted as the appropriate remedy.

Finally, European and American nuclear militarism during the Cold War and after required the Pacific "Basin" to be represented as an empty space. As numerous scholars have pointed out, the Pacific was chosen for nuclear testing in part because small island populations could be relocated with relative ease and were regarded as "exotic, malleable, and, most of all, dispensable."[59] Pikinni (Bikini) atoll, where the first of sixty-seven U.S. nuclear tests took place, was chosen largely because it was removed from commuter or commercial air and sea routes. Pikinni is part of the Republic of the Marshall Islands, which contains more than 1,200 islands extending over 180,000 miles of the northwest Pacific Ocean in two coral atoll chains. The total land mass of the islands is similar to the size of Washington, D.C., and none rise more than six meters or twenty feet above high tide. With its limited land and expansive oceanic territory, U.S. nuclear, economic, and demographic priorities rendered Marshallese lives "ungrievable."[60] The latter sentiment was perhaps most famously demonstrated by U.S. National Security Advisor and Secretary of State Henry Kissinger, who proclaimed, "There are only 90,000 people out there. Who gives a damn?"[61]

Indeed, in the long catalogue of Pacific extinction narratives and the many historical forms of futurelessness imposed on the region, nuclear testing stands out for the extent of its destructive effects. In contrast to Pacific "Rim" states like South Korea, Japan, and Indonesia, the Pacific "Basin" has historically been represented as empty space and its islands as isolated and contained.[62] In "The Myth of Isolates," critical ocean and island studies scholar Elizabeth M. DeLoughrey discusses how this logic of isolation provided a conceptual rubric through which the U.S. Atomic Energy Commission viewed nuclear weapons testing in the Marshall Islands. American nuclear militarism drew on old colonial logics of the island as laboratory as well as newer scientific ecosystem theories of nature as a closed system to rationalize nuclear test bombing from 1946 to 1958. American nuclear militarism was "sustained by the concept of an isolated and ultimately disposable laboratory" in which the consequences of testing could be both contained and left behind.[63] But, of course, nuclear contamination is far from containable, either in space or time. These nuclear histories of futurelessness continue into the present, visible in the absence of former islands like Elugelab, which was blasted from existence by test bombs, and in irradiated bodies across the Pacific.

The threat inaugurated by sea level rise compounds and is layered over these earlier, ongoing histories of futurelessness. Nuclear history epitomizes, though it does not have monopoly over, narratives in which the future of places outside the Pacific is produced in tandem with the excision of the Pacific from a shared future.[64] Pacific extinction narratives thus do not so much describe an inevitable future as they work to impose one: colonial diseases, predatory capitalism, nuclear bombing, and most recently, fossil-fueled sea level rise all posit the Pacific as futureless while actually working to produce and impose such foreclosures on Pacific peoples and their islands.

Many climate documentaries reveal this palimpsestic history of violence in the Pacific. Parts of Torrice's documentary *Rising Waters*, for instance, connect current forms of sea level rise to the history of American nuclear testing in the Marshall Islands. It includes black and white historical footage from mid-century, when residents of Pikinni atoll were evacuated ahead of the Castle Bravo test bomb. Castle Bravo, set off over the atoll on March 1, 1954, was the largest thermonuclear bomb ever detonated by the United States and approximately 1,000 times more powerful than the bomb dropped on Hiroshima.[65] The residents of Rongelap and Utrik atolls, hundreds of miles east of Pikinni, were also evacuated, but only after being exposed to heavy fallout as winds blew radioactive particles from the bomb toward their islands.[66] Historical footage from these evacuations plays on screen as the narrative voice-over in *Rising Waters* notes that the Marshallese "worry that in the not-too-distant future, they may have to leave their homes. Those fears come from a sense of history repeating itself."[67] Thus, through voice-over narration and visual repetition, *Rising Waters* suggests that the threat climate change poses to the Pacific is as dangerous and destructive as earlier waves of nuclear test bombing. By implication, the film also draws parallels between the overt violence of exploding bombs and the more indirect, but equally destructive, effects of sea level rise.

This is a point that Anote Tong dwells on explicitly toward the end of Rytz's documentary *Anote's Ark*. In a voice-over monologue that takes up about a minute of the documentary, Tong lays out a theory of climate change as war:

> What is war? If North Korea was to explode bombs which are highly radioactive and which then they float over to South Korea, what would that constitute? It's virtually an act of war because it would damage their health, and it would kill people in South Korea, maybe even Japan. And it's not the kind of thing that anybody, any country, close by would accept. Yet all of this, all of these emissions are being sent our way. All of the water that's resulting from climate change are being sent our way. Countries which are burning coal, which are very high carbon footprints, are doing it at our cost. If the countries know that their act is detrimental to the health and the life of our people, yet they continue to do it, what is that? This is an act of war.[68]

Like the footage in *Rising Waters*, Tong's commentary here compares climate change to war, arguing that the effects of carbon emissions and sea level rise are just as destructive as more conventional and obviously violent acts like the dropping of a bomb. Indeed, Tong's monologue is a crucial moment of epistemological reorientation for viewers of the film. For as Tong speaks, the film shows footage onscreen from cyclone Winston, which hit Fiji in 2016 and was the most powerful cyclone ever recorded in the Southern Hemisphere. The camera pans over scenes of total devastation: demolished buildings, uprooted trees, churned earth, and intermittent fires blazing against an inky sky. Though this destruction is from the cyclone, the scale and severity of the damage also look like the aftermath of a bomb blast, and Tong's voice-over encourages viewers to shift their understanding of the scene, to see it not as the aftermath of a natural disaster but as the aftermath of an act of war being waged on the Pacific through climate change.

Tong's analogy is not melodramatic. His emphasis on the violence of climate change is only an extension and intensification of the way climate change is already understood in the Anthropocene: as the product of human action. Though the effects of greenhouse gas emissions are not always politicized so overtly, in the Pacific the consequence of emissions is indeed targeted destruction. The futurelessness of sea level rise is happening in specific places and to specific peoples first, traceable to the carbon emissions of industrial economies just as the obliteration of a bomb blast can be traced to the plane that dropped it. Indeed, the scene that immediately follows Tong's monologue and the footage from Fiji is shot from the view of a cockpit, which visually reinforces the analogy between emissions and war. Though this plane drops no bombs, the plane's droning engine emits fossil fuels, and viewers have been primed to think of the fuel as akin to a bomb even though there is no explosion.

Another climate documentary, which focuses on Tuvalu, also suggests continuities between climate change and earlier practices of colonialism and militarism, though more obliquely. The title of Christopher Horner's *The Disappearing of Tuvalu: Trouble in Paradise* (2004) suggests that it will address the problem of fossil fuel-induced sea level rise. The film, however, largely ignores climate change until its ending segments, abstractly linking Tuvalu's disappearance with Western consumer culture instead and then fetishistically depicting Tuvaluans as a quaint, nonmodern people oriented around family and community. Climate change only appears toward the end of the film, when formal disjunctures between the film's soundtrack and image track ironically connect past losses imposed on Tuvalu with current sea level rise.

One of the reasons Tuvalu is so vulnerable to sea level rise is that its land was dredged by the U.S. military to build a landing strip.[69] During WWII, Tuvalu was a British Crown Colony and was used on the frontlines of Allied efforts against Japanese expansion in the Pacific. Though perhaps not as spectacular as Cold War nuclear militarism in the Marshall Islands, ordinary militarism in Tuvalu has nonetheless intensified the vulnerability of the islands to sea level rise in the present. The film initially downplays this history, depicting the landing strip as a depoliticized space. With four flights a week, it is dominated not by air traffic but by everyday sociality: soccer practice, police drills, and community gatherings. Only later does Toaripi Lauti, who served as the first prime minister of Tuvalu, recount that the earth for the airstrip came from "borrow pits"—so called because the earth from them was borrowed for use in the air strip. He notes that these borrow pits take up about half of the atoll of Funafuti, which is home to Tuvalu's capital and is the most populated of the nation's nine islands. As he puts it, "It's quite a big damaging [sic], if I should say."[70] He goes on in what appears to be a critical vein; yet in a pattern of auditory and visual disjuncture that happens repeatedly in the film, most of his commentary is dubbed over by another sound. In this instance, it is a chorus of children singing. Lauti can still be seen talking onscreen, but his words have literally been silenced and replaced with a manufactured sound of harmony. This disjuncture between the film's images and the soundtrack happens randomly many times throughout the documentary. The unintended effect of such track divergence and auditory dubbing is to replicate colonial silencing.

Another especially notable instance of these disjunctures occurs toward the end of the film. The scene opens with Jonathan Gayton, director of Tuvalu's Marine Training School, standing outside one of the oldest buildings in Tuvalu, a school that was built below the water line. He says critically, "The question I have to ask is: why did they build this house in an area where it floods, when if they built it a couple of meters to the left, or ten meters out to the right, it would have been above the water line?"[71] As he continues talking, the camera cuts to a faded plaque that identifies the school as the First Boy's Mission School of the London Missionary Society in Tuvalu. Gayton continues walking around this crumbling British colonial era institution, situated without care or attention to the water line. Such infrastructural choices make flood vulnerability an actual part of the building's foundations.

Then, though Gayton remains visible onscreen, gesticulating and visibly upset, the soundtrack cuts out his words for a woman's voice that recounts how Tuvalu has recently experienced more erratic weather and intensified environmental vulnerability. This is the voice of Hilia Vavae, who works at the Tuvaluan Meteorological Service and appears several times in the documentary. She points out, "We're seeing more droughts, more tropical cyclones, more intense sea water flooding . . . more than that, we have seen more erosion."[72] As her words sound, the mission school is still onscreen, and its visual reference points to the violence of British colonialism and infrastructural negligence; meanwhile, Vavae's voice-over about erosion brings to mind the "big damaging" of the borrow pits and earlier practices of American militarism while also commenting directly on the intensifying effects of climate change. The disjunctive visual and auditory elements in this scene bring historic damage imposed on Tuvalu from British colonialism and American militarism together with present climate vulnerabilities.

None of these connections are made explicitly by the documentary's narrator or recorded subjects. Indeed, DeLoughrey has noted that this and other films about Tuvalu tend to "bracket out modernity and technology from island life . . . mourning about the loss of a subsistence mode of living in which capitalism and empire, including carbon colonialism, are only distantly implicated."[73] And since these track divergences happen erratically throughout the entire documentary, it seems unlikely that they were intentional on the part of the filmmakers. In fact, in this section of the film, almost all the speakers onscreen are shown with a different part of the soundtrack, as when a woman's voice is heard but a man is onscreen, two different men's voices are heard though only one is visible onscreen, and so on. Also, not all the speakers say things about climate change or past colonial institutions, which suggests that this is not a savvy editorial technique but only poor sound engineering. In a review article of Tuvaluan climate films, ethnographers Anne Chambers and Keith Chambers describe this editorial sloppiness euphemistically as the way "concise voiceover narration structures the first half of the film but gradually diminishes, leaving a wide range of English-speaking Tuvaluans to express the film's concluding message."[74] The kind of striking and recurrent disjunctures between *The Disappearing of Tuvalu*'s image track and soundtrack nonetheless produce connections between old practices of futurelessness or earlier extinction narratives and current experiences of sea level rise that threaten Tuvalu. Along with other climate films, *The Disappearance of Tuvalu* thus draws out continuities between different waves of futurelessness in the Pacific, where history has been a palimpsest of colonial, military, and now climate violence, and narratives of extinction are layered one on top of the other.

Surviving the Future in *Iep Jāltok*

As Pacific texts respond to violent pasts that continue and accumulate in the present, they sometimes transform these bad aggregations. For histories of futurelessness are also histories of recursion, accumulations that undermine, diverge from, and counter each other to challenge the progressive destruction they otherwise record. To this end, Kathy Jetñil-Kijiner's poetry collection *Iep Jāltok: Poems from a Marshallese Daughter* (2017) takes up, only to dispute, histories of futurelessness in the Marshall Islands. Jetñil-Kijiner is the daughter of current Marshallese president Hilda Cathy Heine, and *Iep Jāltok* is the first collection of Marshallese poetry to be published in English.[75] In it, Jetñil-Kijiner represents Pacific history as a sedimented accumulation that "is not a series but an *interlocking* of presents, pasts, and futures that retain their depths of other presents, pasts, and futures, each age bearing, altering, and maintaining the previous ones."[76] Such a notion of fluid, recursive, and nonsynchronous time casts the past as always carried forward into, and part of the composition of, the present. But while documentaries like *Rising Waters* and *The Disappearing of Tuvalu* reveal these historic impositions to critique the violence they have wrought in the Pacific, Jetñil-Kijiner's temporal refiguring enacts something like utopian method. It turns existing circumstances to new ends by recuperating past predictions of regional extinction. In Jetñil-Kijiner's poetry, impossible futures in the Pacific are chronicled instead as Pacific histories of surviving the future.

Throughout her collection, Jetñil-Kijiner weaves extinction narratives, especially nuclear militarism, into a recursive account of the Marshall Islands, where the very bodies now threatened by sea level rise become the traveling repositories of a history that is not even past, much less prematurely ended.

Writing from the vantage of a past's future that was never supposed to arrive, whether because of nuclear fallout or sea level rise, Jetñil-Kijiner's poems offer a lineage or temporal genealogy of surviving closed futures. In doing so, *Iep Jāltok* poses sea level rise as the very *kind* of bad future that has *already* been faced and survived in the Pacific. Her poems situate sea level rise within a longer lineage of impossible futures so that, in *Iep Jāltok*, extinction becomes part of Pacific history rather than its end. Jetñil-Kijiner's poetry therefore speaks from the place of an impossible subject, a subject of history whom history was anticipated to wipe out. This Pacific subject does not signify nothing, but articulates an irrevocable something—or rather, a sometime—that rewrites the teleological thrust of extinction and refugeeism and even the singularity of futurity itself as construed in notions of sequential time.

Beginning with Marshallese founding myths that include the invention of the sail and the birth of Marshallese seafaring, the collection then moves on to chart postwar Marshallese experience. Linking the historic with the autobiographical, the collection's second section, "History Project," chronicles the islands' material deprivation after World War II and the onset of international aid before unraveling the history of regional nuclear testing. The section's eponymous poem "History Project" opens as an exercise in self-education and political consciousness raising as the speaker, an unnamed Marshallese girl loosely based on Jetñil-Kijiner herself, declares, "Time to learn my own history."[77]

This poem highlights the horrific physical consequences of nuclear fallout on Marshallese bodies: "I glance at a photograph / of a boy, peeled skin" and "I read firsthand accounts / of what we call / jelly babies."[78] The poem is more than an act of historical witnessing and exposure, though, as it is bookended by two poems about nuclear fallout that extend its temporal, formal, and spatial edges. "History Project" is surrounded by two other poems, "The Letter B is For" and "Fishbone Hair," that bring the physical consequences of fallout into the somatic immediacy of ongoing radiation and formally beyond a single poem's containment.

Given the extensive half-lives of nuclear isotopes and thus the multigenerational effects of radiation poisoning, it is not surprising that Jetñil-Kijiner represents the consequences of the bomb outside the boundedness of a single poem. Attention to the secondary effects of radiation after the initial spectacle of a bomb's explosion is not unusual, but this series of poems highlights the way nuclear radiation's aftermath works as a perverse confirmation of the failure of extinction. Evidenced in the slow death of bodies generations removed from the initial tests and spatially remote from the islands, somatic decay, repeated from "jelly babies" to the speaker's niece Bianca, is proof of uncontained and ongoing history, rather than its ending.

Hence, the visually fluid form of "The Letter B is For," which immediately precedes "History Project," appropriately plays with its own borders and boundaries. More pointedly, the poem is formally ironic. Presented as a dictionary entry, it only records its own inability to contain the meanings of the very word it sets out to define:

baaṃ (baham). From Engl. 2(inf, tr
. . . .
                Are you contaminated
                              with radioactive fallout?[79]

As the poem's staggered typography mimics the way the consequences of the bomb slide or fall away from the moment of initial contact, the bomb becomes redefined as somatic residue rather than temporal finale. It diffuses threat to an anonymous "you" that could be anybody and thus grafts an unruly excess onto the bomb's fatal relation to Pacific bodies.

The concluding poem in this sequence, "Fishbone Hair," parallels the diffused possibility of fallout with the particularity of its effects on an individual, the speaker's niece. "There had been a war/raging inside Bianca's six year old bones," and her fallen hair becomes the emblem of radioactive fallout in the present.[80] But this poem then also gestures to the collection's later concerns with climate change, yoking the former impossible future of nuclear radiation with the current impossible future of sea level rise. In "Fishbone Hair" the somatic effects of nuclear testing and Pacific expendability manifest as *"rootless* hair/that hair without a home."[81] Loss moves from the somatic to the collective in the later poem "Dear Matafele Peinam," where islanders are once again framed as expendable. In the later poem, however, they are not the victims of Western nuclear colonialism but an unchecked and largely external carbon economy:

Men say that one day
that lagoon will devour you
. . . .

They say you, your daughter
and your granddaughter, too
will wander
rootless
with only
a passport
to call home.[82]

Here, rootlessness is not a symptom of nuclear militarism in the Pacific but a product of sea level rise brought on by industrialized greenhouse gas accumulations and other anthropogenic climate changes. Linked references like these across Jetñil-Kijiner's poetic sequences work to concatenate past and present injustices, expand the temporal, spatial, and affective horizons of Pacific injury, and underscore islander continuity in the face of repeated foreclosures.

Critics M. L. Rosenthal and Sally M. Gall have suggested that such affective effects and dynamics are the primary mark of modern poetic sequence. While they also suggest that such "feeling involving a number of radiant centers" may be "progressively liberated from a narrative or thematic framework," *Iep Jāltok* does not prioritize affect at the expense of narrative cohesion.[83] Indeed, its task of revealing and recuperating deleterious Pacific histories depends on reproducing the legibility and narratability of ongoing harm. That is, in *Iep Jāltok* emotive impact adheres precisely in the poems' narratives, their chronicling of individual and collective experiences, and their attention to the particular space of the Pacific as a wasting ground of repeated violence. The point is, though, that *Iep Jāltok* mobilizes a formal hallmark like poetic affect precisely in its sociohistoric task of renarrating history and reconceptualizing Pacific time. Affect accumulates from and through the residuum of former Pacific extinctions and so produces a sense of Marshallese places and peoples as always-already having had to endure the impossible.

Because of this, *Iep Jāltok* makes clear that Pacific extinction narratives can be considered not only (neo)colonial ideology, but perverse precedent. In Jetñil-Kijiner's poems, rather than the linearity of extinction, past harms and present endurance meld together in contradictory overlaps that upset the certainty of bad endings.[84] In being made historical, in offering a lineage of futures that were never supposed to come to pass, Pacific extinction narratives conversely testify to the real resilience of islanders in the face of a ruinous history of Euro-American encounters. More importantly, they suggest something like the impossibility of a totally closed future. Futurelessness as precedent overturns the very world-ending connotations of the term. By turning extinction into antecedent, the ending of the future becomes itself a kind of Pacific worlding, and *Iep Jāltok* aspires utopically toward an unknown future that is otherwise and otherwhen from the end.

Iep Jāltok thus recuperates Pacific futures by rethinking the limits of extinction. But it also works to pluralize the futures that can be imagined from the flood-threatened present in two related climate poems, "Dear Matafele Peinam" and "Two Degrees." Jetñil-Kijiner performed "Dear Matafele Peinam" at the opening of the 2014 United Nations Climate Summit in New York. In one of the world's major centers of fossil capital, Jetñil-Kijiner denounced the inequalities of risk and wealth perpetuated by those "hidden behind platinum titles/who like to pretend/that we don't exist."[85] On the world's largest climate stage, she both chastised her audience and invited them to respond to the urgency of climate change. Her poem suggested that substantial climate action can only happen through collective effort, and while international negotiations make up part of such action, so too do "families biking, recycling, reusing, / engineers dreaming, designing, building, / artists paining, dancing, writing."[86]

"Dear Matafele Peinam" is a poem of climate protest that pursues a concretely utopian vision. It calls for direct action from many parties, but also declares the future it wants by naming the future it does not:

> no one's moving
> no one's losing
> their homeland
> no one's gonna become
> a climate change refugee.[87]

In their negative content, these lines limn the opposite: a concretely utopian future where people can stay where they are, preserve their homelands, and continue to be citizens rather than refugees. These lines turn the negative valences of the present to their positive potentials, mapping an obverse future. They exemplify utopian method by naming a better alternative world that must be imagined against the grain of impending inundation and displacement. The poem ends, finally, on lines of transformative resolution: "because we won't let you down // you'll see" as Jetñil-Kijiner invites kin, international and national leaders, transnational activists, and ordinary people to all fight against climate change in their own ways.[88] Written to her infant daughter Matafele Peinam, the epistolary mode of "Dear Matafele Peinam" is a call to action in the present. But it also sets its horizon of national and international action as retroactive promise, one whose fulfillment is implied by its address to an older Matafele Peinam as future reader.

The later poem, "Two Degrees," also works to imagine concrete utopias of futurity outside inundation. But while "Dear Matafele Peinam" makes confident declarations and calls to action, "Two Degrees" is precariously suspended between hopes for a better future and fears of loss. "Two Degrees" begins with a scene of domestic distress and personal sentiment: "The other night my 1-year-old was a fever / pressed against my chest."[89] In the autobiographical mode of motherly worry, Jetñil-Kijiner's speaker tells readers that "LiPeinam" // "[. . .] drapes / across my lap, listless" and the speaker

> [. . .] think[s]
> what a difference
> a few degrees
> can make.[90]

In the next stanza, LiPenam's fever is yoked to the heating of the planet, as "a few degrees" touches off terrifying statistics about mass extinctions and extreme weather that are predicted to happen in a warmer world. The two degrees of "Two Degrees" turns out to be a multiscalar transition from the domestic to the planetary, the intimate to the international.

The difference of a few degrees becomes terrain for epistemological contestations and struggles for power. First it marks the minimum medical definition of fever:

> technically
> 100.4
> is a fever
> but I can see her flushed face

and the speaker's initial resistance to medical dismissal is echoed later when the speaker as activist, rather than mother, insists:

> At a climate change conference
> a colleague tells me 2 degrees
> is just a benchmark for negotiations
> I tell him for my islands 2 degrees
> is a gamble
> at 2 degrees my islands
> will already be under water
> this is why our leaders push
> for 1.5.[91]

At this point in the poem, the difference between 2 and 1.5 degrees does not merely signify a diplomatic, statistical, or scientific quibble. At this point in the poem, half a degree also signifies the looming loss of the Marshall Islands themselves, concretized and personalized through the affective purchase of LiPeinam's fever and her mother's worry, which counteract the effect of seemingly abstract numbers. The tacit neutrality and benign distance of "a benchmark for negotiations" collapses, as personal and national losses are conflated to disrupt the international consensus of "negotiations" where action never comes fast enough. In this way, Jetñil-Kijiner's poem dramatizes the individual and intimate stakes of climate inaction.

As figurative child, LiPeinam personifies the costs of climate inaction and underscores the innocence and blamelessness of those whose lives will be destroyed by rising oceans. Such details, the poem posits, will make it:

> So that people
> remember
> that beyond
> the discussions
> numbers
> and statistics
> there are faces
> all the way out here.⁹²

Indeed, the poem takes special pains to concretize LiPeinam and her home through visual and sonic detail. Home is where LiPeinam can "[stomp] squeaky/yellow light up shoes/across the edge of a reef."⁹³ The other people who live on this reef, symbolized in LiPeinam's yellow shoes, are individuals with whom readers might identify, faces presented within idioms of local place, filial love, and childhood joy proffered as universally recognizable.

Against the possibility that all this might be lost, the poem then offers a counter in LiPenam's recovery, where a few degrees have inaugurated a sea change: "Today LiPeinam is feeling better."⁹⁴ Just as LiPeinam's fever was an allegory for planetary warming, her recovery also signifies beyond herself: her shift from sickness to health and from listlessness to liveliness figures the difference two degrees can make for the life of the Marshall Islands and the planet as a whole. The poem thus symbolically suspends LiPeinam and with her, the planet, between possible futures. The planet, like the speaker's daughter, might recover. There is still time, a space for action concentrated in the poem's closing stanza, which is only two lines: "not yet/under water."⁹⁵ Jetñil-Kijiner's spatial pause here is akin to the potentiality before closure, where multiple futures are possible because none have yet been definitively chosen. Through its figural child as emblem of the future, the poem simultaneously posits two antithetical endings: the irrevocable loss of vibrant individuality and grounded communal place and a possible future where these things will continue to exist. In the face of anticipated losses, Jetñil-Kijiner's poem works fiercely to pluralize the future. In "Two Degrees" the "not yet" of the poem's ending lines—"not yet/under water" holds open a space for potential climate action. In the wake of the 2015 Paris Agreement and its goal of keeping planetary warming to 1.5°C greenhouse gas–producing companies, countries, and individuals are in a space of suspension that is also a space of action. "Two Degrees," like the protest poem "Dear Matafele Peinam," is committed to imagining what might happen between now and then, between the present and a much warmer world that is fast approaching on the back of climate inertia. We can still change this trajectory, turn from this future.⁹⁶ But will we? And when?

Speculation as Policy

Pluralizing the future is not only a tactic in the arsenal of writers and activists. It has also been used by Pacific leaders seeking to provide concrete utopias of desirable futurity beyond inundation and, indeed, a sense of futurity at all to their citizens. As discussed earlier, Pacific states have mobilized a range of powers from discipline to diplomacy in the face of sea level rise. Some, however, have also used more unconventional tools. This section returns to Anote Tong's climate plan Migration with Dignity, which was discussed earlier for its repurposing of Kiribati labor migration. But Migration with Dignity also had more radical implications, ones that are not readily apparent from a straightforward reading of the policy. And, while Migration with Dignity's more unusual potentials become apparent through utopian method, they actually exceed even the contours of a concretely utopian future.

As noted, Migration with Dignity proposed to turn I-Kiribati into labor migrants before they became displaced peoples. In some ways, this seemed complicit with fossil inertia and neoliberal capital's view of labor. Contrarily, this policy also offered a concrete utopian vision. It aspired to preserve Kiribati community and deflect the losses of climate migration. These interpretations do not, however, exhaust the ways in which Migration with Dignity can be read. For Migration with Dignity also suggested something radically new: an alternate, speculative state form. Without people or territory, MWD logically implied something like a dissolved state, an idea that is itself a contradiction in terms. Along with specific territory over which they have exclusive jurisdiction, modern states are defined by an effective government, a permanent population, and the capacity to enter into relations with other states.[97] Kiribati has worked within this internationally recognized system of statehood in its climate advocacy, at forums like the United Nations' annual Conference of the Parties to the Framework Convention on Climate Change (COP meetings), and in the Alliance of Small Island States (AOSIS), where, with other island nations, it has long advocated for action on greenhouse emissions. In these international fora, state conventions are working bedrock.

But these same conventions of modern statehood, especially those of bounded territories and static populations, are being brought radically into question by sea level rise. Unlike states that are incorporated into, conquered by, or secede from other states, the kind of physical and demographic dissolution facing Pacific atoll nations is unprecedented in international law and modern politics.[98] By deliberately jettisoning one foundational component of statehood—a static population—in response to the threat that sea level rise already poses to another—national territory—MWD suggests a dissolved state that chips away at Kiribati's own coherence. By implying its own dissolution within currently recognized definitions of statehood, MWD interrupts conventional statehood with an impossible, alternative version that does not exist. But in doing so, it also contests the inadequate conditions of statehood in which Pacific politics must be imagined today and in which Pacific state protection, citizenship, and existence itself are being rendered impossible thoughts.

This critical edge is not readily apparent from a straightforward or conventional reading of Kiribati's plan, which seems to play into the hands of neoliberal labor exploitation. It is also not quite revealed by reading for concrete utopias. MWD does not specify what kind of alternate state could come to replace its present one. Unlike the other alternatives states discussed in this book, Migration with Dignity's implied future state is vague and not defined by content; the policy instead pursues radical newness beyond the bounds of concreteness. Migration with Dignity's dissolved state contests the policy's other tendencies to draw on familiar alternatives or "usable pasts" such as labor migration and diaspora. In contrast to the concreteness of these visions, its dissolved state is a state form that is highly speculative and hardly imaginable in the present. That is, Kiribati's dissolved state pushes beyond the boundaries of what constitutes an imaginable state to defamiliarize the givenness of how statehood is conceived at all.

Perhaps because of this, Migration with Dignity seems almost ludicrous. Even more questionable than its potential complicity with labor exploitation is the fact that it makes no sense within the political norms of the present. But this problematic quality is key to the work Migration with Dignity does beyond its content—as a radically utopian act, rather than a concretely utopian vision. For MWD's political nonsense actually replicates a feature of speculation that is familiar from theories of fiction, if not common in policy. It produces what science fiction scholar Darko Suvin has described as the central attribute of science fiction: cognitive estrangement.[99] Speculative and science fictions commonly present different futures to make the norms and systems of any particular historical moment seem epistemologically unfamiliar and therefore changeable. Migration with Dignity does this to statehood, imaginatively stretching the bounds of what counts as a state in the present to make the defining norms of statehood seem contingent. Migration with Dignity's dissolved state cognitively estranges us from modern conceptions of statehood by pointing out the limits of statehood in the present and pushing us to imagine alternatives, even if the contours of those alternatives cannot quite be filled in. Thus, Migration with Dignity works finally as a speculative act—not through its concrete utopian visions but through the inconceivability of its implied state form. The failure of its policy in a conventional view *is* its speculative, cognitively estranging work. This failure makes up its push against the limitations of existing political rules and its demand for other conditions in which Pacific futurity might still be imagined. Though MWD is policy rather than fiction, the work of imaginative stretching and cognitive estrangement that it does repeats the tenets of, and becomes legible through, the way literary scholars have long theorized speculation in fiction. MWD's unthinkable state doubles as a speculation about the supersession of the present that makes existing political structures, such as today's state system of bounded territories and immobile populations, thinkable as constructs with limits rather than unchangeable or inevitable political forms.[100] In this way MWD's dissolved state rejects statehood in the present and gestures to a radically unimaginable, rather than a concretely utopian, alternative.

In the climate documentary *Anote's Ark*, there is a moment where Tong himself describes his climate plans this way: "And there was a time when there was a deep sense of depression. But I had to overcome that. And to overcome that, you've got to really throw away everything. *Don't think in straight, linear terms. Take it all apart.*"[101] Without using the word "speculation," here Tong is describing the cognitive affordances of speculation: to take apart present assumptions and imagined limits so they may be reimagined. To imagine futures beyond what is deemed inevitable in the present. To venture beyond the linearity of inundation → refugeeism. In conventional terms, the gap between present regimes of statehood and MWD's proposal for a dissolved state makes MWD doomed to fail. But the point here is that such failure opens the way for cognitive estrangement and radical thought. It gestures to a version of the state that contests and takes apart existing limits to statehood and, in doing so, defamiliarizes these as the limits of the real, the possible, or the imaginable.

Postcolonial theorist Leela Gandhi has made a similar argument about the "ethics of inconsequence."[102] Inconsequence, she suggests, can serve as a critique of existing circumstances because it "appears as strictly ungenerative and as a type of symbolic celibacy."[103] As such it amounts to a "refusal to participate in any perpetuation of the status quo."[104] Inconsequence appears as such precisely because it fails to conform to existing criteria of effectiveness or sense. While this failure to conform is what makes an inconsequential action appear as such, that very departure from a given realm of consequence is also a way of calling the given into question. As an inconsequential proposal, imaginative limit, or radically utopic alternative to territorial statehood, MWD's dissolved state acts as a stringent condemnation of the very political conditions that make its state form unimaginable. As a utopic proposal, the idea of a dissolved and dispersed state dramatizes the unjust requirements of statehood in the present, requirements that will make the welfarist provisions of Pacific states and indeed some Pacific states themselves obsolete after sea level rise. This is a future state that militates against the way small islands are consigned to positions of sacrifice for the greater good of large fossil fuel emitters or to the function of "canaries in the coalmine" for a warming climate future that can only count the Pacific as already lost.

Yet even the kind of speculative, cognitively estranging alternative proposed by Migration with Dignity is far from isolated. Migration with Dignity's dissolved state is one of a number of alternative state forms that are being proposed in the face of climate change. Legal scholar Maxine Burkett, for instance, has argued that climate change will require a "new category of international actors" she dubs the "Nation *Ex-Situ*."[105] Though Tong does not cite this idea, Migration with Dignity's speculative state in many ways dovetails with the nation ex-situ: "It would protect the peoples forced from their original place of being by serving as a political entity that remains constant even as its citizens establish residence in other states . . . a government framework that could exercise authority over a diffuse people."[106] Like Migration with Dignity, the nation ex-situ has been proposed explicitly because of the challenges that climate change is posing to hegemonic, currently accepted ideas of statehood.

Like Migration with Dignity, the nation ex-situ seeks to maintain national coherence and offer protection for peoples who will lose their territory or whose land will become uninhabitable as the atmosphere warms and the climate changes. Both the nation ex-situ and Migration with Dignity's dissolved state underscore the point that utopic states are not about actual achievement, but rather about pointing up the inadequacies of the present in order to conceive alternatives beyond the limitations of existing political structures and imaginaries, in "counter-move[s] to the badly existing."[107] In the Pacific, this pursuit of better polities entails providing frames through which futures might be imagined at all, given the foreclosure of the future seemingly inaugurated by sea level rise. Migration with Dignity and the nation ex-situ approach this task by stretching the contours of imaginable future states, and in doing so they utopically seek to envision futures in which Pacific states and their peoples might continue to exist at all.

Our / Other Futures

In the face of unprecedented futures, the boundaries between speculation and the real and between literature and politics become fuzzy. New forms of political and social organization arise to confront climate challenges, offering conceptual tools to leaders looking to safeguard their peoples in a world where old regimes are on the verge of change. In Keri Hulme's dizzying mixed-genre short story collection *Stonefish* (2004), speculative futures and more realist representations are also in conversation. This collection explicitly takes on the epistemological challenge that Pacific states, even Kiribati, are at pains to avoid: that sea level rise might indeed lead to Pacific futurelessness. *Stonefish* raises the problem of a futureless world, however, as a cognitive conjuring trick. For if old worlds of climate stability have ended, new ones shaped by anthropogenic climate change, resource depletion, intensifying storms, and rising seas have already arrived. The collection suggests that it is only former worlds of stable climate that have become futureless or untenable. Epistemological commitments to these foregone worlds foreclose one's awareness of the new real world of changed climate, and *Stonefish* suggests that such failures of consciousness and subsequently of action will indeed lead to dead ends. Therefore, *Stonefish* works to show how old epistemologies must be replaced with new kinds of awareness commensurate with the new climate reality of the Anthropocene. To this end it suggests a new ethos for living within the climate-changed present. Such cognitive challenges position the Pacific not as purged from a common future but as a vanguard of the futures coming for all.

In this vein *Stonefish* opens in a futuristic world shaped by floods and ends in a world not noticeably different from that inhabited by twenty-first century readers. Its first story, "Floating Words," is a meditation on proper perceptions of, and action in response, to drastic environmental change. It provides an example of how to live well with such change by relinquishing the prevailing ethos of "man on top" that supports human consumption and domination vis-à-vis other humans, nonhuman species, and the planet's resources.[108] The exhausted world and pervasive but unexplained blight of its last story, "Midden Mine," can by contrast be seen as *Stonefish*'s warning about the consequences of climate inaction.

Stonefish's opening and closing stories are best read within literary scholar Forrest Ingram's definition of the short story cycle: *"a book of short stories so linked to each other by their author that the reader's successive experience on various levels of the pattern of the whole significantly modifies his experience of each of its component parts."*[109] I argue that these two stories must be read as linked within the collection as a whole, as the critique of the later story is only apprehensible by reading it against the first. In particular, "Midden Mine" comes to appear as a failed doubling of the successful climate adaptation staged in "Floating Words," and so only together do they clarify the need for climate action in the present. More importantly, by coming at the end of the collection, "Midden Mine" produces an epistemological gap between the collection's readers and the story's own narrator. In doing so, *Stonefish* positions readers outside a denialist present to beg the question that is the disavowed horizon of Pacific politics: how to live after the flood.

Maori New Zealand author Keri Hulme is perhaps best known for her 1985 Booker Prize–winning *The Bone People*, a novel that put New Zealand literature on the global literary map and cemented Hulme's place as one of New Zealand's most important contemporary writers.[110] *Stonefish*, an eclectic collection of poetry and short stories released about two decades later, has by contrast garnered remarkably little critical attention. Elizabeth DeLoughrey has produced some of the few scholarly engagements with the collection. In "Ordinary Futures," she argues that "Hulme depicts creeping sea level rise in terms that emphasize mutation and adaptation rather than the spectacular tone of apocalypse" and thus posits "the sea, climate change, mutation, and the submarine as profoundly ordinary."[111] For DeLoughrey, the collection's "ethics of environmental adaptability" is most apparent in "Floating Words," which in part plumbs the task of the writer in the face of climatic change.[112] Drawing on this first story's formal movements between narrative present and past, DeLoughrey reads the story's narrative flux as symptom and hermeneutic for living with climate change. The narrator makes this ethos of mutation and flexibility explicit as well:

> We knew—the television told us, the radio mentioned it often—that the oceans would rise, the greenhouse effect would change the weather, and there could be rumblings and distortion along the crustal plates as Gaia adjusted to a different pressure of water. *And we understood it to be one more ordinary change in the everlasting cycle of life.*[113]

Such conceptions of cyclical rather than cataclysmic change echo Maori conceptions of time "that position the past in front while the future is behind."[114] Such temporal understandings do not work to diffuse the threat of climate change because change is not perceived as a threat of future loss. Instead, environmental change, however drastic, can be incorporated within Indigenous ontologies of continuous transformation and relation with the nonhuman world.[115] These invocations of immense geological scale within a conception of the ordinary approach what anthropologist Elizabeth Povinelli has called "geontology," and what DeLoughrey explain as "a mutually constitutive biography/geology" that "[incorporates] the subject into planetary networks of kinship."[116] Thus *Stonefish*'s invocations of adaptation, mutation, and planetary intimacy offer ethical models for living large with climatic change rather than seeking to minimize or resist its threat.

"Floating Words" begins with its narrator balanced between land and water and between past and present: "THINKING BACK (I am balanced on the end bollard, the slip-rope in my hand) there were omens all along."[117] In the story's concluding paragraphs readers find that this state of suspension is spatial as well as temporal, for the narrator has been about to "drift away" from her home on a makeshift raft bound for open water.[118] But between these moments of imminent departure the narrator thinks back to an earlier moment of asking: "Change, change, change. Where is solidity? Where is the rock?"[119] In this earlier moment, she had not yet learned to embrace the new normal of a climate-altered world. Eventually, the unnamed narrator accepts that there is no metaphorical bedrock for living: "Nothing is static, settled, or permanent anymore."[120] This conclusion about her world's mutating nature is also a commentary on the place and role of writers like herself, for "storytellers never stay in one place for long."[121]

The narrator-writer is not only an imminent wanderer, however. For though she decides to leave home and embrace fluidity, having read "the tide in microcosm" and "[recognized] a sign when [she] is given one so clearly," it becomes clear that she is also a guide for those who, like her former self, cling to the "rock" of what counted as sober action in an old world of stable climate.[122] The narrator therefore leaves her repository of books—or signs—as a "FREE LIBRARY" available to "any reader."[123] Readers are never told exactly what the narrator writes, but she disperses missives into the ether, participating in an economy of words. She sends chapters from *"The Neverending Novel"* off in a weekly mail blimp "well-established and dependable. I never did find out who started it, how credit was established, but it worked."[124] In exchange for words she requests and receives foodstuffs; such an exchange of individual interiority for material provision may seem to be an allegory of modern governmentality, but this traveling blimp also makes her weekly missives available to the itinerant, floating bubble cities and mobile populations that have come to populate the future world of "Floating Words." The missives she leaves span an openness toward environmental change, but they are also premised upon exchange and relationality.

More significantly, *Stonefish* is concerned with addressing the costs of failing to adapt—that is, the risks of not giving up the old system that preceded and produced the altered climate of its futuristic opening. Hulme's collection is aware that proposing an alternative ethos is one challenge; acting on it and learning to give up hegemonic forms of worlding grounded in destructive resource use and human species hubris is a different and equally difficult project.

These concerns are funneled through the relationship between "Floating Words" and the collection's last story, "Midden Mine," which is set close to readers' own climate present. *Stonefish* produces the decaying present of its last story, "Midden Mine," as a mirror of the twenty-first-century present and as a failed double of the mutable future in "Floating Words." Together, these linked stories offer a timely critique of the vicissitudes of our present as readers in and of the Anthropocene. "Midden Mine" unfolds around an archaeological dig by a team of international academics, Dave, Bea, and Cam, who search for remnants of past civilizations and attempt to interpret their meaning. The archaeological plot gives way to concern for a changing climate, which is revealed piecemeal. This happens as the story formally and thematically stages its characters' failures to read signs of environmental change that are as profound as the more fantastical ones in "Floating Words."

Following *Stonefish*'s episodic narrative structure, all three protagonists are plagued by personal losses and chronic, deadly illnesses that are never fully explained. Their illnesses at first glance may seem to resurrect the extinction narrative of dying races that has historically overdetermined the Pacific, but Hulme turns such bodily exhaustion to other purposes here, where fragmentation is both theme and heuristic. Their dig reveals a layer of charcoal that testifies to past human disruptions—"Where did they get all the wood?"—and amidst these remnants of trees are human remains.[125] It is unclear if the charcoal is from deforestation or from the practice of human sacrifice. But in twinning past human interspecies violence (burned trees) and intraspecies violence (human death), "Midden Mine" sketches for readers a scene ripe for interpretation. Readers are primed to expect this when we are told early in the story that the main narrator, Dave, gets "feelings about sites."[126] But instead of fulfilling the injunction to read the signs of brutality that have produced the story's titular midden or heap of refuse, Dave comes up against an epistemological limit. He fails to understand the midden as evidence of deadly violence toward other humans and nonhuman species alike, as well as the continuity of these patterns in his present.

This staging of failed knowledge is symptomatic of the kinds of cognitive limits that, over the course of the story, produce an ironic critique of climate denialism. For example, even though there are ample signs of climate change, in "Midden Mine" Dave can only interpret them as the stuff of nightmares. Dave is startled "awake, wet with fear-sweat, wondering why the waves were phosphorescent green—."[127] He does not understand the glowing waves of his dream. Conversely, glowing waves in the time of "Floating Words" fit into that narrator's understanding of an altered climate, for one of the major signs of climate change is a strange, multi-colored mushroom the narrator finds "glowing with minute blue sine waves."[128] The narrator of "Floating Words" understands the glowing signs of climate change around her, but the narrator of "Midden Mine" does not. More mundane signs of climate change abound in "Midden Mine" and are ignored as well: "It is gusty and chill, *most unusual* for December. Well, for the Decembers I remember from the decades past";

"We've had huge storm surges where a simple southerly *would have been ordinary*, would have been enough."[129] Here, Dave's epistemological commitments to a vanished world dampen his sense of disquiet, diminishing also the possibility of a changed climate consciousness.

Such linked references in turn produce epistemological gaps or dramatic irony between the narrator of "Midden Mine" and the collection's readers. For the reader of "Midden Mine" is also the reader of *Stonefish* as a whole, and the environmental knowledge gained from reading the preceding stories positions readers outside the present illustrated in "Midden Mine." From the perspective of enlightened readers, then, the old world to which Dave still clings appears as false consciousness. In other words, while "Midden Mine"'s narrator is the avatar of a conservative status quo, one characterized by climate denialism and inaction, "Midden Mine"'s readers are of a different epistemological and indeed temporal cast. In representing a dying present that subsequently places its readers in a future form of awareness, "Midden Mine" is a provocation beyond the limited epistemologies, cognitive failures, and old-world climate commitments that it stages.

Hulme's stories and this chapter's other texts make clear that submersion and refugeeism are only one way of approaching the climate-changed future. Staying or leaving is only one way of thinking about the effects of sea level rise, and inaction is only one future path. Alternate habitations, poised between prediction and speculation, are located in the very processes of thinking the future in its variegated forms and multiplicity of temporal spans. Diverse visions for the future shuttle across the aesthetic and political registers in which Pacific futurity is being imagined in the face of inundation. Pacific state leaders, writers, and activists all work to reconceive the future, deploying utopic methods to live under the impossible time of oceanic erasure. These utopic imaginaries unmoor futurity from its too-obvious determinants. They make visible the incommensurate and unpredictable modes of temporality, art, and thought through which futures beyond climate refugeeism are always being made.

Coda
Utopia beyond Negative Critique

In their speculative nonfiction manifesto *The Collapse of Western Civilization*, historians of science Naomi Oreskes and Erik M. Conway, writing for a public audience, inhabit the perspective of future historians looking back on the early twenty-first century as a "Penumbral Age."[1] From this vantage they argue satirically, but also seriously, for the role of state intervention in the twenty-first century's moment of climate catastrophe and environmental crisis. Their futuristic example is authoritarian China, which by government fiat will have been able to invest in clean energy sources and relocate vulnerable coastal populations. Without endorsing this specific vision, we can, like Oreskes and Conway, recognize that states simultaneously perpetuate bad practices and are sites of important environmental intervention. Despite their violence or failure, states can also contribute to combating climate change and facilitating concrete environmental utopias.

Indeed, *Reading Better States* has shown that we do not need to look to academic fabulation for such plural conceptions of the state: they are envisioned by postcolonial writers and citizens, and, just as importantly, they occur in actually existing state policies, if only we would see them. In Nigeria and India, the postcolonial state once thought about regulating corporations and protecting the environmental needs of vulnerable communities. In South Africa, the state recently produced less consumptive, more water-conscious citizens; and in the Pacific, sea level rise has led leaders to propose new communal and state forms. So far suspended or deferred, quashed or ignored, these concrete utopias illuminate the processual change always underway now, before, and yet to come, and they point to futures where such state-based "Real-Possible[s]" might yet become more real.[2]

The utopian method of reading in *Reading Better States*, like Oreskes and Conway's call to rethink the state, participates in an ongoing debate over the place of negative critique in the humanities. Few objects attract more negativity than the state in humanistic scholarship and theory.[3] Yet, I have made a case for the costs of failing to see beyond the common frameworks of cynical exposure or outright repudiation that postcolonialists, environmental humanists, and others often apply to the state. This book's impetus to reconsider that putatively negative object, the postcolonial state, and the ways in which it is read, was motored in part by broader preoccupations over what the humanities does with critique, what it could do, and indeed what the intellectual and social mission of the field is in the present. Over the past few decades, humanists have grappled with these questions in the midst of a world on fire, a changing academic and cultural landscape that relegates the humanities to the sidelines, and conversely a media arena where disciplinary practices like diagnosis and suspicion are becoming vulgarized and weaponized to bolster climate denialism, environmental racism, white supremacy, and other forces that dismantle the worlds we live in.

In short, like the effects of anthropogenic climate change itself, we in the humanities are being met with the boomeranging and uncontrollable effects of our own past practices.[4] Philosopher of science Bruno Latour identified one of the most dangerous consequences of this destructive return when he noted: "Conspiracy theories are an absurd deformation of our own arguments, but, like weapons smuggled through a fuzzy border to the wrong party, these are our weapons nonetheless."[5] Indeed more bluntly, "What's the real difference between conspiracists and a popularized, that is a teachable version of social critique?"[6] Having come to recognize the limits of negative critique, humanists, myself included, have been prompted to thorny but important self-reflection. What should we do, besides diagnose and reveal? How can we read, if not suspiciously? What are we, if not gadflies?[7] What comes after negative critique? Most responses have been proposals for new methods—that is, new ways of reading: reparative reading, surface reading, distant reading.[8] My utopian method of reading in *Reading Better States* is part of this effort to rethink the purchase and stakes of critical reading in the humanities.

Some of these methods, like queer theorist Eve Sedgwick's reparative reading, emphasize theorizing positive affects and relinquishing a paranoid hermeneutic of suspicion for more egalitarian, less masterful stances toward cultural objects. Critical theorist Rita Felski has suggested a range of affective and ethical responses to reading, such as enchantment, recognition, or knowledge, that attend to the pleasures of reading and could displace suspicion.[9]

Felski and law and literature scholar Elizabeth S. Anker also suggest that new ways of reading will mean reassessing the antagonistic attitude critique has fostered toward the public world, a move that might in turn allow us to offer more positive formulations of the value of the humanities, values that those outside the field could recognize and share.[10] In a related vein, literary scholar Caroline Levine calls for us to read for formal models and generalities that can support more just kinds of collective life.[11] Others critics, like Anna Kornbluh, take the opposite track, calling for us to retain a suspicious emphasis on causal structures and verticality, but nevertheless to also *"build the world up"* with criticism.[12] Indeed, the problem with negative critique is often phrased in this way: how do we not only tear things down, but build things up?

In many ways, utopian method and the plural states I have traced in *Reading Better States* were motivated by an ambition to build things up—or rather, to illuminate the way things are always-already being built up by writers and ordinary people. In the world, outside the schemas of critical theory, oppressive and unjust conditions are rarely totalizing. Utopian method has followed forms of living within damaged circumstances, of newness within constraint, and the pursuit of better futures that are minor and compromised. This book has offered utopian method as a way of reading that attends to causality and violence while also looking beyond those forces. Reading negativity against the grain for its positive potentials does not do away with negativity. Instead, it allows us to hold contradictory imaginaries and effects together in complex entanglement, where one does not obliterate the other. Utopian method lets us see what is produced out of circumstances we know are bad. Utopian method allows us to diagnose those systems that produce injustice while still attending to the way the effects of those systems are not singular.

In fact, I have always seen this book as a response to the crises of environmental harm and climate catastrophe that disproportionately affect the global South, and equally a response to the need to do more with critique than expose and diagnose oppressive forces at work. For literary ways of reading never only theorize the aesthetic realm but offer insights, concepts, and revelations about the social world. Those insights have for too long been negative. My hope is that utopian method gives us one way to gain a wider explanatory purchase on the world's complexity. For utopian method can explain not only the cultural objects produced in slow violent times but yield a more dynamic and nuanced view of the times to which those texts respond. What can we see when we read utopically, when we acknowledge negativity but do not let it limit the horizon of the visible or the imaginable? What lies beyond negative critique in the Anthropocene? Complaints, promises, proposals, alternatives, and antecedents. Suffering and partial redress. Concrete utopias, and perhaps, better states.

So too, utopian method gives us a way of defending the versions of the state that we want. For it reveals that we need not cede the state to its many failures. The state is never only one thing or imagined in one way. It is always imagined and experienced through a plethora of roles and positions, through contradiction rather than singularity. Focusing on the disappointing elements of the state has for too long locked humanists into a feedback loop of pessimism and negativity that makes it nigh impossible to see the state for its potentials. And if this feedback loop is especially potent now, when all institutions, from the university to the state, seem to have become bad actors, utopian method gives us a way to think beyond these patently negative surfaces. No matter how wide the gap between complaint and desire, between promise and fulfillment, utopian method teaches us to never accept the limits of existing institutional forms, and instead to mine them for past antecedents, future possibilities, or existing potentials that can be brought closer to realization. We cannot abandon the state, burn it down, or leave it to be hijacked by the interests of capital. Corporate takeovers and state capture are happening, and they will never yield more livable futures. Through utopian method we can learn to see the state's potentials again, and we can work to reinforce and amplify the versions of the state that we want. For who knows when promises will come to pass, when the interventionist actions of people and institutions, including the state, will actualize deeply desired concrete utopias? Whenever it takes, we cannot stop fighting for the futures that we want. And that means we cannot stop imagining the better states that we want, for ourselves and for the planet.

The debate about humanistic methods and their consequences has not been settled. I cannot say if any of these alternative ways of reading will enjoy the kind of triumphant methodological sway that suspicious reading has held in the past. But it seems that part of the new critical landscape is precisely that we can, as Sedgwick said long ago, have more tools rather than fewer, an "additive and accretive" methodology instead of a monolithic one.[13] Indeed, Sedgwick importantly noted that turning away from negativity and suspicion was not a zero-sum game. Rather, the challenge would be to make suspicion one kind of critical practice among others. Rethinking method is not a trend. It matters in the long term because what we argue depends on how we read. What we conclude depends on what we are able to see. Which methods, then, will allow us to continue reading for contradiction and causation without simply falling back into negative diagnosis? Can we be suspicious and generous?

How can we build things up while holding on to culpability, the mandate, long cherished in the humanities, of speaking back to power? One way to do so is through utopian method, by reading for failure and violence and using them as springboards to reveal the better futures in emergence all around, within the negative valences of what exists.

Acknowledgments

This book has been a long time coming into the world. I have many people to thank for its varied life stages and its final form. First, I thank Benjamin Morgan, Christopher Taylor, and Sonali Thakkar at the University of Chicago, who read this project with patience, care, and critique in its earliest days. I learned from other inspiring teachers as well, including Lauren Berlant, Adrienne Brown, Leela Gandhi, and Deborah Nelson. I must acknowledge the pivotal role of Ian Baucom, whose visiting lecture on the Anthropocene was the catalyst that turned me to the environmental humanities. I also owe deep thanks to Rita Felski, who trained me to look past the limits of negative critique during my undergraduate years at the University of Virginia, Vicki Olwell, who introduced me to postcolonial literature while I was there, and Michael Levenson, who oversaw my first attempts at research. Those halcyon days were also brightened by Pete Capuano, Mrinalini Chakravorty, Farzaneh Milani, Caroline Rody, and Denise Walsh.

Since leaving the University of Chicago, I have been most fortunate to make the University of Illinois Urbana-Champaign my intellectual home. Illinois has been a dream institution—not perfect, as no institution is—but welcoming, collegial, democratic, and supportive in all the ways that matter. My home department of English has provided a rich intellectual space and a wonderful community. Manisha Basu, Eleanor Courtemanche, Tim Dean, Christopher Freeberg, Andrew Gaedtke, Bob Markley, Justine Murison, Lori Newcomb, Tim Newcomb, Bob Parker, and Gillen Wood mentored me, advocated for me, and answered my many questions. Countless other colleagues and friends in the department and across the university have read chapter drafts, offered sage advice, encouraged me, or shaped my thinking, including Teresa Barnes,

Robert Barrett, Siân Butcher, Eric Calderwood, José B. Capino, Lucinda Cole, Catharine Gray, Waïl Hassan, Christopher Kempf, Craig Koslofsky, Melissa Littlefield, Charlesia McKinney, Tess McNulty, David Morris, Deena Rymhs, Ramón Soto-Crespo, Ted Underwood, and Corey van Landingham. Special thanks go to Jessica Greenberg, Jamie Jones, and Dana Rabin, who have shown me so much light; unparalleled friends, colleagues, and mentors, they always pushed me to grow.

The First Book Workshop, run by the Office of the Vice Chancellor for Research and Innovation at UIUC, taught me early on to have faith in revisions. Run by Cynthia Oliver, Gabriel Solis, Carol Symes, Shelley Weinberg, and the outstanding Maria Gillombardo, it was a stellar experience of institutional support. Many other units at UIUC have supported my work by providing spaces of intellectual exchange and inspiration as well, including the Unit for Criticism and Interpretive Theory, the Center for Advanced Study, and the Humanities Research Institute, helmed by the incomparable Antoinette Burton. I have benefited from rigorous feedback on my writing at the Center for African Studies, the Center for South Asian and Middle Eastern Studies, and the IPRH-Mellon Environmental Humanities Working Group, which later became the HRI Environmental Humanities Research Cluster. I am grateful to many colleagues from these communities, and especially to the members of the EH Research Cluster: Leah Aronowsky, John Levi Barnard, Clara Bosak-Schroeder, Carolyn Fornoff, Jamie Jones, Bob Morrissey, James Pilgrim, Pollyanna Rhee, and Rod Wilson. I also owe much to my students, both undergraduate and graduate, at the University of Illinois and the University of Chicago. They have taught me at least as much as I have taught them. Olivia Streitmatter provided excellent research support.

Conferences have offered a different kind of intellectual home, and since resuming after the hiatus of COVID-19, I appreciate the unique energy that comes from being in person with far-flung colleagues more than ever. I am grateful to have presented portions from early and late iterations of this project at ASA, ACLA, APT, ASLE, and MLA with Nasia Anam, Elizabeth Anker, Sarah Arens, Farah Bakaari, Rebecca Ballard, Jacob Berg, Sourit Bhattacharaya, Byron Caminero-Santangelo, Rose Casey, Alex Chambers, Nandini Chandra, Jeremy de Chavez, Kiu-wai Chu, Doron Darnov, Sarah Dimick, Matthew Eatough, Sarah Ensor, Michael Gaffney, Greg Garrard, Carmela Garritano, Alison Glassie, Bina Gogineni, Yogita Goyal, Katherine Hallemeier, Jennifer Hamilton, Katherine Hummel, Joya John, Nudrat Kamal, Robert LaRue, Nick Lu, Ian MacDonald, Alden Sajor Marte-Wood, Juan Meneses, Rituparna Mitra, Astrida Neimanis, Justyna Poray-Wybranowska, Martin Premoli, Erin Prior, Kelly Mee Rich, Laura Ritland,

ACKNOWLEDGMENTS

Bruce Robbins, Taylor Roberts, Matthew Schneider-Mayerson, Lisi Schoenbach, Bassam Sidiki, Ben Jamieson Stanley, Adedoyin Teriba, Philip Tsang, Meg Weisberg, Janet Zong, and many others. I am particularly grateful to Cajetan Iheka, Brian Larkin, Caroline Levine, and Teresa Shewry, whom I first met at conferences. They have generously read chapter drafts and supported my work after those first meetings. Cajetan and Caroline have become especially staunch supporters and letter writers; I cannot thank them enough.

I have grown as a scholar and researcher through the intellectual companionship of many, many others, not all of whom can be named here. Thanks to Alexia Alkadi-Barbaro, Ulka Anjaria, Elizabeth Chatterjee, Elizabeth DeLoughrey, Ursula Heise, Rebecca Hogue, Jessica Hurley, Anna Kornbluh, Rebecca Macklin, Jap-Nanak Makkar, Kalyan Nadiminti, Stephanie Reist, Nicole Rizzuto, Andrew Rose, Kirk Sides, Arielle Stambler, Jennifer Wenzel, and Sevin Yildiz. I am also grateful to Tessa Archambault at the University of Wisconsin-Madison and Jonathan Foster at Stockholm University for inviting me to speak about this work and for their audiences' feedback.

I received financial support for this book from the Humanities Division, Department of English Language and Literature and the Blair Fellowship at the University of Chicago. The English department at the University of Illinois provided valuable release time and a final manuscript workshop. Rachel Havrelock and Supriya Nair were dream manuscript readers; their incisive suggestions and deep enthusiasm helped put the final shine on the project. Finally, the Office of the Vice Chancellor for Research and Innovation at the University of Illinois provided a substantial book subvention to support the publication of *Reading Better States*.

I am incredibly fortunate that so many colleagues are also wonderful friends. But I particularly want to thank Sarah Kunjummen, Katharine Mershon, Mollie McFee, Samuel Rowe, and Cass Turner, who kept me buoyed during that marathon of intellectual sprints that was graduate school. And I am profoundly grateful to my writing and accountability group, the Anti-Burnout Collective. Rebecca Ballard, Lauren Herold, Katharine Mershon, Nicole Morse, and Allison Page read so many drafts with care and attention, taught me to embrace rest and play as much as work, to prioritize self-care, and kept me grounded amidst the rollercoaster of pre-tenure and book stress. I treasure our ABC community and wisdom.

Thanks to Tom Lay and the editorial team at Fordham University Press for their steady support for this book. I am grateful to the two anonymous press reviewers for their meticulous and constructive feedback; it made this book stronger. I am also very grateful to Silvestre Santiago Pejac for granting permission to use his arresting image, "Le Bateau Ivre," on the cover. Finally, I acknowledge permission to reprint material here from other venues. A version of chapter 1 was published as "The Claims of Bodies: Practices of Citizenship After Bhopal in Survivor Testimony and Indra Sinha's Animal's People," in *Interventions: International Journal of Postcolonial Studies* 21, no. 1 (2019): 70–91. A portion of chapter 4 was published as "Making Time: Pacific Futures in Kiribati's Migration with Dignity, Kathy Jetñil-Kijiner's *Iep Jāltok*, and Keri Hulme's *Stonefish*," copyright 2020 Purdue University. This article first appeared in *MFS Modern Fiction Studies*, vol. 66, issue 4 (Winter, 2020): 597–619.

I could not have written this book without the support of my family. My parents, Charles Oh and Kelly Chun-Oh, gave me everything. They fed my endless appetite for books, taught me drive and ambition, and to love learning, work hard, and never stop pursuing my dreams. Diana Jiorle and Edward Oh are the best siblings. I'm proud to have grown together as we follow our own paths. I am grateful to my relatives-in-law Bruce and Janice Sing, Michelle Sing-Ehret, Steve Ehret, Lauren Medina Oh, Ryan Jiorle, and my nephews Peter and Sam Jiorle. And, to our cats Astrid and Ginkgo, thank you for bringing me so much joy.

My most profound thanks go to Charles Sing, spouse and best partner in everything. You anchor me and show me the bright side. Your optimism, empathy, and support kept me going when this journey felt endless. Every day with you is a tenacious adventure, and this book would never have existed without you. I love you always.

Notes

Introduction: Reading Better States

1. Abani, *GraceLand*, 248.
2. Abani, *GraceLand*, 6.
3. Abani, *GraceLand*, 248.
4. Bloch, *Principle of Hope*, 146.
5. Bloch, *Principle of Hope*, 150, 148, emphasis original.
6. Such understandings of utopia are not uncommon. Queer theorists like José Esteban Muñoz have found them in art and everyday intimacy, while historians Michael D. Gordin, Helen Tilley, and Gyan Prakash have argued that utopias were always grounded operations enacted to improve historical circumstances, "concrete practices through which historically situated actors seek to reimagine their present and transform it into a plausible future." Gordin, Tilley, and Prakash, *Utopia/Dystopia*, "Introduction," 2.
7. Bloch, *Principle of Hope*, 145.
8. Bloch, *Principle of Hope*, 145.
9. This phrasing is inspired by Tsing et al., *Arts of Living on a Damaged Planet*.
10. Weber, *Theory of Social and Economic Organization*, 154, emphasis original. Examples from Marx and Engels abound in *The Communist Manifesto*.
11. Agamben, *Homo Sacer*.
12. Mbembe, *Necropolitics*, 70. In *History of Sexuality*, Foucault initially described biopolitics as a more neutral or polyvalent exercise, one that could augment or diminish the population. But he later stressed biopolitics' death-producing and racialized elements. Agamben and Mbembe are perhaps some of the most explicit, but Black, Indigenous, and other scholars working on state biopolitics tend to privilege its violence, as well.
13. Lloyd, "Nationalisms against the State," and Mamdani, *Neither Settler nor Native*.

14. Frank, "Development of Underdevelopment."

15. The destructive effects of SAPs have even been popularized in public-facing books like Klein's *Shock Doctrine*.

16. Hellman, Jones, and Kaufmann, "Seize the State, Seize the Day," 3, emphasis original.

17. State capture has been used to describe corporate meddling in the state but also the capture of state power by individual political elites, such as in Jacob Zuma's South Africa.

18. Partha Chatterjee, *Politics of the Governed*, 37.

19. Chatterjee, *Politics of the Governed*, 3 and 34. For Chatterjee the prevalence of interventionist states is an inheritance from colonialism, since colonial administrations developed the tools for addressing colonial populations according to specific group needs. But he does not primarily condemn this continuity between colonialism and postcolonialism; he instead critiques how particular provisions have overshadowed the pursuit of universal political rights or civic participation.

20. Kaviraj, *Imaginary Institution of India*, 211.

21. Recent literary scholarship on the welfare state has focused on its development in Europe and North America. See Aslami, *Dream Life of Citizens* for the British welfare state in the liberal tradition, where state intervention is theorized in relation to purportedly autonomous subjects and individual freedom. Scholars like Szalay writing about the American welfare state consider the welfare state's relationship to public security, and Robbins, in *Upward Mobility*, suggests that new kinds of social relations are central to welfare states depicted in Euro-American literature. More in line with my own emphasis on the positive qualities of the welfare state is Esteve, *Incremental Realism*, which argues that postwar American writers bolstered the claims of disadvantaged groups on the state through the trope of happiness, and Rich, in *Promise of Welfare*, who explores how the British welfare state has been imagined through post-WWII promises of repair.

22. Barry, *Welfare*, 12.

23. There is little consensus on when the welfare state started, but many historians and political scientists confirm that by the mid-twentieth century, welfare states had emerged in Europe and that they were defined by their large-scale social interventions. For a discussion of the rise of the "social" as a concept and the Jacobin origins of welfare, see Moyn, *Not Enough*. For an account of welfare that arose after wartime in Britain, see Lowe, *Welfare State in Britain*, and Bruce Robbins, *Beneficiary*, 89–90.

24. Moyn, *Not Enough*, 90, 55.

25. In *Exporting American Dreams*, Dudziak shows how the U.S. Bill of Rights influenced the Kenyan Bill of Rights during Kenyan's independence negotiations.

26. Thanks to Waïl Hassan for reminding me of this point.

27. See Cooper, *Citizenship between Empire and Nation*; Wilder, *French Imperial Nation-State*; and Kortenaar, *Debt, Law, Realism*. The disappointing status of the postcolonial state has become something of a taken-for-granted frame in the field.

28. See Getachew, "Welfare World," chap. 5 in *Worldmaking after Empire*.
29. Fanon, *Wretched of the Earth*, 236.
30. Rogan and Madeline, "Utopia Studies (Part II: Theory)."
31. Patel and Moore, "Introduction" and "Cheap Nature," chap. 1 in *Seven Cheap Things*.
32. This is not to discount activist networks, which have also been vital in contesting capitalism's environmental destruction, or UN climate negotiations, which have been global attempts to curb fossil fuels.
33. Lisa Mitchell, *Hailing the State*, 10. Mitchell focuses more narrowly on an Indian context and, rather than textual and cultural objects, considers collective actions like protests and sit-ins as examples of hailing the state.
34. Bourdieu, "Rethinking the State," 53.
35. Robbins, *Upward Mobility*, 7.
36. In this commitment to theorizing a state without a center, traceable in its effects and practices, Abrams is indebted to Foucault, who since at least *History of Sexuality* theorized the dispersal rather than the centralization of state power. This constructivist view of the state contrasts with state functionalists, who take for granted the coherent existence of the state outside civil society and who are then concerned with theorizing its unique functions.
37. Abrams, "Notes on the Difficulty of Studying the State," 82.
38. John Marx's book *Geopolitics and the Anglophone Novel* is another important exception. In chap. 2, "How Literature Administers 'Failed' States," he argues that state failure is normative, not necessarily negative, and not unique to postcolonial states.
39. See Nixon, *Slow Violence*, and Wenzel, *Disposition of Nature*. Postcolonial states have a long history of intervening heavily into the environment, but postcolonial environmental scholars have largely considered the negative effects of these state interventions, such as destructive development or short-term resource extraction. More generally, ecocriticism has traditionally not engaged with the state, and it has only in recent years moved beyond a preoccupation with local nature writing. Heise, in *Sense of Place and Sense of Planet*, pioneered this shift by foregrounding the rise of shared risks across borders. Her horizon, though, was the planetary, and the state level slips out of her influential conceptual expansion from the local to the global.
40. This approach is more established in the social sciences, where anthropologists working on the global South have shown how the state has multiple, contradictory roles and is imagined in a plurality of ways and uses beyond violence. They also record persistent desires for state intervention in a wide range of postcolonial contexts. Some recent examples include Gupta, *Red Tape*; Anand, *Hydraulic City*; Fredericks, *Garbage Citizenship*; and Mitchell, *Hailing the State*.
41. Jameson, "Utopia as Method," 42, emphasis mine.
42. In the more recent long essay *An American Utopia*, Jameson expands on his earlier notions of utopian method to propose the U.S. military and its sophisticated organization of civil services as a model for improving political institutions.

43. Jameson, "Utopia as Method," 26.
44. Oxford English Dictionary Online, "Complaint, n."
45. Cornell Law School LII/Legal Information Institute, "Complaint."
46. Travers, *Empires of Complaints*, looks at the centrality of complaint to the fiscal-juridical state in India, first under Mughal emperors and then under the East India Company. Scase, *Literature and Complaint in England*, also traces the history of complaint in medieval English courts. Though complaints eventually were taken up by poets and used outside the courtroom, she stresses their initial development as a specific kind of legal language.
47. Shortslef, *The Drama of Complaint*, and Kerrigan, *Motives of Woe*, show how in early modern Anglophone literature, complaint became an extra-legal subgenre, used not only in court but deployed on public stages.
48. Ahmed, *Complaint!*, 28.
49. Gupta, *Red Tape*, 100.
50. Fanon, *Wretched of the Earth*, 5.
51. Fanon, *Wretched of the Earth*, 111.
52. Fanon, *Wretched of the Earth*, 112.
53. Fanon, *Wretched of the Earth*, 117.
54. Fanon, *Wretched of the Earth*, 111, emphasis mine.
55. Fanon, *Wretched of the Earth*, 123 and 144.
56. Stoler, *Duress*, 26, emphasis original.
57. Stoler, *Duress*, 27, emphasis original.
58. Scott, *Conscripts of Modernity*, 134–35.
59. See Chakrabarty, *Provincializing Europe*. Craps, *Postcolonial Witnessing*, and Iheka, *African Ecomedia*, discuss postcolonial trauma, which importantly is theorized collectively rather than individually. On Pacific indigenous cyclical time, see DeLoughrey, *Routes and Roots*. See Kanu, "Dimensions of African Cosmology," and Garuba, "Explorations in Animist Materialism," for African cosmologies that emphasize the imbrication of the spirit and material worlds and the nonlinear nature of life and death. Such nonlinearity is also amply demonstrated in novels like Okri, *Famished Road*.
60. Stoler, *Duress*, 23, emphasis mine.
61. Stoler, *Duress*, 26.
62. Benhabib, *Critique, Norm, and Utopia*, 13.
63. Benhabib, *Critique, Norm, and Utopia*, 13, 1.
64. Benhabib, *Critique, Norm, and Utopia*, 41.
65. In *Critique, Norm, and Utopia*, Benhabib argues that there are two kinds of utopic politics—a politics of fulfillment and a politics of transfiguration, the former about fulfilling present needs for justice and the latter about radical breaks.
66. Bloch, "Can Hope Be Disappointed?," 340, emphasis original. Van der Vlies in *Present Imperfect* insightfully discusses Bloch's notion of educated hope in post-apartheid South Africa. My thanks to Katherine Hallemier for alerting me to Van der Vlies's work.
67. Bloch, "Can Hope be Disappointed?," 341, 342.

68. Bloch, "Can Hope be Disappointed?," 341.

69. Bloch, "Can Hope be Disappointed?," 343, emphasis original.

70. With postcolonial critics, BIPOC scholars and activists in North America have been instrumental to the rise of an environmental justice focus in environmental scholarship.

71. "Environmental racism" as a term is usually credited to Benjamin Chavis, former head of the United Church of Christ's Commission on Racial Justice, after he participated in the 1982 protests against the siting of a hazardous waste landfill in Warren County, North Carolina.

72. Summers, quoted in Nixon, *Slow Violence*, 1.

73. DeLoughrey and Handley, *Postcolonial Ecologies*. There are also many environmental histories of colonialism, including Grove, *Green Imperialism*, and Ross, *Ecology and Power*.

74. Lerner, *Sacrifice Zones*. The term "sacrifice zone" now has widespread usage in environmental justice work but was originally coined as "National Sacrifice Zone" during the Cold War to designate areas dangerously contaminated by radiation in the United States.

75. Guha and Martínez-Alier, *Varieties of Environmentalism*, xxi. This understanding of entwined social and environmental concerns has become mainstream, displacing earlier ecocritical views of the environment as separate from human struggles. Likewise, Gadgil and Guha, in *Ecology and Equity*, coined the term "the environmentalism of the poor" to describe the way environmental concerns in the global South are inseparable from social concerns over survival and resources.

76. Cilano and DeLoughrey, "Against Authenticity," 84.

77. Nixon, *Slow Violence*, 2.

78. Schwarz, "Objective Form," 187.

79. Malm and Hornborg, "Geology of Mankind?," and Chakrabarty, "Climate and Capital," among others, have pointed out the need to disaggregate the "Anthropos" in the Anthropocene. Elizabeth Chatterjee, "Asian Anthropocene," argues for Asia's contribution to the Anthropocene.

80. Ghosh, *Nutmeg's Curse*.

81. Anderson, *Imagined Communities*, influentially theorized the nation as an imagined community.

1. Unsettled: Toxicity after Bhopal

1. Iris Bell, quoted in Franklin, "Toxic Cloud Leaks at Carbide Plant."

2. Coleman, "Frequency of Man-Made Disasters," 6.

3. Bloch, *Principle of Hope*, 150, 148.

4. Fortun, *Advocacy after Bhopal*, 15, and Kurzman, *Killing Wind*, 130–31. Accounts of victim numbers vary, but scholarly and activist accounts uniformly place the numbers of dead and injured higher than the government's count.

5. Menon, "Orders (Settlement) of the Supreme Court," in *Documents and Court Opinions on Bhopal Gas Leak Disaster Case*, 288 and 289.
6. Fortun, *Advocacy after Bhopal*, 38.
7. Fortun, *Advocacy after Bhopal*, 146.
8. Fortun, *Advocacy after Bhopal*, 39
9. Petryna, *Life Exposed*, 34.
10. *News18*, "MP HC Raps Centre." See also International Campaign for Justice in Bhopal, "Bhopal Survivors Demand 'Right to Live.'"
11. Panagariya, *India: The Emerging Giant*. A wave of national protections and market restrictions were imposed in the 1960s during Indira Gandhi's first regime. But much of the rest of India's economic policy has been favorable to international investment. Even Nehru recognized the need for some foreign capital and equipment in specific areas, including pesticides. See also Denoon, "Cycles in Indian Economic Liberalization."
12. Kurzman, *Killing Wind*, 21.
13. Panagariya, *India: The Emerging Giant*, 92–94.
14. Champa Devi, quoted in Suroopa Mukherjee, *Surviving Bhopal*, 44.
15. Das, "Moral Orientations to Suffering," in Hanna, Morehouse, and Sarangi, *Bhopal Reader*, 53–54.
16. Everest, *Behind the Poison Cloud*, 46–47.
17. Warren Anderson, quoted in Everest, *Behind the Poison Cloud*, 18.
18. Everest, *Behind the Poison Cloud*, 33.
19. Bhopal and the Niger Delta, examined in chapter 2, have taken on a paradigmatic status among postcolonial critics working on environmental injustice. Nixon, whose *Slow Violence* is perhaps the most important book in the postcolonial environmental humanities from the last fifteen years, discusses both at length. Wenzel, another leading postcolonial environmental humanist, writes extensively about Bhopal and the Niger Delta in *Disposition of Nature*.
20. This is not to say the struggle for justice in Bhopal has ceased or that it is always channeled toward the state. Local NGOs like the Bhopal Medical Appeal offer ongoing medical relief, and international coalitions like the International Campaign for Justice in Bhopal also advocate for gas survivors outside the state.
21. In N. R. Madhava Menon's edited collection of the documents from the Bhopal gas leak disaster, the suit is titled "Civil Suit for Damages filed by Union of India." This suit could be considered a legal complaint in the technical sense, as it did begin India's civil case against Union Carbide. However, since I use "complaint" in ways that go beyond its meaning as a specific kind of legal document throughout the book, I refrain from calling it a complaint here to avoid confusion.
22. Menon, "Processing of Claims Act," 377.
23. Menon, "Processing of Claims Act," 378.
24. Menon, "Processing of Claims Act," 378.
25. Mukherjee, *Surviving Bhopal*, 62.
26. Menon, "Civil Suit for Damages," 76.

27. Menon, "Civil Suit for Damages," 76, emphasis mine.
28. Menon, "Civil Suit for Damages," 76.
29. Menon, "Civil Suit for Damages," 76. In India, Union Carbide operated through Union Carbide India Limited, which was joint-owned by Union Carbide and Indian investors; however, Union Carbide owned a controlling majority of the company, and decisions about the plant's operation came from Union Carbide headquarters in Danbury, Connecticut. After the gas explosion Union Carbide attempted to blame UCIL.
30. Menon, "Civil Suit for Damages," 76.
31. Menon, "Civil Suit for Damages," 76.
32. Menon, "Civil Suit for Damages," 74–76.
33. Menon, "Orders (Settlement) of the Supreme Court," 288.
34. Menon, "Orders (Settlement) of the Supreme Court," 288.
35. Jameson, "Utopia as Method, 32.
36. *Charan Lal Sahu*, 1990 AIR 1480 at 5 (Supreme Court of India, Dec. 22, 1989).
37. Constitution of India, art. 37, emphasis mine. Some scholars point out that the non-enforceable quality of directive principles renders them useless. Abraham and Abraham, "Bhopal Case and the Development of Environmental Law in India," argue that India's judiciary is known for having an activist character.
38. *Charan Lal Sahu*, 1990 AIR 1480 at 6 (Supreme Court of India, Dec. 22, 1989).
39. Benhabib, *Critique, Norm, and Utopia*, 41.
40. Mukherjee, *Surviving Bhopal*, 87.
41. Mukherjee, *Surviving Bhopal*, 88.
42. Chander Singh, quoted in Hanna, Morehouse, and Sarangi, *Bhopal Reader*, 113.
43. Quoted in Fortun, *Advocacy after Bhopal*, 46–49.
44. Petryna, *Life Exposed*, 5.
45. Petryna, *Life Exposed*, 6.
46. Petryna, *Life Exposed*, 6.
47. Benhabib, *Critique, Norm, and Utopia*, 13, 1.
48. Kailasam's title is taken from the Cat Stevens song of the same name.
49. Kailasam, *Where Do the Children Play?*, 00:08:33–00:08:38.
50. Kailasam, *Where Do the Children Play?*, 00:09:01–00:09:11.
51. De and Travers argue that petitioning is "a constitutive element in modern political regimes," especially in South Asia; "Petitioning and Political Cultures in South Asia," 4.
52. Kailasam, *Where Do the Children Play?*, 00:10:48–00:10:53.
53. Kailasam, *Where Do the Children Play?*, 00:10:10–00:10:23.
54. Kailasam, *Where Do the Children Play?*, 00:11:53–00:12:01.
55. Kailasam, *Where Do the Children Play?*, 00:10:53–00:10:56.
56. Benhabib, *Critique, Norm, and Utopia*, 1.

57. Kailasam, *Where Do the Children Play?*, 00:11:21–00:11:30.
58. Kailasam, *Where Do the Children Play?*, 00:11:45–00:11:52.
59. McFarlane and Vasudevan, "Informal Infrastructures," 256. Jantar Mantar is the only remaining public site in New Delhi where Section 144, a law that bans gatherings of more than five people, is not enforced.
60. Kailasam, *Where Do the Children Play?*, 00:52:05.
61. Kailasam, *Where Do the Children Play?*, 00:56:54–00:57:54.
62. Kailasam, *Where Do the Children Play?*, 00:59:10–00:59:12.
63. Kailasam, *Where Do the Children Play?*, 00:59:45–00:59:51.
64. Sinha, *Animal's People*, 106.
65. Sinha, *Animal's People*, 24. Many scholars have noted the politics of dehumanization that are emblematized in Animal's body. See, for example, Nixon, "Slow Violence, Neoliberalism, and the Environmental Picaresque," chap. 1 in *Slow Violence*, and Johnston, "'A Nother World.'"
66. Sinha, *Animal's People*, 108.
67. Sinha, *Animal's People*, 107.
68. Sinha, *Animal's People*, 130, 147.
69. Sinha, *Animal's People*, 366.
70. Sinha, *Animal's People*, 267, 268.
71. Sinha, *Animal's People*, 3, emphasis original.
72. Sinha, *Animal's People*, 22.
73. Sinha, *Animal's People*, 39.
74. Sinha, *Animal's People*, 50.
75. Sinha, *Animal's People*, 50, emphasis mine.
76. Sinha, *Animal's People*, 284.
77. Sinha, *Animal's People*, 3, emphasis original.
78. Rickel, "'The Poor Remain,'" Singh, "Post-Humanitarian Fictions," and Snell, "Assessing the Limitations of Laughter," all discuss how *Animal's People* critiques the fetishization of Bhopal and other global South tragedies by international audiences. O'Loughlin, "Negotiating Solidarity," critiques the NGO-ization of postcolonial literature more generally and interprets *Animal's People* as a refutation of humanitarian pressures on fiction.
79. Sinha, "Chemicals for War and Chemicals for Peace."
80. Sinha, *Animal's People*, 5, 7.
81. Sinha, *Animal's People*, 15.
82. Sinha, *Animal's People*, 105.
83. Sinha, *Animal's People*, 283.
84. Sinha, *Animal's People*, 227, 228.
85. Latour, *Reassembling the Social*.
86. Sinha, *Animal's People*, 314.
87. Sinha, *Animal's People*, 8 and 2.
88. Upamanyu Pablo Mukherjee, *Postcolonial Environments*, 152, makes a similar point about the posthuman, collective quality of Animal's body.

89. Sinha, *Animal's People*, 55.
90. Alaimo, *Bodily Natures*, 4.
91. Sinha, *Animal's People*, 366.
92. Sinha, *Animal's People*, 365.
93. Greenpeace International, *Corporate Crimes*, 4.
94. Greenpeace International, *Corporate Crimes*, 2
95. Greenpeace International, *Corporate Crimes*, 3.
96. Hart, in *Extraterritorial*, argues that states do in fact have mobile borders that exceed national territory. But he argues that these enhance security priorities of surveillance and repression, not welfare.
97. Jameson, "Utopia as Method," 42.
98. Bloch, *Principle of Hope*, 146.
99. Bloch, *Principle of Hope*, 145, 150.
100. Bloch, *Principle of Hope*, 157, emphasis original.

2. Beyond Petrostates: Oil Pollution in the Niger Delta

1. *Deepwater Horizon* was owned by Transocean but leased and operated by BP during the explosion.
2. Barron et al., "Long-Term Ecological Impacts from Oil Spills," 6460–61.
3. Barron et al., "Long-Term Ecological Impacts from Oil Spills," 6457.
4. Amnesty International, "Niger Delta Negligence."
5. Hellman, Jones, and Kaufmann, "Seize the State, Seize the Day."
6. The phrase "black gold" has been used to describe oil around the world. See, for example, Watts, "Oil as Money: The Devil's Excrement and the Spectacle of Black Gold."
7. Coronil, *Magical State*.
8. Watts, "Sweet and Sour," 42–43.
9. Watts, "Chronicle of a Future Foretold," 369.
10. Ekeh, "Structure and Meaning of Federal Character," 36, emphasis original.
11. Apter, *Pan-African Nation*, 39.
12. Saro-Wiwa, *Genocide in Nigeria*, 7.
13. Leton, "Statement" *Ogoni Bill of Rights*.
14. Leton, "Statement" *Ogoni Bill of Rights*.
15. Leton, "Statement" *Ogoni Bill of Rights*.
16. Ghosh, "Petrofiction." Ghosh coined the term "petrofiction" in this review of Abdul Munif's oil novel *Cities of Salt*.
17. By the time the novel ends in 1978, Nigeria's economy had begun suffering from the effects of high spending and crashing oil prices.
18. Okpewho, *Tides*, 26.
19. Okpewho, *Tides*, 84.
20. Okpewho, *Tides*, 126.

21. Okpewho, *Tides*, 6. Though *Tides* is petrofiction, it is also concerned with the role of ethnic conflict and competition in Nigeria.

22. MacArthur, *Extravagant Narratives*, 8, 9.

23. Okpewho, *Tides*, 178.

24. Iheka, "Rethinking Postcolonial Resistance," chap. 3 in *Naturalizing Africa*, also makes this point about *Tides*' ending.

25. United Nations Environment Programme, *Environmental Assessment of Ogoniland*, 10.

26. Mbue, *How Beautiful We Were*, 3.

27. Mbue, *How Beautiful We Were*, 8.

28. Mbue, *How Beautiful We Were*, 22.

29. Mbue, *How Beautiful We Were*, 316.

30. Mbue, *How Beautiful We Were*, 316.

31. Conversely, some political theorists have argued that markets are "complex institutions that must be created and sustained by the visible hand of the government." Vogel, *Marketcraft*, 2.

32. Wenzel does not use the term "state capture," but similarly describes how the Nigerian petro-state "epitomizes neoliberal globalization's repurposing of the state." Wenzel, *Disposition of Nature*, 104.

33. Though Nigeria did not gain full independence from Great Britain until 1960, it took steps toward self-rule before this date; in 1953 the major political parties in Nigeria gathered in London for a Constitutional Conference.

34. Oil Pipelines Act of 1956.

35. *Bodo* [2014], EWHC 1973 (TCC) BAILII at *4.

36. Ribadu, quoted in *Bodo* [2014], EWHC 1973 (TCC) BAILII at *5.

37. Vidal, "Shell Announces £55m Payout."

38. Oil Pipelines Act of 1956, Part 4, § 11.

39. *Bodo* [2014], EWHC 1973 (TCC) BAILII at *40.

40. See Timothy Mitchell, "Machines of Democracy," chap. 1 in *Carbon Democracy*.

41. Williams, *Country and the City*, 125.

42. Heise, *Sense of Place and Sense of Planet*, 121.

43. Constitution of the Federal Republic of Nigeria 1999, ch. 2, § 20.

44. This clause on environmental protection appeared in the unenforceable "Fundamental Objectives and Directive Principles of State Policy," but it was still a noteworthy development. It is part of a larger trend in constitutionally embedded environmental protections. See May and Daly, *Global Environmental Constitutionalism*.

45. As Ebeku notes, "Up until this case, Nigerian judges usually privileged the economic benefits of the country over environmental protection, particularly in relation to oil operations notwithstanding the existence of the legal right to a healthy environment." Ebeku, "Constitutional Right to a Healthy Environment," 316.

46. Faturoti, Agbaitoro, and Onya, "Environmental Protection," 227. Rose Casey has also identified a string of recent cases in which European-based oil companies operating in the Niger Delta are being held accountable by their home countries in "an emergent legal understanding of globally dispersed responsibility for ecological and human harms." Casey, *Aesthetic Impropriety*, 33.

47. *Jonah Gbemre*, Federal High Court Benin City, Climate Change Litigation Databases, at *2.

48. *Jonah Gbemre*, Federal High Court Benin City, Climate Change Litigation Databases, at *29–32.

49. Faturoti, Agbaitoro, and Onya, "Environmental Protection," 235.

50. Weis, "Constitutional Directive Principles."

51. Osaghae, *Crippled Giant*, 22.

52. Movement for the Survival of the Ogoni People, *Ogoni Bill of Rights*, art. 10.

53. Movement for the Survival of the Ogoni People, *Ogoni Bill of Rights*, art. 11 (i–v).

54. Daniel Jordan Smith, *Culture of Corruption*. Other assessments of Nigerian corruption abound. In addition to Smith, see Bayart, *State in Africa*; Pierce, *Moral Economies of Corruption*; Saro-Wiwa, *Month and a Day*; and Griswold, *Bearing Witness*.

55. Ekeh, "Structure and Meaning of Federal Character," 36, emphasis original.

56. Benhabib, *Critique, Norm, and Utopia*, 1.

57. Movement for the Survival of the Ogoni People, *Ogoni Bill of Rights*, emphasis mine.

58. Osaghae, *Crippled Giant*, 115.

59. Constitution of the Federal Republic of Nigeria 1979, ch. 2 § 14(3). A similar principle applies to regional state and local governments in § 14(4).

60. Movement for the Survival of the Ogoni People, *Ogoni Bill of Rights*.

61. Movement for the Survival of the Ogoni People, *Ogoni Bill of Rights*.

62. Movement for the Survival of the Ogoni People, *Ogoni Bill of Rights*, art. 6.

63. Mahmood Mamdani, quoted in Watts, "Sweet and Sour," 41.

64. Mamdani, *Citizen and Subject*, discusses how policies of indirect rule facilitated ethnic competition in Nigeria and have spread across the continent. These follow from the way British administrator Frederick Lugard combined the Northern and Southern protectorates of Nigeria in 1914, combining more than two hundred ethnic groups into one administrative entity.

65. Benhabib, *Critique, Norm, and Utopia*, 1.

66. Achebe, "African Writer and the English Language," 62.

67. Achebe, *Trouble with Nigeria*, 1.

68. Kortenaar, "'Only Connect,'"; Erritouni, "Contradictions and Alternatives"; Wenzel, "Trouble with Narrators."

69. Achebe, *Anthills of the Savannah*, 29, 15.

70. Achebe, *Anthills of the Savannah*, 28. Gikandi, *Reading Chinua Achebe*, Ikegami, "Knowledge and Power," and Iyasere, "Oral Tradition," all discuss elements of oral narrative, style, and form in Achebe's oeuvre.

71. Achebe, *Anthills of the Savannah*, 28.
72. Achebe, *Anthills of the Savannah*, 3.
73. Achebe, *Anthills of the Savannah*, 29–30.
74. Achebe, *Anthills of the Savannah*, 116.
75. Achebe, *Anthills of the Savannah*, 30.
76. Achebe, *Anthills of the Savannah*, 30.
77. Achebe, *Anthills of the Savannah*, 15.
78. Achebe, *Anthills of the Savannah*, 117.
79. Achebe, *Anthills of the Savannah*, 116–17.
80. Kortenaar, "'Only Connect,'" 61.
81. Achebe, *Anthills of the Savannah*, 1.
82. Achebe, *Anthills of the Savannah*, 1.
83. Achebe, *Anthills of the Savannah*, 8, 111.
84. Achebe, *Anthills of the Savannah*, 15.
85. Achebe, *Anthills of the Savannah*, 213.

86. Innes argues that "The Hymn to the Sun" is about "the arrogance and cruelty of naked power." Innes, *Chinua Achebe*, 156. She points out the gendered quality of power in the novel and finds a precursor to Beatrice's leadership in the Myth of Idemili.

87. Jameson famously argued that "*the story of the private individual destiny is always an allegory of the embattled situation of the public third-world culture and society*," a claim many postcolonial scholars have disputed. Jameson, "Third-World Literature," 69, emphasis original.

88. Johns-Putra, "'My Job Is to Take Care of You,'" and Sheldon, *Child to Come*, consider how children are paradigmatic symbols of futurity. For an argument against the historic investment in child-based futurity see Edelman, *No Future*.

89. Achebe, *Anthills of the Savannah*, 211–12.

90. Sackey, "Oral Tradition and the African Novel," discusses how an oral exchange is often used to formally open an oral narration as well as build rapport between speaker and audience.

91. Brady Smith, "Red, Black, and Green," argues that urban settings, as much as rural ones, must be considered environmentally important sites in African novels.

92. Achebe, *Anthills of the Savannah*, 194.
93. Mbue, *How Beautiful We Were*, 226.
94. Mbue, *How Beautiful We Were*, 95.
95. Mbue, *How Beautiful We Were*, 41.
96. Mbue, *How Beautiful We Were*, 10.
97. Mbue, *How Beautiful We Were*, 41.
98. Mbue, *How Beautiful We Were*, 316.
99. Mbue, *How Beautiful We Were*, 187.
100. Mbue, *How Beautiful We Were*, 189.

101. Saro-Wiwa's death at the hands of the Abacha regime "was probably a defining moment for me as a person with a social and political conscience." Mbue,

"Author Imbolo Mbue Explores the Politics of Oil in 'How Beautiful We Were.'" As a child growing up in Limbe in neighboring Camaroon, Mbue also first heard the word "environmentalist" used to describe Saro-Wiwa.

102. Mbue, *How Beautiful We Were*, 316.
103. Bloch, *Principle of Hope*, 150 and 148, emphasis original.
104. Mbue, *How Beautiful We Were*, 313.
105. Mbue, *How Beautiful We Were*, 277.
106. Mbue, *How Beautiful We Were*, 333.
107. Mbue, *How Beautiful We Were*, 334.
108. Mbue, *How Beautiful We Were*, 337.
109. Mbue, *How Beautiful We Were*, 212.
110. Stoler, *Duress*, 26, emphasis original.
111. Brooks, *Reading for the Plot*, 93.
112. Mbue, *How Beautiful We Were*, 360.
113. Muñoz, *Cruising Utopia*, 4, 30.
114. Stoler, *Duress*, 33.
115. Benjamin, *Arcades Project*, 392.

3. Undoing Apartheid: Water Pasts and Futures in Cape Town

1. Central California Area Office, Bureau of Reclamation, "Water Facts."
2. United Nations, "Water—at the Center of the Climate Crisis."
3. See Bakker, "Political Ecology of Water Privatization," and Peter Robbins, "Transnational Corporations." A handful of private companies hold the majority of contracts for water and sanitation projects. For example, Thames Water, England's largest water supply company, has 25 million customers on four continents.
4. Ahlers, "Fixing and Nixing," 219.
5. Robbins, "Transnational Corporations," 1079–80.
6. Muehlebach, *Vital Frontier*.
7. Anand, "Introduction," in *Hydraulic City*.
8. Shepherd, "Making Sense of 'Day Zero,'" 4.
9. The idea of an Anthropocene conjuncture draws on the way disaster studies scholars have argued that natural disasters interact with preexisting social vulnerabilities. See Neil Smith, "There's No Such Thing as a Natural Disaster."
10. Rubenstein, *Public Works*, shows that public water utilities, gas, and electricity were foundational to twentieth-century imaginaries of development and the state elsewhere, as in Ireland.
11. Chance, *Living Politics*, 43.
12. Gordon, *Apartheid in South Africa*, and Maylam, *South Africa's Racial Past*, note that racial segregation far preceded apartheid, and there is some debate about whether apartheid simply continued earlier segregationist policies laid down during the early colonial era. But apartheid is also generally acknowledged as a regime with

new, starker policies beginning in the 1950s under the leadership of Hendrick Verwoerd.

13. Welsh, "Cultural Dimension of Apartheid," 51.
14. Von Schnitzler, *Democracy's Infrastructure*, 14–15.
15. Von Schnitzler discusses the deeply infrastructural quality of apartheid, and hence also of apartheid protests and post-apartheid relationships with the state, in her monograph *Democracy's Infrastructure*.
16. South African Government, "Growth, Employment and Redistribution."
17. Bond, *Elite Transition*. See also Adelzadeh, "From the RDP to GEAR," for the argument that GEAR is basically a homegrown SAP policy.
18. Shepherd, "Making Sense of 'Day Zero,'" 6.
19. On suspension, see Habib, *South Africa's Suspended Revolution*; on incomplete liberation, see Chance, *Living Politics*.
20. Comaroff and Comaroff, "Figuring Crime," 233.
21. Chance, "Ashes to Ashes, Dust to Dust," chap. 4 in *Living Politics*.
22. Von Schnitzler, "Infrastructure, Apartheid Technopolitics," in *Promise of Infrastructure*, ed. Anand, Gupta, and Appel, 133.
23. Alexander, "Rebellion of the Poor," 37.
24. Lemanski, "Infrastructural Citizenship," 590.
25. Hemson and Owusu-Ampomah, "A Better Life for All?," 512.
26. Attwell and Harlow, "Introduction: South African Fiction after Apartheid," 3.
27. Attwell and Harlow, "Introduction: South African Fiction after Apartheid," 2, 3.
28. Byrne, "'Policing Borders,'" 87.
29. Byrne, "'Policing Borders,'" 87. Byrne notes that by contrast, insects have often had important spiritual and cultural significance for Black African writers.
30. Rose-Innes, *Nineveh*, 101.
31. Williams, "Life Among the Vermin," 427.
32. Rose-Innes, *Nineveh*, 20, 32.
33. Rose-Innes, *Nineveh*, 17, 20.
34. Rose-Innes, *Nineveh*, 27.
35. Cracks in a coherent whole have long signified national fragmentation in postcolonial literature, perhaps most canonically in the cracked face of Saleem Sinai, the protagonist of Salman Rushdie's *Midnight's Children*. Saleem is commonly interpreted to allegorize the Indian nation and its trials and fragmentation after independence.
36. Rose-Innes, *Nineveh*, 150.
37. Duiker published two novels during his life, *Thirteen Cents* and *The Quiet Violence of Dreams*. His third novel, *The Hidden Star*, was incomplete when he died but published posthumously.
38. Zakes Mda, quoted in Obi-Young, "Remembering K. Sello Duiker."
39. Duiker, *Thirteen Cents*, 49, emphasis original.
40. Duiker, *Thirteen Cents*, 1.
41. Duiker, *Thirteen Cents*, 1.

42. Samuelson, "Anomalous, Containerized and Inundating Waters," 466.

43. Duiker, *Thirteen Cents*, 35. Njovane similarly argues that Azure's body "reflects colonial, apartheid, and post-transitional manifestations of unmitigated violence against those who inhabit black bodies." Njovane, "'My Mother Was a Fish,'" 174.

44. Samuelson, in "Anomalous, Containerized and Inundating Waters," argues that Azure's perspective infuses the novel with "blue focalization." For Samuelson this is not about representations of water as I discuss, but watery qualities of the narrative like fluidity and chaotic mixture.

45. Duiker, *Thirteen Cents*, 19.

46. Duiker, *Thirteen Cents*, 125.

47. Vandana Shiva, quoted in Samuelson, "Anomalous, Containerized and Inundating Waters," 468.

48. Duiker, *Thirteen Cents*, 9.

49. Crutzen and Stoermer, "'Anthropocene.'"

50. Duiker, *Thirteen Cents*, 163.

51. Duiker, *Thirteen Cents*, 160.

52. Green, "Rock: Cape Town's Natures," chap. 1 in *Rock/Water/Life*.

53. Robins, "Defence of the Commons," 6. Despite the accusations of activists, it should be noted that Cape Town has not, like other areas in South Africa, actually privatized water or turned water provision over to corporations. Laila Smith, "Murky Waters," argues that Cape Town has been subject to a more subtle form of neoliberal expansion as the local government increasingly frames its own provision through ideas of consumption and cost recovery over earlier discourses and practices that prioritized water as a common good. This has not been totally uniform, though, and so battles continue over private and public framings of water in Cape Town's government.

54. Robins, "Defence of the Commons," 25.

55. African National Congress, Reconstruction and Development Programme (RDP), 1.1.1.

56. African National Congress, Reconstruction and Development Programme (RDP), 1.2.1 and 1.2.4.

57. African National Congress, Reconstruction and Development Programme (RDP), 2 and 2.1.1.

58. African National Congress, Reconstruction and Development Programme (RDP), 1.2.9.

59. African National Congress, Reconstruction and Development Programme (RDP), 2.5.4.

60. African National Congress, Reconstruction and Development Programme (RDP), 2.5.7.

61. African National Congress, Reconstruction and Development Programme (RDP), 2.6.6. and 2.6.7.

62. Constitution of the Republic of South Africa, Preamble.

63. Constitution of the Republic of South Africa, § 26 (1) and 27 (1)(b).
64. African National Congress, Reconstruction and Development Programme (RDP), 2.6.6. and 2.6.7.
65. Constitution of the Republic of South Africa, § 26 (1) and 26 (2), emphasis mine.
66. Constitution of the Republic of South Africa, § 27.
67. Van der Vlies, *Present Imperfect*, also draws on the way grammatical tenses describe the South African present.
68. Benhabib, *Critique, Norm, and Utopia*, 13.
69. Rose-Innes, *Nineveh*, 193.
70. Rose-Innes, *Nineveh*, 167, 61.
71. Rose-Innes, *Nineveh*, 59, 58.
72. Rose-Innes, *Nineveh*, 193, 193–94.
73. Oldfield and Greyling, "Waiting for the State," 1100.
74. Oldfield and Greyling, "Waiting for the State," 1100.
75. Oldfield and Greyling, "Waiting for the State."
76. Oldfield and Greyling, "Waiting for the State," 1102.
77. Oldfield and Greyling, "Waiting for the State," 1107.
78. Oldfield and Greyling, "Waiting for the State," 1103.
79. Quoted in Oldfield and Greyling, "Waiting for the State," 1108, ellipsis original.
80. Berlant, *Cruel Optimism*.
81. Charlton and Meth, "Lived Experiences of State Housing," 92 and 93.
82. Oldfield and Greyling, "Waiting for the State," 1108.
83. Oldfield and Greyling, "Waiting for the State," 1109.
84. Charlton and Meth, "Lived Experiences of State Housing," 96.
85. Florence, quoted in Charlton and Meth, "Lived Experiences of State Housing," 97, ellipses original.
86. Bolina, quoted in Charlton and Meth, "Lived Experiences of State Housing," 97, ellipses original.
87. Oldfield and Greyling, "Waiting for the State," 1109.
88. Sfiso, quoted in Charlton and Meth, "Lived Experiences of State Housing," 107.
89. Rodina and Harris, "Water Services, Lived Citizenship," 337.
90. Rodina and Harris, "Water Services, Lived Citizenship," 345.
91. Quoted in Rodina and Harris, "Water Services, Lived Citizenship," 345.
92. Rodina and Harris, "Water Services, Lived Citizenship," 345.
93. Quoted in Rodina and Harris, "Water Services, Lived Citizenship," 346.
94. In Cape Town, pro-poor water measures have only been partly successful, and their implementation is often uneven. In 2005, for instance, a grant program was put in place to subsidize water beyond the free basic minimum for indigent households, and a progressive tariff structure was put in place where payment above the free basic amount would rise gradually. Census data, however, shows that in Site C, an area in Khayelitsha's northern side, only 50 percent of households have water

in their dwellings or yards, and taps are often dirty or broken. Providing the infrastructure is one challenge, maintaining it another.

95. Chance, *Living Politics*, 46, 45.
96. Chance, *Living Politics*, 45.
97. Duiker, *Thirteen Cents*, 69.
98. Duiker, *Thirteen Cents*, 7.
99. Even during apartheid, when they had no political rights, Black South Africans primarily interacted with the state via infrastructure and administration: "The state was also the provider and landlord of plots and houses, infrastructures and basic services, and collector of payments and rents." Von Schnitzler, *Democracy's Infrastructure*, 14.
100. Duiker, *Thirteen Cents*, 19.
101. Duiker, *Thirteen Cents*, 126.
102. Cape Town's water is supplied by six dams, the largest of which is the Theewaterskloof Dam.
103. Baker, "Cape Town Is 90 Days Away." Ben Jamieson Stanley argues conversely that these "emergency narratives" created panic and facilitated repressive measures; Stanley, *Precarious Eating*, 171.
104. Robins, "Defence of the Commons," 28.
105. Davis, "#CapeWaterGate." The idea of Day Zero did not emerge immediately with the drought but was suggested late in 2017 by former Democratic Alliance leader Tony Leon's public relations company, Resolve. The Democratic Alliance, an ANC rival, is the ruling party in Western Cape.
106. Robins, "Defence of the Commons," 17.
107. Stodel, quoted in Monteiro, "Water Crisis Grips Cape Town."
108. De Villiers, "How Cape Town Avoided Day Zero."
109. Joubert and Ziervogal, *Day Zero: One City's Response*, 28.
110. Robins, "Defence of the Commons," 18.
111. De Lille, "Cape Town Will Reach Day Zero."
112. De Lille, "Cape Town Will Reach Day Zero."
113. De Lille, "Cape Town Will Reach Day Zero."
114. Moffett, "1001 Ways to Save Water."
115. Moffett, "1001 Ways to Save Water."
116. "Critical Water Shortages Disaster Plan."
117. Indeed, this cross-subsidizing has been described as a "Robin Hood" approach to water provision, taking money from wealthy residents to finance water to the townships; Joubert and Ziervogal, *Day Zero: One City's Response*, 11. However, they have also been critiqued for burdening lower-middle-class residents.
118. Riddel, *Cape Town*, 15:37–40.
119. Canavan, "Introduction: If This Goes On," 13, emphasis original.
120. Goodbody, "Cli-Fi—Genre of the Twenty-First Century?" notes that climate fictions tend to be concerned with bridging the gap between knowledge and action in response to climate change. However, not all climate fiction is speculative.

Realist climate fictions also often convey the existing reality of climate change and scientific knowledge.

121. "Critical Water Shortages Disaster Plan."
122. Zille, "From the Inside."
123. De Lille, "Day Zero Now Likely to Happen."
124. "Critical Water Shortages Disaster Plan."
125. Enqvist and Ziervogel, in "Water governance and justice in Cape Town," make a similar point about avoiding Phase Three.
126. *City of Cape Town Climate Change Action Plan*, § 2.
127. Mackay, "Spotlight: An Interview with Alistair Mackay."
128. Mackay, *It Doesn't Have to Be This Way*, 57.
129. Canavan, "Introduction: If This Goes On," 13.
130. Mackay, *It Doesn't Have to Be This Way*, 15.
131. Mackay, *It Doesn't Have to Be This Way*, 71.
132. Mackay, *It Doesn't Have to Be This Way*, 72–73.
133. Von Schnitzler, *Democracy's Infrastructure*, 15.
134. See Cremer, "'It's a privilege to call it a crisis'"; Fisher, "Finally, we have a crisis"; and Stanley, "Purity and Porosity," chap. 5 in *Precarious Eating*.

4. Making Time: Pacific Futurity and Rising Seas

1. Boyd, "Louisiana's First Climate Refugees."
2. Church and White, "20th Century Acceleration in Global Sea-Level Rise."
3. Rott et al., "Climate Talks End on a First-Ever Call."
4. Rowlatt, "UAE Planned to Use COP28 Climate Talks."
5. Loginova and Cassel, in "Leaving the Island," cover a number of setbacks and missteps that have occurred between the tribe and U.S. government, including a reduction in the number of tribal members eligible for relocation.
6. National Resources Defense Council, "Bangladesh: A Country Underwater."
7. Sarwar and Khan, "Sea Level Rise," 375.
8. Davenport and Robertson, "Resettling the First American 'Climate Refugees.'"
9. These islands are not alone. Tokelau, the Carteret islands of Papua New Guinea, and the Maldives in the Indian Ocean also face imminent inundation.
10. Dreher and Voyer, "Climate Refugees or Migrants?," offers an overview of the rise and prevalence of the climate refugee frame. See also Farbotko and Lazrus, "First Climate Refugees?"
11. Ahuja, *Planetary Specters*, argues that climate refugeeism is not new or unique but only a continuation of discourses of racialization and border policing that have accompanied the figure of the migrant or refugee over time. Yet climate refugeeism does differ in that its drivers are not only economic and social but environmental, and that in some cases the lands from which climate refugees move will literally cease to exist.

12. Tina Stege, quoted in Batrawy, "What It Means for an Oil Producing Country."
13. American Chemical Society, "Keeling Curve."
14. Lindsey, "Climate Change: Atmospheric Carbon Dioxide."
15. Rytz, *Anote's Ark*, 00:11:16–00:11:35.
16. Rytz, *Anote's Ark*, 00:02:50–00:02:57.
17. Corneloup and Mol, "Small Island Developing States."
18. Rytz, *Anote's Ark*, 00:11:37–00:11:57.
19. IPCC, 2023: Summary of Policymakers, 21.
20. IPCC, 2023: Summary of Policymakers, 11.
21. Yamin, "Kyoto Protocol," 113.
22. Torrice, *Rising Waters*, 35:33–35:44.
23. Rytz, *Anote's Ark*, 00:33:29–00:33:40.
24. Rytz, *Anote's Ark*, 00:13:04–00:13:18.
25. Shenk, *Island President*, 1:00:36.
26. Government of Tuvalu, *Te Kaniva*, Foreword.
27. Government of Tuvalu, *Te Kaniva*, Foreword.
28. Farbotko, Stratford, and Lazrus, "Climate Migrants and New Identities?," 535. There are a range of responses to migration in all Pacific states, and some Tuvaluans do want to leave.
29. Farbotko, Stratford, and Lazrus, "Climate Migrants and New Identities?," 535, emphasis original.
30. Farbotk, Stratford, and Lazrus, "Climate Migrants and New Identities?," 540.
31. Stratford, Farbotko, and Lazrus, "Tuvalu, Sovereignty and Climate Change," 69–70. Many other Pacific languages have similar terms that designate people and place together.
32. Hau'ofa, "Our Sea of Islands."
33. Government of Tuvalu, *Te Kaniva*, 25.
34. Chakrabarty, chap. 2, "Two Histories of Capital" and chap. 4, "Minority Histories, Subaltern Pasts," both in *Provincializing Europe*.
35. Government of Tuvalu, *Te Kavina*, 26.
36. McAdam, "'Disappearing States,'" notes that one state can technically exist inside another.
37. Burkett, "Nation *Ex-Situ*," discusses examples like governments in exile, which operate without territory.
38. Rytz, *Anote's Ark*, 00:24:04–00:24:09. Tong's administration oversaw the purchase of 20 sq km on Vanua Levu, Fiji's second-largest island in 2014.
39. Phelps, "As Waters Rise."
40. McKenzie, "Remittances in the Pacific," 100.
41. Maclellan, "Kiribati's Policy for 'Migration with Dignity.'"
42. Tessie Lambourne, quoted in Maclellan, "Kiribati's Policy for 'Migration with Dignity.'"

43. Anote Tong, quoted in Pashley, "Climate-Induced Migration Is 5 Years Away."
44. Anote Tong, quoted in Maclellan, "Kiribati's Policy for 'Migration with Dignity.'"
45. Tessie Lambourne, quoted in Maclellan, "Kiribati's Policy for 'Migration with Dignity.'"
46. Farquhar, "'Migration with Dignity,'" notes that migration would also relieve the burdens of overcrowding and unemployment that threaten the welfare of citizens remaining at home.
47. Government of Kiribati, "Relocation." The original site has been discontinued.
48. About 12 percent of Kiribati's GDP was from overseas remittances in 2005. McKenzie, "Remittances in the Pacific," 100.
49. Brooks, "On Creating a Usable Past."
50. Felli and Castree, in "Neoliberalising Adaptation to Environmental Change," argue similarly.
51. Bloch, *Principle of Hope*, 146.
52. Wolfe, "Settler Colonialism and the Elimination of the Native," discusses how colonialism rests on the physical and cultural erasure of Indigenous peoples.
53. The devastation European diseases wrought on Indigenous populations without immunity was part of colonial encounters across the globe. For a longer history of fatal impact's Pacific genealogy in particular, see Edmond, *Representing the South Pacific*.
54. Keown, *Pacific Islands Writing*, 40.
55. Keown, "Europeans in the Pacific," chap. 2 in *Pacific Islands Writing*. These writers at times critiqued various aspects of European exploitation of Indigenous populations, but this does not erase their contribution to fatal impact narratives.
56. Tuvalu voted for independence with only a British second-hand cargo ship in its terms of separation. Lazrus interprets this as part of a Tuvaluan ethos of "perseverance in the face of opposition" and conversely as a sign of British skepticism over Tuvalu's (then the Ellice Islands) willingness to pursue independence. Lazrus, "Shifting Tides," in *Anthropology and Climate Change*, ed. Crate and Nuttall, 225.
57. Fry, "Framing the Islands," 25.
58. Fry, "Framing the Islands," 26.
59. Teaiwa, "Bikinis and Other S/pacific N/oceans," 20.
60. Butler, *Precarious Life*, xiv.
61. Henry Kissinger, quoted in Teaiwa, "Bikinis and Other S/pacific N/oceans," 25.
62. DeLoughrey discusses how the empty Pacific "Basin" has been made to stand in contrast to the active Pacific "Rim" states in "Vessels of the Pacific," chap. 2 of *Routes and Roots*.
63. DeLoughrey, "Myth of Isolates," 173. DeLoughrey, *Allegories of the Anthropocene*, 171, likewise discusses how the Atomic Energy Commission represented Micronesians as primitive to justify their sacrifice to nuclear testing.

64. Hurley, *Infrastructures of Apocalypse*, details the way Black, Indigenous, and other minoritized groups in the United States were excised from the shared future of the nation by Cold War nuclear plans and infrastructures.

65. National Security Archive, "Castle BRAVO at 70."

66. Twenty-three crew members of the Japanese fishing vessel *Daigo Fukuryū Maru* were also exposed to heavy fallout. Johnston, "Atomic Times in the Pacific," offers an overview of U.S. test bombing and its aftermath in the Marshall Islands.

67. Torrice, *Rising Waters*, 28:37–28:46.

68. Rytz, *Anote's Ark*, 1:08:22–1:09:39.

69. DeLoughrey, *Allegories of the Anthropocene*, 188, notes that dredging in Funafuti's lagoon to make room for wartime ships also contributed to the island's climate vulnerability.

70. Horner, *Disappearing of Tuvalu*, 00:30:48–00:30:52.

71. Horner, *Disappearing of Tuvalu*, 00:55:59–00:56:12.

72. Horner, *Disappearing of Tuvalu*, 00:56:50–00:57:04.

73. DeLoughrey, *Allegories of the Anthropocene*, 188.

74. Chambers and Chambers, "Five Takes on Climate and Cultural Change in Tuvalu," 297.

75. Heine was president of the Marshall Islands from 2016 to 2020 and was reelected for a second term in January 2024.

76. Mbembe, *On the Postcolony*, 16.

77. Jetñil-Kijiner, *Iep Jāltok*, 20.

78. Jetñil-Kijiner, *Iep Jāltok*, 20.

79. Jetñil-Kijiner, *Iep Jāltok*, 19.

80. Jetñil-Kijiner, *Iep Jāltok*, 25.

81. Jetñil-Kijiner, *Iep Jāltok*, 24, emphasis mine.

82. Jetñil-Kijiner, *Iep Jāltok*, 70, emphasis mine.

83. Rosenthal and Gall, *Modern Poetic Sequence*, 11.

84. Bernstein, in *Foregone Conclusions*, warns against the dangers of historical determinism or foreshadowing, as well as "backshadowing," its corollary wherein the past is too smoothly reconstructed from present circumstances, eliding the contingency of both present and past.

85. Jetñil-Kijiner, *Iep Jāltok*, 71–72.

86. Jetñil-Kijiner, *Iep Jāltok*, 72.

87. Jetñil-Kijiner, *Iep Jāltok*, 71.

88. Jetñil-Kijiner, *Iep Jāltok*, 73.

89. Jetñil-Kijiner, *Iep Jāltok*, 76.

90. Jetñil-Kijiner, *Iep Jāltok*, 76.

91. Jetñil-Kijiner, *Iep Jāltok*, 76 and 77, emphasis original.

92. Jetñil-Kijiner, *Iep Jāltok*, 78–79.

93. Jetñil-Kijiner, *Iep Jāltok*, 79.

94. Jetñil-Kijiner, *Iep Jāltok*, 77.

95. Jetñil-Kijiner, *Iep Jāltok*, 79.

96. Scientists agree that some amount of planetary warming would occur even if all greenhouse gas emissions ceased immediately. But how much more warming will occur is contested and often modeled through a range of possible scenarios. See, for example, IPCC, 2023: Summary of Policymakers, 9–13.

97. University of Oslo Faculty of Law, "Montevideo Convention on the Rights and Duties of States." These rules are also not always followed; military and humanitarian interventions contravene principles of non-intervention, and some state-like entities, like the Order of Malta, operate without territory.

98. Burkett, "Nation *Ex-Situ*," and McAdam, "'Disappearing States,'" argue that climate change poses a challenge to the very foundations of international law.

99. Suvin, "On the Poetics of the Science Fiction Genre."

100. Similar work can be accomplished through historical fiction or historical inquiry, which like future speculation reveals the impermanence of present structures, systems, or forms of culture, since these have changed throughout time.

101. Rytz, *Anote's Ark*, 00:40:00–00:40:14, emphasis mine.

102. Gandhi, *Common Cause*, 122.

103. Gandhi, *Common Cause*, 127.

104. Gandhi, *Common Cause*, 127.

105. Burkett, "Nation *Ex-Situ*," emphasis original.

106. Burkett, "Nation *Ex-Situ*," 346.

107. Bloch, *Principle of Hope*, 148.

108. Hulme, *Stonefish*, 32. Hulme's gender dynamics should also be noted. Those characters most amenable to adaptability and non-dominance in her stories are women or recognizably gendered female, while men, especially in "The Pluperfect Pā-Wā," remain committed to practices of human species isolation and destruction.

109. Ingram, *Representative Short Story Cycles*, 19, emphasis original.

110. Caffin, "Aotearoa/New Zealand," 52.

111. DeLoughrey, "Ordinary Futures," 357.

112. DeLoughrey, "Ordinary Futures," 353

113. Hulme, *Stonefish*, 18, emphasis mine.

114. DeLoughrey, "Ordinary Futures," 359.

115. DeLoughrey situates her argument about Indigenous cyclical time and material mutability in contrast to Dipesh Chakrabarty's argument about the ontological impossibility of understanding human species-being in his "Climate of History."

116. DeLoughrey, "Ordinary Futures," 354.

117. Hulme, *Stonefish*, 5.

118. Hulme, *Stonefish*, 18.

119. Hulme, *Stonefish*, 6.

120. Hulme, *Stonefish*, 16.

121. Hulme, *Stonefish*, 17.

122. Hulme, *Stonefish*, 17.

123. Hulme, *Stonefish*, 15, 17.

124. Hulme, *Stonefish*, 17, 8.
125. Hulme, *Stonefish*, 192.
126. Hulme, *Stonefish*, 193.
127. Hulme, *Stonefish*, 215.
128. Hulme, *Stonefish*, 17.
129. Hulme, *Stonefish*, 189 and 217, emphasis mine.

Coda: Utopia beyond Negative Critique

1. Oreskes and Conway, *Collapse of Western Civilization*, 1.
2. Bloch, *Principle of Hope*, 146.
3. This intellectual tendency is not, however, universal. Some social science disciplines, such as anthropology, tend to diagnose less and describe more; indeed, I first learned to see the state dynamically and plurally by reading ethnographic accounts of the global South where states were clearly not working well and yet were still being used by disempowered people for their own purposes. Hull's *Government of Paper* and Gupta's *Red Tape* were especially influential.
4. Davis and Todd describe climate change's effects as a returning "shockwave" that is now "hitting" the global North in "On the Importance of a Date," 774.
5. Latour, "Why Has Critique Run out of Steam?," 230.
6. Latour, "Why Has Critique Run out of Steam?," 228. Latour notably makes this critique in relation to climate denialism's weaponization of social constructivism.
7. Caroline Levine diagnoses humanist criticism as a "gadfly" that "agitates and unsettles, but it does not push us to imagine how we might sustain collectives differently." Levine, "Model Thinking," 638.
8. See, for instance, Best and Marcus on "Surface Reading" and Moretti on distant reading, "Conjectures on World Literature."
9. Felski has developed these ideas in *Limits of Critique* and *Uses of Literature*.
10. Anker and Felski, *Critique and Postcritique*.
11. Levine, "Model Thinking."
12. Kornbluh, "Extinct Critique," 775, emphasis original. In fact, Kornbluh notes that Karl Marx, a foundational figure for suspicious criticism, was equally interested in building things up and offering positive constructs.
13. Sedgwick, "Paranoid Reading and Reparative Reading," 27–28.

Works Cited

Abani, Christopher. *GraceLand*. New York: Picador, 2004.
Abraham, C. M., and Sushila Abraham. "The Bhopal Case and the Development of Environmental Law in India." *International and Comparative Law Quarterly* 40, no. 2 (1991): 334–65. https://doi.org/10.1093/iclqaj/40.2.334.
Abrams, Philip. "Notes on the Difficulty of Studying the State." *Journal of Historical Sociology* 1, no. 1 (1988): 58–89. https://doi.org/10.1111/j.1467-6443.1988.tb00004.x.
Achebe, Chinua. "The African Writer and the English Language." In *Morning Yet on Creation Day: Essays*, 55–62. London: Heinemann, 1975.
———. *Anthills of the Savannah*. New York: Anchor Press, 1988.
———. *Arrow of God*. London: Heinemann, 1964.
———. *A Man of the People*. London: Heinemann, 1966.
———. *No Longer at Ease*. London: Heinemann, 1960.
———. *Things Fall Apart*. New York: Anchor Books, 1994. Originally published by Heinemann in 1958.
———. *The Trouble with Nigeria*. London: Heinemann, 1983.
Adelzadeh, Asghar. "From the RDP to GEAR: The Gradual Embracing of Neo-Liberalism in Economic Policy." Braamfontein, South Africa: National Institute for Economic Policy, 1996.
Adichie, Chimamanda Ngozi. *Half of a Yellow Sun*. New York: Knopf, 2006.
African National Congress. Reconstruction and Development Programme (RDP). South African History Online. Accessed August 2, 2025. https://sahistory.org.za/archive/reconstruction-and-development-programme-rdp.
Agamben, Giorgio. *Homo Sacer: Sovereign Power and Bare Life*. Stanford, CA: Stanford University Press, 1998.
Ahlers, Rhodante. "Fixing and Nixing: The Politics of Water Privatization." *Review of Radical Political Economics* 42, no. 2 (2010): 213–30. https://doi.org/10.1177/0486613410368497.

Ahmed, Sara. *Complaint!* Durham, NC: Duke University Press, 2021.
Ahuja, Neel. *Planetary Specters: Race, Migration, and Climate Change in the Twenty-First Century.* Chapel Hill: University of North Carolina Press, 2021.
Alaimo, Stacy. *Bodily Natures: Science, Environment, and the Material Self.* Bloomington: Indiana University Press, 2010.
Alexander, Peter. "Rebellion of the Poor: South Africa's Service Delivery Protests—A Preliminary Analysis." *Review of African Political Economy* 37, no. 123 (2010): 25–40. https://doi.org/10.1080/03056241003637870.
American Chemical Society. "The Keeling Curve: Carbon Dioxide Measurements at Mauna Loa." Accessed June 18, 2024. https://www.acs.org/education/whatischemistry/landmarks/keeling-curve.html.
Amnesty International. "Niger Delta Negligence." March 16, 2018. https://www.amnesty.org/en/latest/news/2018/03/Niger-Delta-Oil-Spills-Decoders/.
Anand, Nikhil. *Hydraulic City: Water and the Infrastructures of Citizenship in Mumbai.* Durham, NC: Duke University Press, 2017.
Anderson, Benedict. *Imagined Communities: Reflections on the Origin and Spread of Nationalism.* 2nd ed. London: Verso, 2006.
Anker, Elizabeth S., and Rita Felski, eds. *Critique and Postcritique.* Durham, NC: Duke University Press, 2017.
Apter, Andrew. *The Pan-African Nation: Oil and the Spectacle of Culture in Nigeria.* Chicago: University of Chicago Press, 2005.
Armah, Ayi Kwei. *The Beautyful Ones Are Not Yet Born.* London: Heinemann, 1989.
Ashe, John W., Robert van Lierop, and Anilla Cherian. "The Role of the Alliance of Small Island States (AOSIS) in the Negotiation of the United Nations Framework Convention on Climate Change (UNFCCC)." *Natural Resources Forum* 23, no. 3 (1999): 209–20. https://doi.org/10.1111/j.1477-8947.1999.tb00910.x.
Aslami, Zarena. *The Dream Life of Citizens: Late Victorian Novels and the Fantasy of the State.* New York: Fordham University Press, 2012.
Atwood, Margaret. *The Year of the Flood.* New York: Anchor Books, 2010.
Attwell, David, and Barbara Harlow. "Introduction: South African Fiction after Apartheid." *Modern Fiction Studies* 46, no. 1 (2000): 1–9. https://doi.org/10.1353/mfs.2000.0006.
Bacigalupi, Paolo. *The Water Knife.* New York: Knopf, 2015.
Baker, Aryn. "Cape Town Is 90 Days Away from Running Out of Water." *TIME*, January 15, 2018. https://time.com/5103259/cape-town-water-crisis/.
Bakker, Karen J. "A Political Ecology of Water Privatization." *Studies in Political Economy,* 70 no. 1 (2003): 35–58. https://doi.org/10.1080/07078552.2003.11827129.
Barron, Mace G., Deborah N. Vivian, Ron A. Heintz, and Un Hyuk Yim. "Long-Term Ecological Impacts from Oil Spills: Comparison of Exxon Valdez, Hebei Spirit, and Deepwater Horizon." *Environmental Science & Technology* 54, no. 11 (2020): 6456–67. https://doi.org/10.1021/acs.est.9b05020.
Barry, Norman. *Welfare.* Milton Keynes: Open University Press, 1990.

Batrawy, Aya. "What It Means for an Oil Producing Country, the UAE, to Host U.N. Climate Talks." *NPR*, December 9, 2023. https://www.npr.org/2023/12/09/1217970348/what-it-means-for-an-oil-producing-country-the-uae-to-host-un-climate-talks.

Bayart, Jean-François. *The State in Africa: The Politics of the Belly*. 2nd ed. Cambridge: Polity, 2009.

Beck, Ulrich. *Risk Society: Towards a New Modernity*. London: Sage, 1992.

Benhabib, Seyla. *Critique, Norm, and Utopia: A Study of the Foundations of Critical Theory*. New York: Columbia University Press, 1986.

Benjamin, Walter. *The Arcades Project*. Translated by Howard Eiland and Kevin McLaughlin. Edited by Rolf Tiedemann. Cambridge, MA: Belknap Press of Harvard University Press, 1999.

Berlant, Lauren. *Cruel Optimism*. Durham, NC: Duke University Press, 2011.

Bernstein, Michael André. *Foregone Conclusions: Against Apocalyptic History*. Berkeley: University of California Press, 1994. https://doi.org/10.2307/jj.15552470.

Best, Stephen, and Sharon Marcus. "Surface Reading: An Introduction." *Representations* 108, no. 1 (2009): 1–21. https://doi.org/10.1525/rep.2009.108.1.1.

"The Bhopal Gas Leak Disaster (Processing of Claims) Act, 1985." In *Documents and Court Opinions on Bhopal Gas Leak Disaster Case*, edited by N. R. Madhava Menon, 377–80. Bangalore: National Law School of India University, 1991.

Bloch, Ernst. "Can Hope Be Disappointed?" In *Literary Essays*, translated by Andrew Joron, 339–45. Stanford, CA: Stanford University Press, 1998.

———. *The Principle of Hope*. Vol. 1. Cambridge, MA: MIT Press, 1995.

Bodo Community and Others v. Shell Petroleum Development Company of Nigeria Limited, HT-13-295 and HT-13-339 to 350 [2014] EWHC 1973 BAILII (TCC Jun. 20, 2014).

Bond, Patrick. *Elite Transition: From Apartheid to Neoliberalism in South Africa*. London: Pluto Press, 2000.

Bourdieu, Pierre. "Rethinking the State: Genesis and Structure of the Bureaucratic Field." In *State/Culture: State-Formation after the Cultural Turn*, edited by George Steinmetz, 53–75. Ithaca, NY: Cornell University Press, 1999. https://www.jstor.org/stable/10.7591/j.ctv1nhjcg.6.

Bowers, Mike. "'Pacific Climate Warriors' Blockade Newcastle Harbour—in Pictures." *Guardian*, October 17, 2014. http://www.theguardian.com/australia-news/gallery/2014/oct/17/pacific-climate-warriors-blockade-newcastle-coal-port-in-pictures.

Boyd, Robynne. "The People of the Isle de Jean Charles Are Louisiana's First Climate Refugees—but They Won't Be the Last." National Resources Defense Council, September 23, 2019. https://www.nrdc.org/stories/people-isle-jean-charles-are-louisianas-first-climate-refugees-they-wont-be-last.

Brooks, Peter. *Reading for the Plot: Design and Intention in Narrative*. New York: Vintage Books, 1985.

Brooks, Van Wyck. "On Creating a Usable Past." *Dial* 64, no. 11 (1918): 337–41.
Burkett, Maxine. "The Nation *Ex-Situ*: On Climate Change, Deterritorialized Nationhood and the Post-Climate Era." *Climate Law* 2, no. 3 (2011): 345–74. https://doi.org/10.1163/CL-2011-040.
Butler, Judith. *Precarious Life: The Powers of Mourning and Violence*. London: Verso, 2004.
Byrne, Deirdre. "'Policing Borders': Extermination and Relocation of Insects in Three South African Texts." *Journal of Literary Studies* 36, no. 4 (2020): 86–104. https://doi.org/10.1080/02564718.2020.1822603.
Caffin, Elizabeth. "Aotearoa/New Zealand." In *The Novel in Australia, Canada, New Zealand, and the South Pacific since 1950*. Volume 12 of *The Oxford History of the Novel in English*, edited by Coral Ann Howells, Paul Sharrad, and Gerry Turcotte, 46–60. Oxford: Oxford University Press, 2018. https://doi.org/10.1093/oso/9780199679775.003.0006.
Canavan, Gerry. "Introduction: If This Goes On." In *Green Planets: Ecology and Science Fiction*, edited by Gerry Canavan and Kim Stanley Robinson, 1–21. Middletown, CT: Wesleyan University Press, 2014.
Casey, Rose. *Aesthetic Impropriety: Property Law and Postcolonial Style*. New York: Fordham University Press, 2025.
Central California Area Office, Bureau of Reclamation. "Water Facts—Worldwide Water Supply." Updated November 4, 2020. https://www.usbr.gov/mp/arwec/water-facts-ww-water-sup.html.
Chakrabarty, Dipesh. "Climate and Capital: On Conjoined Histories." *Critical Inquiry* 41, no. 1 (2014): 1–23. https://doi.org/10.1086/678154.
——. "The Climate of History: Four Theses." *Critical Inquiry* 35, no. 2 (2009): 197–222. https://doi.org/10.1086/596640.
——. *Provincializing Europe: Postcolonial Thought and Historical Difference*. Reissue. Princeton: Princeton University Press, 2008. See esp. chap 2, "Two Histories of Capital" and chap. 4, "Minority Histories, Subaltern Pasts."
Chambers, Anne, and Keith S. Chambers. "Five Takes on Climate and Cultural Change in Tuvalu." *Contemporary Pacific* 19, no. 1 (2007): 294–306. https://doi.org/10.1353/cp.2007.0004.
Chance, Kerry Ryan. *Living Politics in South Africa's Urban Shacklands*. Chicago: University of Chicago Press, 2018.
Charan Lal Sahu v. Union of India. 1990 AIR 1480 (Supreme Court of India, Dec. 22, 1989).
Charlton, Sarah, and Paula Meth. "Lived Experiences of State Housing in Johannesburg and Durban." *Transformation: Critical Perspectives on Southern Africa* 93, no. 1 (2017): 91–115. https://doi.org/10.1353/trn.2017.0004.
Chatterjee, Elizabeth. "The Asian Anthropocene: Electricity and Fossil Developmentalism." *Journal of Asian Studies* 79, no. 1 (2020): 3–24. https://doi.org/10.1017/S0021911819000573.

Chatterjee, Partha. *The Politics of the Governed: Reflections on Popular Politics in Most of the World*. New York: Columbia University Press, 2006.

Church, John A., and Neil J. White. "A 20th Century Acceleration in Global Sea-Level Rise." *Geophysical Research Letters* 33, no. 1 (2006), L01602. https://doi.org/10.1029/2005GL024826.

Cilano, Cara, and Elizabeth DeLoughrey. "Against Authenticity: Global Knowledges and Postcolonial Ecocriticism." *ISLE: Interdisciplinary Studies in Literature and Environment* 14, no. 1 (2007): 71–87. https://doi.org/10.1093/isle/14.1.71.

City of Cape Town Climate Change Action Plan. City of Cape Town Communications Department. Accessed May 29, 2025. https://resource.capetown.gov.za/documentcentre/Documents/City%20strategies%2C%20plans%20and%20frameworks/CCT_Climate_Change_Action_Plan.pdf.

"Civil Suit for Damages filed by Union of India (5th September, 1986)." In *Documents and Court Opinions on Bhopal Gas Leak Disaster Case*, edited by N. R. Madhava Menon, 73–78. Bangalore: National Law School of India University, 1991.

Coleman, Les. "Frequency of Man-Made Disasters in the 20th Century." *Journal of Contingencies & Crisis Management* 14, no. 1 (2006): 3–11. https://doi.org/10.1111/j.1468-5973.2006.00476.x.

Comaroff, Jean, and John L. Comaroff. "Figuring Crime: Quantifacts and the Production of the Un/Real." *Public Culture* 18, no. 1 (2006): 209–46. https://doi.org/10.1215/08992363-18-1-209.

Constitution of the Federal Republic of Nigeria, 1979. ConstitutionNet. Accessed July 12, 2019. http://constitutionnet.org/vl/item/constitution-federal-republic-nigeria-1979.

Constitution of the Federal Republic of Nigeria, 1999. National Library of Nigeria. Accessed August 13, 2024. https://nigeriareposit.nln.gov.ng/items/a1eb9942-661f-41d7-969e-01e69a6c8c5d/full.

Constitution of India, 2024 (English Version). Legislative Department. Accessed July 25, 2024. https://legislative.gov.in/constitution-of-india.

Constitution of the Republic of South Africa, 1996. South African Government. Accessed July 25, 2024. https://www.gov.za/documents/constitution/constitution-republic-south-africa-04-feb-1997.

Cooper, Frederick. *Citizenship between Empire and Nation: Remaking France and French Africa, 1945–1960*. Princeton: Princeton University Press, 2014.

Cornell Law School. "Complaint." LII / Legal Information Institute. Accessed June 18, 2024. https://www.law.cornell.edu/wex/complaint.

Corneloup, Inés de Águeda, and Arthur P. J. Mol. "Small Island Developing States and International Climate Change Negotiations: The Power of Moral 'Leadership.'" *International Environmental Agreements: Politics, Law and Economics* 14, no. 3 (2014): 281–97. https://doi.org/10.1007/s10784-013-9227-0.

Coronil, Fernando. *The Magical State: Nature, Money, and Modernity in Venezuela*. Chicago: University of Chicago Press, 1997.

Craps, Stef. *Postcolonial Witnessing: Trauma out of Bounds.* New York: Palgrave Macmillan, 2013.

Cremer, Teresa. "'It's a Privilege to Call It a Crisis': Improvised Practices and Socio-Economic Dynamics of Cape Town's Water Shortage (2015–2018)." MA thesis, University of Cologne, 2020. https://kups.ub.uni-koeln.de/36339/.

"Critical Water Shortages Disaster Plan—Public Summary." City of Cape Town, Safety and Security Department, October 2017. https://resource.capetown.gov.za/documentcentre/Documents/City%20strategies%2C%20plans%20and%20frameworks/Critical%20Water%20Shortages%20Disaster%20Plan%20Summary.pdf.

Crutzen, Paul J., and Eugene F. Stoermer. "The 'Anthropocene.'" *IGBP Global Change Newsletter* 41 (May 2000): 17–18.

Das, Veena. "Moral Orientations to Suffering: Legitimation, Power, and Healing." In *The Bhopal Reader: Twenty Years of the World's Worst Industrial Disaster,* edited by Bridget Hanna, Ward Morehouse, and Satinath Sarangi, 51–59. New York: Apex Press 2005.

Davenport, Coral, and Campbell Robertson. "Resettling the First American 'Climate Refugees.'" *New York Times,* May 3, 2016. https://www.nytimes.com/2016/05/03/us/resettling-the-first-american-climate-refugees.html.

Davis, Heather, and Zoe Todd. "On the Importance of a Date, or, Decolonizing the Anthropocene." *ACME: An International Journal for Critical Geographies* 16, no. 4 (December 20, 2017): 761–80. https://doi.org/10.14288/acme.v16i4.1539.

Davis, Rebecca. "#CapeWaterGate: In the End, What Was Day Zero All About?" *Daily Maverick,* March 14, 2018, https://www.dailymaverick.co.za/article/2018-03-14-capewatergate-in-the-end-what-was-day-zero-all-about/.

De, Rohit, and Robert Travers. "Petitioning and Political Cultures in South Asia: Introduction." *Modern Asian Studies* 53, no. 1 (2019): 1–20. https://doi.org/10.1017/S0026749X18000537.

DeLoughrey, Elizabeth M. *Allegories of the Anthropocene.* Durham, NC: Duke University Press, 2019.

———. "The Myth of Isolates: Ecosystem Ecologies in the Nuclear Pacific." *Cultural Geographies* 20, no. 2 (2013): 167–84. https://doi.org/10.1177/1474474012463664.

———. "Ordinary Futures: Interspecies Worldings in the Anthropocene." In *Global Ecologies and the Environmental Humanities: Postcolonial Approaches,* edited by Elizabeth M. DeLoughrey, Jill Didur, and Anthony Carrigan, 352–72. New York: Routledge, 2015.

———. *Routes and Roots: Navigating Caribbean and Pacific Island Literatures.* Honolulu: University of Hawaii Press, 2007. See esp. chap. 2, "Vessels of the Pacific."

DeLoughrey, Elizabeth M., and George B. Handley. "Introduction: Toward an Aesthetics of the Earth." In *Postcolonial Ecologies: Literatures of the Environment,* edited by Elizabeth M. DeLoughrey and George B. Handley. New York: Oxford University Press, 2011.

Dening, Greg. "Sea People of the West." *Geographical Review* 97, no. 2 (2007): 288–301. https://www.jstor.org/stable/30034167.
Denoon, David B. H. "Cycles in Indian Economic Liberalization, 1966–1996." *Comparative Politics* 31, no. 1 (1998): 43–60. https://doi.org/10.2307/422105.
Dreher, Tanja, and Michelle Voyer. "Climate Refugees or Migrants? Contesting Media Frames on Climate Justice in the Pacific." *Environmental Communication* 9, no. 1 (2015): 58–76. https://doi.org/10.1080/17524032.2014.932818.
Dudziak, Mary L. *Exporting American Dreams: Thurgood Marshall's African Journey.* Princeton: Princeton University Press, 2008. https://www.jstor.org/stable/j.ctt7t6nf.
Duiker, K. Sello. *The Hidden Star.* Roggebaai, South Africa: Umuzi, 2006.
———. *The Quiet Violence of Dreams.* Cape Town: Kwela Books, 2001.
———. *Thirteen Cents.* Cape Town: Ink Inc., 2000.
Ebeku, Kaniye S. A. "Constitutional Right to a Healthy Environment and Human Rights Approaches to Environmental Protection in Nigeria: Gbemre v. Shell Revisited." *Review of European Community & International Environmental Law* 16, no. 3 (2007): 312–20. https://doi.org/10.1111/j.1467-9388.2007.00570.x.
Edelman, Lee. *No Future: Queer Theory and the Death Drive.* Durham, NC: Duke University Press, 2004.
Edmond, Rod. *Representing the South Pacific: Colonial Discourse from Cook to Gauguin.* Cambridge: Cambridge University Press, 1997.
Ekeh, Peter P. "The Structure and Meaning of Federal Character in the Nigerian Political System." In *Federal Character and Federalism in Nigeria*, edited by Peter P. Ekeh and Eghosa E. Osaghae, 19–44. Ibadan: Heinemann Educational Books (Nigeria), 1989.
Enqvist, Johan P., and Gina Ziervogel. "Water Governance and Justice in Cape Town: An Overview." *WIREs Water* 6, no. 4 (2019): 1–15. https://doi.org/10.1002/wat2.1354.
Erritouni, Ali. "Contradictions and Alternatives in Chinua Achebe's *Anthills of the Savannah*." *Journal of Modern Literature* 29, no. 2 (2006): 50–74. http://www.jstor.org/stable/3831792.
Esteve, Mary. *Incremental Realism: Postwar American Fiction, Happiness, and Welfare-State Liberalism.* Stanford, CA: Stanford University Press, 2021.
Everest, Larry. *Behind the Poison Cloud: Union Carbide's Bhopal Massacre.* Chicago: Banner, 1985.
Fanon, Frantz. *Black Skin, White Masks.* Translated by Richard Philcox. New York: Grove Press, 2008.
———. *The Wretched of the Earth.* Translated by Richard Philcox. New York: Grove Press, 2004.
Farbotko, Carol, and Heather Lazrus. "The First Climate Refugees? Contesting Global Narratives of Climate Change in Tuvalu." *Global Environmental Change* 22, no. 2 (2012): 382–90. https://doi.org/10.1016/j.gloenvcha.2011.11.014.
Farbotko, Carol, Elaine Stratford, and Heather Lazrus. "Climate Migrants and New Identities? The Geopolitics of Embracing or Rejecting Mobility." *Social &*

Cultural Geography 17, no. 4 (2016): 533–52. https://doi.org/10.1080/14649365.2015.1089589.

Farquhar, Harriet. "'Migration with Dignity': Towards a New Zealand Response to Climate Change Displacement in the Pacific." *Victoria University of Wellington Law Review* 46, no. 1 (2015): 29–56. https://doi.org/10.26686/vuwlr.v46i1.4936.

Faturoti, Bukola, Godswill Agbaitoro, and Obinna Onya. "Environmental Protection in the Nigerian Oil and Gas Industry and Jonah Gbemre v. Shell PDC Nigeria Limited: Let the Plunder Continue?" *African Journal of International and Comparative Law* 27, no. 2 (2019): 225–45. https://doi.org/10.3366/ajicl.2019.0270.

Felli, Romain, and Noel Castree. "Neoliberalising Adaptation to Environmental Change: Foresight or Foreclosure?" *Environment and Planning A: Economy and Space* 44, no. 1 (2012): 1–4. https://doi.org/10.1068/a44680.

Felski, Rita. *The Limits of Critique*. Chicago: University of Chicago Press, 2015.

———. *Uses of Literature*. Malden, MA: Blackwell, 2008.

Fisher, Ryland. "Finally, We Have a Crisis on Our Hands That Affects All." *Ryland Fisher* (blog). January 27, 2018. https://www.rylandfisher.com/blog/2018/3/6/finally-we-have-a-crisis-on-our-hands-that-affects-all.

Fortun, Kim. *Advocacy after Bhopal: Environmentalism, Disaster, New Global Orders*. Chicago: University of Chicago Press, 2001.

Foucault, Michel. *The History of Sexuality*. Volume 1. Translated by Robert Hurley. New York: Vintage Books, 1988.

———. *Society Must Be Defended: Lectures at the Collège de France, 1975–76*. Edited by Mauro Bertani and Alessandro Fontana. Translated by David Macey. New York: Picador, 2003.

Frank, Andre Gunder. "The Development of Underdevelopment." In *Sociological Worlds: Comparative and Historical Readings on Society*, edited by Stephen K. Sanderson, 135–41. New York: Routledge, 2013.

Franklin, Ben A. "Toxic Cloud Leaks at Carbide Plant in West Virginia." *New York Times*, August 12, 1985. https://www.nytimes.com/1985/08/12/us/toxic-cloud-leaks-at-carbide-plant-in-west-virginia.html.

Fredericks, Rosalind. *Garbage Citizenship: Vital Infrastructures of Labor in Dakar, Senegal*. Durham, NC: Duke University Press, 2018.

Fry, Greg. "Framing the Islands: Knowledge and Power in Changing Australian Images of the South Pacific." In *Voyaging Through the Contemporary Pacific*, edited by David L. Hanlon and Geoffrey M. White, 25–63. Lanham, MD: Rowman & Littlefield, 2000.

Gadgil, Madhav, and Ramachandra Guha. *Ecology and Equity: The Use and Abuse of Nature in Contemporary India*. New Delhi: Penguin Books India, 1995.

Gandhi, Leela. *The Common Cause: Postcolonial Ethics and the Practice of Democracy, 1900–1955*. Chicago: University of Chicago Press, 2014.

Garuba, Harry. "Explorations in Animist Materialism: Notes on Reading/Writing African Literature, Culture, and Society." *Public Culture* 15, no. 2 (2003): 261–85. https://muse-jhu-edu.proxy2.library.illinois.edu/article/42967/pdf.

Getachew, Adom. *Worldmaking after Empire: The Rise and Fall of Self-Determination*. Princeton: Princeton University Press, 2019. See esp. chap. 5, "Welfare World."

Ghosh, Amitav. *The Nutmeg's Curse: Parables for a Planet in Crisis*. Chicago: University of Chicago Press, 2021.

———. "Petrofiction: The Oil Encounter and the Novel." *New Republic*, March 2, 1992, 29–33.

Gikandi, Simon. *Reading Chinua Achebe: Language & Ideology in Fiction*. London: J. Currey, 1991.

Goodbody, Axel. "Cli-Fi—Genre of the Twenty-First Century? Narrative Strategies in Contemporary Climate Fiction and Film." In *Green Matters: Ecocultural Functions of Literature*, edited by Maria Löschnigg and Melanie Braunecker, 131–53. Leiden: Brill, 2019. https://doi.org/10.1163/9789004408876_008.

Gordin, Michael D., Helen Tilley, and Gyan Prakash. "Introduction: Utopia and Dystopia beyond Space and Time." In *Utopia/Dystopia: Conditions of Historical Possibility*, edited by Michael D. Gordin, Helen Tilley, and Gyan Prakash, 1–18. Princeton: Princeton University Press, 2010, http://www.jstor.org/stable/j.ctt7t5gs.3.

Gordon, David M. *Apartheid in South Africa: A Brief History with Documents*. Boston: Bedford/St. Martin's, 2017.

Government of Kiribati. "Relocation." Kiribati Climate Change. Accessed August 28, 2022. http://www.climate.gov.ki/category/action/relocation/. (Original site discontinued.)

Government of Tuvalu. *Te Kaniva: Tuvalu Climate Change Policy 2012–2021*. https://www.tuvaluclimatechange.gov.tv/sites/default/files/documents/Te%20Kaniva%20Tuvalu%20Climate%20Change%20Policy%202012_0.pdf.

Green, Lesley. *Rock/Water/Life: Ecology and Humanities for a Decolonial South Africa*. Durham, NC: Duke University Press, 2020. See esp. chap. 1, "Rock: Cape Town's Natures."

Greenpeace International. *Corporate Crimes*. August 2002, https://www.greenpeace.org/static/planet4-netherlands-stateless-release/2018/06/corporate-crimes-the-need-fo.pdf.

Griswold, Wendy. *Bearing Witness: Readers, Writers, and the Novel in Nigeria*. Princeton: Princeton University Press, 2000.

Grote, Jenny. "The Changing Tides of Small Island States Discourse—A Historical Overview of the Appearance of Small Island States in the International Arena." *Verfassung und Recht in Übersee/Law and Politics in Africa, Asia and Latin America* 43, no. 2 (2010): 164–91. http://www.jstor.org/stable/43239555.

Grove, Richard. *Green Imperialism: Colonial Expansion, Tropical Island Edens, and the Origins of Environmentalism, 1600–1860*. Cambridge: Cambridge University Press, 1995.

Guha, Ramachandra, and Juan Martínez-Alier. *Varieties of Environmentalism: Essays North and South*. London: Earthscan, 1997.

Gupta, Akhil. *Red Tape: Bureaucracy, Structural Violence, and Poverty in India.* Durham, NC: Duke University Press, 2012.
Habib, Adam. *South Africa's Suspended Revolution: Hopes and Prospects.* Athens: Ohio University Press, 2013.
Hanna, Bridget, Ward Morehouse, and Satinath Sarangi. *The Bhopal Reader: Twenty Years of the World's Worst Industrial Disaster.* New York: Apex Press, 2005.
Hart, Matthew. *Extraterritorial: A Political Geography of Contemporary Fiction.* New York: Columbia University Press, 2020. https://doi.org/10.7312/hart18838.
Hau'ofa, Epeli. "Our Sea of Islands." *Contemporary Pacific* 6, no. 1 (1994): 148–61. https://www.jstor.org/stable/23701593.
Heise, Ursula K. *Sense of Place and Sense of Planet: The Environmental Imagination of the Global.* Oxford: Oxford University Press, 2008.
Hellman, Joel S., Geraint Jones, and Daniel Kaufmann. "Seize the State, Seize the Day: State Capture, Corruption, and Influence in Transition." Policy Research Working Paper 2444, The World Bank, September 2000. https://documents.worldbank.org/en/publication/documents-reports/documentdetail/537461468766474836/seize-the-state-seize-the-day-state-capture-corruption-and-influence-in-transition.
Hemson, David, and Kwme Owusu-Ampomah. "A Better Life for All? Service Delivery and Poverty Alleviation." In *State of the Nation: South Africa 2004–2005*, edited by John Daniel, Roger Southall, and Jessica Lutchman, 511–40. Cape Town: HSRC Press, 2005.
Horner, Christopher, dir. *The Disappearing of Tuvalu: Trouble in Paradise.* Documentary Educational Resources. 2004. Streaming video. Alexander Street, 1 hr., 13 min.
Hull, Matthew S. *Government of Paper: The Materiality of Bureaucracy in Urban Pakistan.* Berkeley: University of California Press, 2012.
Hulme, Keri. *The Bone People.* Baton Rouge: Louisiana State University Press, 1985
———. *Stonefish.* Wellington: Huia, 2004.
Hurley, Jessica. *Infrastructures of Apocalypse: American Literature and the Nuclear Complex.* Minneapolis: University of Minnesota Press, 2020.
Iheka, Cajetan. *African Ecomedia: Network Forms, Planetary Politics.* Durham, NC: Duke University Press, 2021.
———. *Naturalizing Africa: Ecological Violence, Agency, and Postcolonial Resistance in African Literature.* Cambridge: Cambridge University Press, 2017. See esp. chap. 3, "Rethinking Postcolonial Resistance."
Ikegami, Robin. "Knowledge and Power, the Story and the Storyteller: Achebe's *Anthills of the Savannah.*" *Modern Fiction Studies* 37, no. 3 (1991): 493–507. https://www.jstor.org/stable/26283158.
Ingram, Forrest L. *Representative Short Story Cycles of the Twentieth Century.* The Hague: Mouton, 1971.
Innes, Catherine Lynette. *Chinua Achebe.* Cambridge: Cambridge University Press, 1990.

International Campaign for Justice in Bhopal. "Bhopal Survivors Demand 'Right to Live,' Condemn Heartless Inaction of the BJP State Government." February 19, 2007. https://www.bhopal.net/bhopal-survivors-demand-right-to-live-condemn-heartless-inaction-of-the-bjp-state-government/.

IPCC, 2023: Summary for Policymakers. In Climate Change 2023: Synthesis Report. Contribution of Working Groups I, II, and III to the Sixth Assessment Report of the Intergovernmental Panel on Climate Change [Core Writing Team, H. Lee and J. Romero (eds.)]. IPCC, Geneva, Switzerland, pp. 1–34. doi: 10.59327/IPCC/AR6-9789291691647.001..

Iyasere, Solomon O. "Oral Tradition in the Criticism of African Literature." *The Journal of Modern African Studies* 13, no. 1 (1975): 107–19. https://www.jstor.org/stable/159699.

Jameson, Fredric. *An American Utopia: Dual Power and the Universal Army*. Edited by Slavoj Žižek. London: Verso, 2016.

———. *Archaeologies of the Future: The Desire Called Utopia and Other Science Fictions*. New York: Verso, 2005.

———. "Third-World Literature in the Era of Multinational Capitalism." *Social Text*, no. 15 (October 1, 1986): 65–88. https://doi.org/10.2307/466493.

———. "Utopia as Method or, The Uses of the Future." In *Utopia/Dystopia*, edited by Michael D. Gordin, Helen Tilley, and Gyan Prakash, 21–44. Princeton: Princeton University Press, 2010. http://www.jstor.org/stable/j.ctt7t5gs.

Jetñil-Kijiner, Kathy. *Iep Jāltok: Poems from a Marshallese Daughter*. Tucson: University of Arizona Press, 2017.

Johns-Putra, Adeline. "'My Job Is to Take Care of You': Climate Change, Humanity, and Cormac McCarthy's *The Road*." *Modern Fiction Studies* 62, no. 3 (2016): 519–40. https://www.jstor.org/stable/26421875.

Johnston, Barbara Rose. "Atomic Times in the Pacific." *Anthropology Now* 1, no. 2 (2009): 1–9. https://www.jstor.org/stable/41203536.

Johnston, Justin Omar. "'A Nother World' in Indra Sinha's Animal's People." *Twentieth Century Literature* 62, no. 2 (2016): 118–44. https://doi.org/10.1215/0041462X-3616552.

Jonah Gbemre v. Shell Petroleum Development Company Nigeria Limited and Others, FHC/B/CS/53/05 (Federal High Court Benin City, Nov. 14, 2005). Climate Change Litigation Databases. Accessed June 12, 2024. https://climatecasechart.com/wp-content/uploads/non-us-case-documents/2005/20051130_FHCBCS5305_judgment.pdf.

Joubert, Leonie, and Gina Ziervogel. *Day Zero: One City's Response to a Record-Breaking Drought*. Cape Town, 2019. https://dayzero.org.za/Day-Zero.pdf.

Kailasam, Bala, dir. *Vaastu Marabu*. Watertown, MA: Documentary Educational Resources. 2004. Streaming video. Alexander Street, 52 min.

———. *Where Do the Children Play?* India: Geetha Kailasam, 2019. Vimeo, 1 hr., 3 min.

Kanu, Ikechukwu Anthony. "The Dimensions of African Cosmology." *Filosofia Theoretica: Journal of African Philosophy, Culture and Religion* 2, no 2 (2013): 533–55. https://www.ajol.info/index.php/ft/article/view/109700.

Kaviraj, Sudipta. *The Imaginary Institution of India: Politics and Ideas.* New York: Columbia University Press, 2010.

Keown, Michelle. *Pacific Islands Writing: The Postcolonial Literatures of Aotearoa/New Zealand and Oceania.* Oxford: Oxford University Press, 2007. See esp. chap. 2, "Europeans in the Pacific."

Kerrigan, John. *Motives of Woe: Shakespeare and "Female Complaint."* Oxford: Clarendon Press, 1991.

Klein, Naomi. *The Shock Doctrine.* New York: Picador, 2007.

Kornbluh, Anna. "Extinct Critique." *South Atlantic Quarterly* 119, no. 4 (2020): 767–77. https://doi.org/10.1215/00382876-8663675.

Kortenaar, Neil ten. *Debt, Law, Realism: Nigerian Writers Imagine the State at Independence.* Montreal: McGill-Queen's University Press, 2021.

——. "'Only Connect': 'Anthills of the Savannah' and Achebe's Trouble with Nigeria." *Research in African Literatures* 24, no. 3 (1993): 59–72. https://www.jstor.org/stable/3820113.

Kumar, Ravi, dir. *Bhopal: A Prayer for Rain.* 2014. Mumbai: Sahara Movie Studios, 2014. Streaming video. Amazon, 1 hr., 41 min.

Kurzman, Dan. *A Killing Wind: Inside Union Carbide and the Bhopal Catastrophe.* New York: McGraw-Hill, 1987.

Latour, Bruno. *Reassembling the Social: An Introduction to Actor-Network-Theory.* Oxford: Oxford University Press, 2005.

——. "Why Has Critique Run out of Steam? From Matters of Fact to Matters of Concern." *Critical Inquiry* 30, no. 2 (2004): 225–48. https://doi.org/10.1086/421123.

Lazrus, Heather. "Sea Change: Island Communities and Climate Change." *Annual Review of Anthropology* 41 (January 1, 2012): 285–301. https://doi.org/10.1146/annurev-anthro-092611-145730.

——. "Shifting Tides: Climate Change, Migration, and Agency in Tuvalu." In *Anthropology and Climate Change: From Actions to Transformations*, 2nd ed., edited by Susan A. Crate and Mark Nuttall, 220–27. New York: Routledge, 2016.

Lemanski, Charlotte. "Infrastructural Citizenship: The Everyday Citizenships of Adapting and/or Destroying Public Infrastructure in Cape Town, South Africa." *Transactions of the Institute of British Geographers* 45, no. 3 (2020): 589–605. https://doi.org/10.1111/tran.12370.

Lerner, Steve. *Sacrifice Zones: The Front Lines of Toxic Chemical Exposure in the United States.* Cambridge, MA: MIT Press, 2010.

Leton, G. B. "Statement." *Ogoni Bill of Rights.* Movement for the Survival of the Ogoni People (MOSOP) & Ogoni News and Resources. Accessed August 13, 2024. https://www.mosop.org/2015/10/10/ogoni-bill-of-rights/.

Levine, Caroline. "Model Thinking: Generalization, Political Form, and the Common Good." *New Literary History* 48, no. 4 (2017): 633–53. https://doi.org/10.1353/nlh.2017.0033.

Lille, Patricia de. "Cape Town Will Reach Day Zero If Stubborn Residents Continue to Use Water Excessively." City of Cape Town, December 3, 2017. https://resource.capetown.gov.za/documentcentre/Documents/Speeches%20and%20statements/3%20December%2017%20Cape%20Town%20will%20reach%20Day%20Zero.pdf.

———. "Day Zero Now Likely to Happen—New Emergency Measures." City of Cape Town, January 18, 2018. https://resource.capetown.gov.za/documentcentre/Documents/Speeches%20and%20statements/18%20January%2018-%20Day%20Zero%20new%20emergency%20measures.pdf.

Lindsey, Rebecca. "Climate Change: Atmospheric Carbon Dioxide." NOAA Climate.gov. April 9, 2024. http://www.climate.gov/news-features/understanding-climate/climate-change-atmospheric-carbon-dioxide.

Lloyd, David. "Nationalisms against the State." In *The Politics of Culture in the Shadow of Capital*, edited by Lisa Lowe and David Lloyd, 173–97. Durham, NC: Duke University Press, 1997.

Loginova, Olga, and Zak Cassel. "Leaving The Island: The Messy, Contentious Reality of Climate Relocation." *Honolulu Civil Beat*, August 18, 2022. https://www.civilbeat.org/2022/08/leaving-the-island-the-messy-contentious-reality-of-climate-relocation/.

Lowe, Rodney. *The Welfare State in Britain since 1945*. 3rd ed. Houndmills, Hampshire: Palgrave Macmillan, 2005.

MacArthur, Elizabeth Jane. *Extravagant Narratives: Closure and Dynamics in the Epistolary Form*. Princeton: Princeton University Press, 1990.

Mackay, Alastair. *It Doesn't Have to Be This Way*. Cape Town: Kwela, 2022.

———. "Spotlight: An Interview with Alistair Mackay about His Debut Novel, 'It Doesn't Have to Be This Way.'" Interview by Gary Hartley. *Scaffold*, accessed July 24, 2024. https://www.scaffold-culture.com/developments/spotlight-an-interview-with-alistair-mackay-about-his-debut-novel-it-doesnt-have-to-be-this-way.

Maclellan, Nic. "Kiribati's Policy for 'Migration with Dignity.'" *Devpolicy Blog from the Development Policy Centre* (blog), January 11, 2012. https://devpolicy.org/kiribati_migration_climate_change20120112/.

Malm, Andreas, and Alf Hornborg. "The Geology of Mankind? A Critique of the Anthropocene Narrative." *Anthropocene Review* 1, no. 1 (2014): 62–69. https://doi.org/10.1177/2053019613516291.

Mamdani, Mahmood. *Citizen and Subject: Contemporary Africa and the Legacy of Late Colonialism*. Princeton Studies in Culture/Power/History. Princeton: Princeton University Press, 1996.

———. *Neither Settler nor Native: The Making and Unmaking of Permanent Minorities*. Cambridge, MA: Belknap Press of Harvard University Press, 2020.

Marx, John. *Geopolitics and the Anglophone Novel, 1890–2011*. Cambridge: Cambridge University Press, 2012. See esp. chap. 2, "How Literature Administers 'Failed' States."

Marx, Karl, and Friedrich Engels. *The Communist Manifesto*. Edited by Jeffrey C. Isaac. New Haven: Yale University Press, 2012. http://www.jstor.org/stable/j.ctt5vm1x2.

Mathai Mahesh, dir. *Bhopal Express*. 1999; Los Angeles: Cinebella Home Entertainment, 2004. DVD. 1 hr., 40 min.

May, James R., and Erin Daly. *Global Environmental Constitutionalism*. Cambridge: Cambridge University Press, 2014.

Maylam, Paul. *South Africa's Racial Past: The History and Historiography of Racism, Segregation, and Apartheid*. Aldershot: Ashgate, 2001.

Mbembe, Achille. *Necropolitics*. Translated by Steve Corcoran. Durham, NC: Duke University Press, 2019.

———. *On the Postcolony*. Berkeley: University of California Press, 2001.

Mbue, Imbolo. "Author Imbolo Mbue Explores the Politics of Oil in 'How Beautiful We Were.'" Interview by Arun Venugopal. *FreshAir*, NPR, April 29, 2021. https://www.npr.org/2021/04/29/991956171/author-imbolo-mbue-explores-the-politics-of-oil-in-how-beautiful-we-were.

———. *Behold the Dreamers*. New York: Random House, 2016.

———. *How Beautiful We Were*. New York: Random House, 2021.

McAdam, Jane. "'Disappearing States,' Statelessness and the Boundaries of International Law." In *Climate Change and Displacement: Multidisciplinary Perspectives*, edited by Jane McAdam, 105–30. Oxford: Hart Publishing, 2010.

McFarlane, Colin, and Alex Vasudevan. "Informal Infrastructures." In *The Routledge Handbook of Mobilities*, edited by Peter Adey, David Bissell, Kevin Hannam, Peter Merriman, and Mimi Sheller, 256–64. London: Routledge, 2013. https://www-taylorfrancis-com.proxy2.library.illinois.edu/chapters/edit/10.4324/9781315857572-28/informal-infrastructures-colin-mcfarlane-alex-vasudevan?context=ubx&refId=65967d19-edaf-4b7e-a5ba-d3df5b60026f.

McKenzie, David J. "Remittances in the Pacific." In *Immigrants and Their International Money Flows*, edited by Susan Pozo, 99–122. Kalamazoo: W. E. Upjohn Institute for Employment Research, 2007.

Menon, N. R. Madhava, ed. *Documents and Court Opinions on Bhopal Gas Leak Disaster Case*. Bangalore: National Law School of India University, 1991.

Miller, George, dir. *Mad Max: Fury Road*. 2015. Burbank, CA: Warner Brothers, 2015. Streaming video. Amazon, 1 hr., 54 min.

Mitchell, Lisa. *Hailing the State: Indian Democracy between Elections*. Durham, NC: Duke University Press, 2023.

Mitchell, Timothy. *Carbon Democracy: Political Power in the Age of Oil*. London: Verso, 2013. See esp. chap. 1, "Machines of Democracy."

Moffett, Helen. "1001 Ways to Save Water: A Start." *Helen Moffett* (blog). January 19, 2018. https://www.helenmoffett.com/green-hat/2018/1/19/1001-ways-to-save-water-a-start.

Monteiro, Catie. "Water Crisis Grips Cape Town, South Africa, after Drought Stretching Years." *NBC News*, January 29, 2018. https://www.nbcnews.com/news/world/water-crisis-hits-cape-town-south-africa-day-zero-looms-n841881.

Moretti, Franco. "Conjectures on World Literature." *New Left Review* 1, no. 1 (2000): 54–68. https://newleftreview.org/issues/ii1/articles/franco-moretti-conjectures-on-world-literature.

Movement for the Survival of the Ogoni People. *Ogoni Bill of Rights*. Movement for the Survival of the Ogoni People (MOSOP) & Ogoni News and Resources. Accessed July 24, 2024. http://www.mosop.org/2015/10/10/ogoni-bill-of-rights/.

Moyn, Samuel. *Not Enough: Human Rights in an Unequal World*. Cambridge, MA: Belknap Press of Harvard University Press, 2018.

Muehlebach, Andrea. *A Vital Frontier: Water Insurgencies in Europe*. Durham, NC: Duke University Press, 2023.

Mukherjee, Suroopa. *Surviving Bhopal: Dancing Bodies, Written Texts, and Oral Testimonials of Women in the Wake of an Industrial Disaster*. New York: Palgrave Macmillan, 2010.

Mukherjee, Upamanyu Pablo. *Postcolonial Environments: Nature, Culture and the Contemporary Indian Novel in English*. Houndsmills, Basingstroke: Palgrave Macmillan, 2010.

Muñoz, José Esteban. *Cruising Utopia: The Then and There of Queer Futurity*. New York: New York University Press, 2009.

National Resources Defense Council. "Bangladesh: A Country Underwater, a Culture on the Move." September 13, 2018. https://www.nrdc.org/stories/bangladesh-country-underwater-culture-move.

National Security Archive. "Castle BRAVO at 70: The Worst Nuclear Test in U.S. History." Accessed June 18, 2024. https://nsarchive.gwu.edu/briefing-book/nuclear-vault/2024-02-29/castle-bravo-70-worst-nuclear-test-us-history.

Nayar, Pramod K. *Bhopal's Ecological Gothic: Disaster, Precarity, and the Biopolitical Uncanny*. Lanham, MD: Lexington Books, 2017.

News18. "MP HC Raps Centre, Seeks Compliance Report on 1984 Gas Tragedy Dedicated Hospital Next Month." Updated December 21, 2021. https://www.news18.com/news/india/mp-hc-raps-centre-seeks-compliance-report-on-1984-gas-tragedy-dedicated-hospital-next-month-4579088.html.

Nixon, Rob. *Slow Violence and the Environmentalism of the Poor*. Cambridge, MA: Belknap Press of Harvard University Press, 2011.

Njovane, Thando. "'My Mother Was a Fish': Racial Trauma, Precarity, and Grief in K. Sello Duiker's *Thirteen Cents*." *Research in African Literatures* 51, no. 4 (2021): 173–89. muse.jhu.edu/article/798059.

Obi-Young, Otosirieze. "Remembering K. Sello Duiker, Great Writer of South Africa's Post-Apartheid Generation, Who Would Have Been 45 This Month." *Brittle Paper*, April 19, 2019. https://brittlepaper.com/2019/04/remembering-k-sello-duiker-great-writer-of-south-africas-post-apartheid-generation-who-would-have-been-45-this-month/.

Oil Pipelines Act of 1956. The Complete 2004 Laws of Nigeria. Accessed August 28, 2022. http://lawsofnigeria.placng.org/view2.php?sn=425.

Okpewho, Isidore. *Tides*. Harlow, Essex: Longman, 1993.

Okri, Ben. *The Famished Road*. New York: N. A. Talese, 1992.

Oldfield, Sophie, and Saskia Greyling. "Waiting for the State: A Politics of Housing in South Africa." *Environment and Planning A: Economy and Space* 47, no. 5 (2015): 1100–1112. https://doi.org/10.1177/0308518X15592309.

O'Loughlin, Liam. "Negotiating Solidarity: Indra Sinha's Animal's People and the 'NGO-ization' of Postcolonial Narrative." *Comparative American Studies: An International Journal* 12, no. 1–2 (2014): 101–13. https://doi.org/10.1179/1477570014Z.00000000073.

"Orders (Settlement) of the Supreme Court on the Special Leave Petitions (14–15 February, 1989)." In *Documents and Court Opinions on Bhopal Gas Leak Disaster Case*, edited by N.R. Madhava Menon, 288–89. Bangalore: National Law School of India University, 1991.

Oreskes, Naomi, and Erik M. Conway. *The Collapse of Western Civilization: A View from the Future*. New York: Columbia University Press, 2014.

Osaghae, Eghosa E. *Crippled Giant: Nigeria since Independence*. Bloomington: Indiana University Press, 1998.

Oxford English Dictionary. "Complaint." Accessed June 18, 2024. https://www.oed.com/dictionary/complaint_n?tab=meaning_and_use#8826085.

———. "Parens Patriae." Accessed June 21, 2019. https://doi.org/10.1093/OED/6005207148.

Panagariya, Arvind. *India: The Emerging Giant*. New York: Oxford University Press, 2008.

Pashley, Alex. "Kiribati President: Climate-Induced Migration Is 5 Years Away." *Climate Home News*, February 18, 2016. https://www.climatechangenews.com/2016/02/18/kiribati-president-climate-induced-migration-is-5-years-away/.

Patel, Raj, and Jason W. Moore. *A History of the World in Seven Cheap Things: A Guide to Capitalism, Nature, and the Future of the Planet*. Oakland: University of California Press, 2017. See esp. "Introduction" and chap. 1, "Cheap Nature."

Petryna, Adriana. *Life Exposed: Biological Citizens after Chernobyl*. Princeton: Princeton University Press, 2002.

Phelps, Erin D. "As Waters Rise: A Race to Migrate with Dignity." *Migrationist* (blog), February 9, 2015. https://themigrationist.wordpress.com/2015/02/09/as-waters-rise-a-race-to-migrate-with-dignity/.

Pierce, Steven. *Moral Economies of Corruption: State Formation and Political Culture in Nigeria*. Durham, NC: Duke University Press, 2016.

Povinelli, Elizabeth A. *Geontologies: A Requiem to Late Liberalism*. Durham, NC: Duke University Press, 2016.

Rich, Kelly M. *The Promise of Welfare in the Postwar British and Anglophone Novel: States of Repair*. Oxford: Oxford University Press, 2023.

Rickel, Jennifer. "'The Poor Remain': A Posthumanist Rethinking of Literary Humanitarianism in Indra Sinha's Animal's People." *Ariel: A Review of International English Literature* 43, no. 1 (2012). https://journalhosting.ucalgary.ca/index.php/ariel/article/view/35244.

Riddel, Juliet, dir. *Cape Town: Life without Water*. Cape Town: Financial Times Films, 2018. YouTube. Streaming video, 17 minutes. https://www.youtube.com/watch?v=78B-wQQutjU.

Robbins, Bruce. *The Beneficiary*. Durham, NC: Duke University Press, 2017.

———. *Upward Mobility and the Common Good: Toward a Literary History of the Welfare State*. Princeton: Princeton University Press, 2007.

Robbins, Peter T. "Transnational Corporations and the Discourse of Water Privatization." *Journal of International Development* 15, no. 8 (2003): 1073–82. https://doi.org/10.1002/jid.1054.

Robins, Steven. "'Day Zero,' Hydraulic Citizenship and the Defence of the Commons in Cape Town: A Case Study of the Politics of Water and Its Infrastructures (2017–2018)." *Journal of Southern African Studies* 45, no. 1 (2019): 5–29. https://doi.org/10.1080/03057070.2019.1552424.

Rodina, Lucy, and Leila M Harris. "Water Services, Lived Citizenship, and Notions of the State in Marginalised Urban Spaces: The Case of Khayelitsha, South Africa." *Water Alternatives* 9, no. 2 (2016): 336–55. https://www.water-alternatives.org/index.php/alldoc/articles/319-a9-2-9/file.

Rogan, Davis, and Alcena Madeline. "Utopian Studies (Part II: Theory)." In *The Routledge Companion to Science Fiction*, edited by Mark Bould, Andrew Butler, Adam Roberts, and Sherryl Vint. New York: Routledge, 2009. https://www.proquest.com/encyclopedias-reference-works/31-utopian-studies-part-ii-theory/docview/2137959474/se-2.

Rose-Innes, Henrietta. *Nineveh*. Los Angeles: Unnamed Press, 2016.

———. "Poison." *Guardian*, July 9, 2008. https://www.theguardian.com/books/2008/jul/09/caineprize.

Rosenthal, M. L., and Sally M. Gall. *The Modern Poetic Sequence: The Genius of Modern Poetry*. New York: Oxford University Press, 1983.

Ross, Corey. *Ecology and Power in the Age of Empire: Europe and the Transformation of the Tropical World*. Oxford: Oxford University Press, 2017.

Rott, Nathan, Rebecca Hersher, Jeff Brady, Lauren Sommer, Alejandra Borunda, and Julia Simon. "Climate Talks End on a First-Ever Call for the World to Move Away from Fossil Fuels." *NPR*. Updated December 13, 2023. https://www.npr.org/2023/12/13/1218125835/climate-talks-end-on-a-first-ever-call-for-the-world-to-move-away-from-fossil-fu.

Rowlatt, Justin. "UAE Planned to Use COP28 Climate Talks to Make Oil Deals." *BBC*, November 27, 2023. https://www.bbc.com/news/science-environment-67508331.

Rubenstein, Michael. *Public Works: Infrastructure, Irish Modernism, and the Postcolonial*. Notre Dame, Ind: University of Notre Dame Press, 2010.

Rushdie, Salman. *Midnight's Children*. New York: Random House Trade Paperbacks, 2006.
Rytz, Matthieu, dir. *Anote's Ark*. EyeSteel Film and Documentary Channel. 2018. Streaming video. Alexander Street, 1 hour and 17 min.
Sackey, Edward. "Oral Tradition and the African Novel." *Modern Fiction Studies* 37, no. 3 (1991): 389–407. https://www.jstor.org/stable/26283152.
Samuelson, Meg. "Anomalous, Containerized and Inundating Waters: Thinking from the Cape and through Blue Focalization with K. Sello Duiker's Thirteen Cents." *Interventions* 24, no. 3 (2022): 463–78. https://doi.org/10.1080/1369801X.2021.2015706.
Saro-Wiwa, Ken. *Genocide in Nigeria*. Port Harcourt, Nigeria: Saros International, 1992.
———. *A Month and a Day & Letters*. Banbury, Oxfordshire: Ayebia Clarke, 1995.
———. *Sozaboy*. Port Harcourt, Nigeria: Saros International, 1985.
Sarwar, Golam Mahabub, and Mamunul H. Khan. "Sea Level Rise: A Threat to the Coast of Bangladesh." *Internationales Asienforum* 38, no. 3–4 (2007): 375–97.
Scase, Wendy. *Literature and Complaint in England, 1272–1553*. Oxford: Oxford University Press, 2007.
Schnitzler, Antina von. *Democracy's Infrastructure: Techno-Politics and Protest after Apartheid*. Princeton: Princeton University Press, 2016.
———. "Infrastructure, Apartheid Technopolitics, and Temporalities of 'Transition.'" In *Promise of Infrastructure*, edited by Nikhil Anand, Akhil Gupta, and Hannah Appel, 133–54. Durham, NC: Duke University Press, 2018.
Schwarz, Roberto. "Objective Form: Reflections on the Dialectic of Roguery." In *Literary Materialisms*, edited by Mathias Nilges and Emilio Sauri, 185–99. New York: Palgrave Macmillan, 2013. https://doi.org/10.1057/9781137339959_11.
Scott, David. *Conscripts of Modernity: The Tragedy of Colonial Enlightenment*. Durham, NC: Duke University Press, 2004.
Sedgwick, Eve Kosofsky. "Paranoid Reading and Reparative Reading; or, You're So Paranoid, You Probably Think This Introduction Is About You." In *Novel Gazing: Queer Readings in Fiction*, edited by Eve Kosofsky Sedgwick, 1–37. Durham, NC: Duke University Press, 1997.
Sharma, Aradhana, and Akhil Gupta, eds. *The Anthropology of the State: A Reader*. Malden, MA: Blackwell, 2006.
Sheldon, Rebekah. *The Child to Come: Life after the Human Catastrophe*. Minneapolis: University of Minnesota Press, 2016.
Shenk, John, dir. *The Island President*. AfterImage Public Media, 2011. Streaming video. Amazon, 1 hr., 41 min.
Shepherd, Nick. "Making Sense of 'Day Zero': Slow Catastrophes, Anthropocene Futures, and the Story of Cape Town's Water Crisis." *Water* 11, no. 9 (2019): 1744. https://doi.org/10.3390/w11091744.
Shortslef, Emily. *The Drama of Complaint: Ethical Provocations in Shakespeare's Tragedy*. Oxford: Oxford University Press, 2023.

Singh, Julietta. "Post-Humanitarian Fictions." *Symplokē* 23, no. 1–2 (2015): 137–52. https://doi.org/10.5250/symploke.23.1-2.0137.

Sinha, Indra. *Animal's People*. New York: Simon & Schuster, 2007.

———. "Chemicals for War and Chemicals for Peace: Poison Gas in Bhopal, India, and Halabja, Kurdistan, Iraq." *Social Justice* 41, no. 1–2 (2014): 125–45. https://www.jstor.org/stable/24361594.

———. *The Cybergypsies: A True Tale of Lust, War, and Betrayal on the Electronic Frontier*. New York: Viking, 1999.

———. *The Death of Mr. Love*. New York: HarperCollins, 2004.

Smith, Brady. "Red, Black and Green: Ecology, Economy and the Contemporary African Novel." PhD diss., University of Chicago, 2015. ProQuest (3687171).

Smith, Daniel Jordan. *Culture of Corruption: Everyday Deception and Popular Discontent in Nigeria*. Princeton: Princeton University Press, 2007.

Smith, Laila. "The Murky Waters of the Second Wave of Neoliberalism: Corporatization as a Service Delivery Model in Cape Town." *Geoforum* 35, no. 3 (2004): 375–93. https://doi.org/10.1016/j.geoforum.2003.05.003.

Smith, Neil. "There's No Such Thing as a Natural Disaster." Items, Social Science Research Council. June 11, 2006. https://items.ssrc.org/understanding-katrina/theres-no-such-thing-as-a-natural-disaster/.

Snell, Heather R. "Assessing the Limitations of Laughter in Indra Sinha's Animal's People." *Postcolonial Text* 4, no. 4 (2008): 1–15. https://www.postcolonial.org/index.php/pct/article/view/990.

South African Government. "Growth, Employment and Redistribution: A Macroeconomic Strategy for South Africa (GEAR)." Accessed May 17, 2024. https://www.gov.za/documents/other/growth-employment-and-redistribution-macroeconomic-strategy-south-africa-gear-18.

Stanley, Ben Jamieson. *Precarious Eating: Narrating Environmental Harm in the Global South*. Minneapolis: University of Minnesota Press, 2024. See esp. chap. 5, "Purity and Porosity."

Stoler, Ann Laura. *Duress: Imperial Durabilities in Our Times*. Durham, NC: Duke University Press, 2016.

Stratford, Elaine, Carol Farbotko, and Heather Lazrus. "Tuvalu, Sovereignty and Climate Change: Considering Fenua, the Archipelago and Emigration." *Island Studies Journal* 8, no. 1 (2013): 67–83.

Suvin, Darko. "On the Poetics of the Science Fiction Genre." *College English* 34, no. 3 (1972): 372–82. https://doi.org/10.2307/375141.

Szalay, Michael. *New Deal Modernism: American Literature and the Invention of the Welfare State*. Durham, NC: Duke University Press, 2000.

Teaiwa, Teresia K. "Bikinis and Other S/pacific N/oceans." In *Militarized Currents: Toward a Decolonized Future in Asia and the Pacific*, new ed., edited by Setsu Shigematsu and Keith L. Camacho, 15–32. Minneapolis: University of Minnesota Press, 2010. http://www.jstor.org/stable/10.5749/j.ctttv7q0.7.

Thiong'o, Ngũgĩ wa. *Petals of Blood*. London: Heinemann, 1977.

———. *Wizard of the Crow*. New York: Pantheon Books, 2006.

Torrice, Andrea, dir. *Rising Waters: Global Warming and the Fate of the Pacific Islands*. Bullfrog Films. 2000. Streaming video. Alexander Street, 57 min.

Travers, Robert. *Empires of Complaints: Mughal Law and the Making of British India, 1765–1793*. Cambridge: Cambridge University Press, 2022.

Tsing, Anna, Heather Swanson, Elaine Gan, and Nils Bubandt, eds. *Arts of Living on a Damaged Planet*. Minneapolis: University of Minnesota Press, 2017.

United Nations. "Water—at the Center of the Climate Crisis." Accessed June 19, 2024. https://www.un.org/en/climatechange/science/climate-issues/water.

United Nations Environment Programme. *Environmental Assessment of Ogoniland*. 2011. https://www.unep.org/resources/report/environmental-assessment-ogoniland.

University of Oslo Faculty of Law. "Montevideo Convention on the Rights and Duties of States." Treaty Database. Accessed July 24, 2024. https://www.jus.uio.no/english/services/library/treaties/01/1-02/rights-duties-states.html.

Vidal, John. "Shell Announces £55m Payout for Nigeria Oil Spills." *Guardian*, January 7, 2015. https://www.theguardian.com/environment/2015/jan/07/shell-announces-55m-payout-for-nigeria-oil-spills.

Villiers, James de. "How Cape Town Avoided Day Zero and Cut Its Water Usage by 50% in 3 Years—It Took Melbourne 12 Years to Do the Same." *News24*, March 7, 2018. https://www.news24.com/news24/bi-archive/how-cape-town-cut-its-water-usage-by-50-in-3-years-it-took-melbourne-12-years-to-do-the-same-2018-3.

Vlies, Andrew van der. *Present Imperfect: Contemporary South African Writing*. Oxford: Oxford University Press, 2017.

Vogel, Steven K. *Marketcraft: How Governments Make Markets Work*. New York: Oxford University Press, 2018. https://doi.org/10.1093/oso/9780190699857.001.0001.

Watts, Michael J. "Chronicle of a Future Foretold: The Complex Legacies of Ken Saro-Wiwa." *Extractive Industries and Society* 2, no. 4 (2015): 635–44. https://doi.org/10.1016/j.exis.2015.08.002.

———. "Oil as Money: The Devil's Excrement and the Spectacle of Black Gold." In *Reading Economic Geography*, edited by Trevor J. Barnes, Jamie Peck, Eric Sheppard, and Adam Tickell. Malden, 205–19. Malden, MA: Blackwell, 2004.

———. "Sweet and Sour." In *Curse of the Black Gold: Fifty Years of Oil in the Niger Delta*, edited by Michael Watts, 36–61. Brooklyn, NY: PowerHouse, 2008.

Weber, Max. *The Theory of Social and Economic Organization*. Translated by A. M. Henderson and Talcott Parsons. Edited by Talcott Parsons. New York: Oxford University Press, 1974.

Weis, Lael K. "Constitutional Directive Principles." *Oxford Journal of Legal Studies* 37, no. 4 (2017): 916–45. https://doi.org/10.1093/ojls/gqx015.

Welsh, David. "The Cultural Dimension of Apartheid." *African Affairs* 71, no. 282 (1972): 35–53. https://www.jstor.org/stable/720362.

Wenzel, Jennifer. *The Disposition of Nature: Environmental Crisis and World Literature*. New York: Fordham University Press, 2019.

———. "The Trouble with Narrators." In *Emerging Perspectives on Chinua Achebe*, edited by Ernest N. Emenyonu, 1:319–32. Trenton, NJ: Africa World Press, 2003.

Wilder, Gary. *The French Imperial Nation-State: Negritude & Colonial Humanism between the Two World Wars*. Chicago: University of Chicago Press, 2005.

Williams, Daniel. "Life Among the Vermin: Nineveh and Ecological Relocation." *Studies in the Novel* 50, no. 3 (2018): 419–40. https://www.jstor.org/stable/48559281.

Williams, Raymond. *The Country and the City*. New York: Oxford University Press, 1975.

Wolfe, Patrick. "Settler Colonialism and the Elimination of the Native." *Journal of Genocide Research* 8, no. 4 (2006): 387–409. https://doi.org/10.1080/14623520601056240.

Yamin, Farhana. "The Kyoto Protocol: Origins, Assessment and Future Challenges." *Review of European Community & International Environmental Law* 7, no. 2 (1998): 113–27. https://doi.org/10.1111/1467-9388.00138.

Young, Crawford. *The Postcolonial State in Africa: Fifty Years of Independence, 1960–2010*. Madison: The University of Wisconsin Press, 2012.

Zille, Helen. "From the Inside: The Countdown to Day Zero." *Daily Maverick*, January 21, 2018. https://www.dailymaverick.co.za/opinionista/2018-01-22-from-the-inside-the-countdown-to-day-zero/.

Index

Abacha, Sani, 64, 88, 180n101
Abani, Chris 1–2, 11; *GraceLand*, 1–2, 13
Abrams, Philip, 10–11, 171n36
Abu Dhabi National Oil Company (ADNOC), 125
Achebe, Chinua, 78–79; *Anthills of the Savannah*, 78–86; *Arrow of God*, 79; *A Man of the People*, 79; mentioned, 22; *No Longer at Ease*, 79; *Things Fall Apart*, 79; *The Trouble with Nigeria*, 79
Adichie, Chimamanda Ngozi, 78; *Half of a Yellow Sun*, 78
African National Congress, 93, 96–97, 105–7, 110, 114; uMkhonto weSizwe, 123. *See also* post-apartheid South Africa
Agamben, Giorgio, 4, 169n12
Ahmed, Sarah, 13; *Complaint!*, 13
Ahuja, Neel, 186n11
Alaimo, Stacey, 54; trans-corporeal, 54
Al-Jaber, Sultan, 125
Alliance of Small Island States (AOSIS), 129, 151
Amnesty International, 51, 60
Anand, Nikhil, 93, 171n40
Anderson, Benedict, 24, 173n81
Anderson, Warren, 26, 32
Animal's People (Sinha), 42, 47–55; mentioned, 21
Anker, Elizabeth S., and Rita Felski, 162
Anote's Ark (Rytz), 128–30, 141, 153; mentioned, 23

Anthills of the Savannah (Achebe), 78–86; mentioned, 22
Anthropocene, 22, 102–3, 141, 173n79
Anthropocene conjuncture, 23, 94–95, 98, 103–4, 181n9
anti-statism, 4–6, 11, 161–63
apartheid, 93–96, 123–24; continuities of, 95–102, 104, 107–8, 113, 124; Group Areas Act of 1950, 96; and infrastructure, 93–98, 106; mentioned, 23; relocation, 96–97, 99
Apter, Andrew, 63
Archaeologies of the Future (Jameson), 12
Armah, Ayi Kwei, 5
Arts of Living on a Damaged Planet (Tsing et al.), 169n9
Aslami, Zarena, 170n21
Attwell, David, and Barbara Harlow, 98
Atwood, Margaret, 119

Babangida, Ibrahim, 74, 75
Bacigalupi, Paolo, 119; *The Water Knife*, 119
Bangladesh, 126
Bayart, Jean-François, 179n54
Benhabib, Seyla, 16–17, 42, 105, 107; *Critique, Norm, and Utopia*, 172n65
Bernstein, Michael André, 189n84
Best, Stephen, and Sharon Marcus, 191n8
Bhopal: A Prayer for Rain, 31
Bhopal civil suit, 33–37, 57, 174n21
Bhopal gas disaster, 19–21, 25–32, 53; Bhopal Medical Appeal, 174n20; mentioned, 12,

215

Bhopal gas disaster (*continued*)
  16. *See also* methyl isocyanate (MIC); Union Carbide Corporation
Bhopal Gas Leak Disaster (Processing of Claims) Act, 33–37; mentioned, 21
Bhopal Principles on Corporate Responsibility, 56–57
Bhopal settlement, 28–32, 35–36, 57; mentioned 12, 21
Bhopal survivors, 25–31, 39–42; complaints, 31, 39–44, 49–50; testimony, 31, 39–44; toxicity, 25, 28–30, 40–41, 43, 47–48, 51–55; water contamination, 29, 44, 46–49
Biloxi-Chitimacha-Choctaw tribe, 125
biological citizenship, 41
black gold, 62–63, 177n6
Bloch, Ernst, 2–3, 17–18, 27, 57, 88; "Can Hope be Disappointed?," 17–18, 172n66; *The Principle of Hope*, 2–3, 57, 88, 138, 154, 160
Bodo Community v. The Shell Petroleum Development Company of Nigeria Limited, 69–70
Bond, Patrick, 97
Bourdieu, Pierre, 10
Burkett, Maxine, 154, 187b37, 190n98
Byrne, Deirdre, 98–99, 182n29

Canavan, Gerry, 119
Cape Flats, 101
Cape Town Critical Water Shortages Disaster Plan, 119–20
Casey, Rose, 179n46
Chakrabarty, Dipesh, 132, 172n59, 173n79, 190n115; mentioned, 15
Chambers, Anne, and Keith S. Chambers, 144
Chance, Kerry Ryan, 112–13
Charan Lal Sahu v. Union of India, 37–39
Charlton, Sarah, and Paula Meth, 110–11
Chatterjee, Elizabeth, 173n79
Chatterjee, Partha, 6, 170n19
Chernobyl, 41
climate action, 23, 120–23, 128–31, 148, 150, 155
climate apocalypse, 115, 119–21, 156
climate change: and adaptation, 131–38, 156–59, 160; and colonialism, 22–24, 102–3, 138–43, 145–46; Global South and, 2–3, 8–9, 18–20, 162; injustice of, 94, 98, 100–4, 128–31, 149–50; and protest 122–23, 130; and state intervention, 7–9, 16, 22–24; as war, 140–42; and water struggles, 92–95, 100–4, 125–30
climate denialism, 155–59, 191n6
climate displacement, 125–28; and staying in place, 127–35, 148–50; and voyaging, 131–32
climate fiction, 119–23, 185n120
climate migration, 133–38
climate refugeeism: mainstream narratives of, 23, 126–27, 186n10; Pacific resistance to, 126–38, 146–54
cognitive estrangement, 152–55
Cold War, 139–42, 173n74, 189n64
Collapse of Western Civilization, The (Oreskes and Conway), 160–61
Comaroff, Jean, and John L. Comaroff, 97
complaint. *See* Utopian method
concrete utopia: Ernst Bloch and, 2, 27, 57, 88; bodily care as, 3, 21, 26–28, 33–34, 40–41, 43–44, 52–53, 113–14; corporate accountability as, 3, 9, 21, 32–37, 56–58, 69–73; definition of, 2–4; discussion of, 8–12, 27–28, 56–57, 91, 160, 163, 169n6; drawing on state frameworks, 1–4, 10–11, 37–41, 43–47, 74–78; imaginable futures as, 3, 39–42, 78, 135, 137, 152–54, 162–63; infrastructural expansion as, 105–14; political inclusion as, 9, 74–75, 77–78, 94–95, 112–13, 124; and protection from oil, 69–73; service delivery as, 97–98, 112–14; and state responses, 49–51, 73–78, 82–85, 88–89, 105–14, 132–38; staying in place as, 130–35, 148; undoing apartheid as, 94–95, 105–11, 123–24
Conference of the Parties to the United Nations Framework Convention on Climate Change (COP), 125–26, 128, 151; COP15, 128; COP28, 125–26, 128
Constitution of India, 38
Constitution of the Federal Republic of Nigeria, 1979, 74–77
Constitution of the Federal Republic of Nigeria, 1999, 72–74
Constitution of the Republic of South Africa, 106–7
Cooper, Frederick, 7
Craps, Stef, 172n59

INDEX

Critique, Norm, and Utopia (Benhabib), 172n65
Crutzen, Paul J., and Eugene F. Stoermer., 22, 102–3

Das, Veena, 31
Davis, Heather, and Zoe Todd, 191n4
Day Zero, 94–95, 104, 114–21, 123–24; as apartheid legacy, 124; Capetonian responses to, 115–18; media coverage of, 115; mentioned 22–23; prevention of, 115–20; state surveillance during, 116; water restrictions during, 104, 115–20
De, Rohit, and Robert Travers, 175n51
Deepwater Horizon, 59, 177n1
defamiliarization, 152–53
DeLoughrey, Elizabeth M., 140, 143, 156, 172n59, 188nn62–63, 189n69, 190n115
DeLoughrey, Elizabeth M., and George Handley, 18
Denoon, David B. H., 174n11
desertification, 92
diaspora 137–38
Disappearing of Tuvalu: Trouble in Paradise, The (Horner), 142–44
Dreher, Tanja, and Michelle Voyer, 186n10
Dudziak, Mary, 170n25
Duiker, K. Sello, 101, 182n37; *The Hidden Star*, 182n37; mentioned, 23; *The Quiet Violence of Dreams*, 182n37; *Thirteen Cents*, 98, 101–4, 113–14
Duress (Stoler), 15
Dutch colonization, 103–4; Dutch East India Company, 103

Ebeku, Kaniye S. A., 178n45
Edelman, Lee, 180n88
Edmond, Rod, 188n53
Ekeh, Peter P., 63
Elugelab, 140
environmental justice, 18–19, 173n70
environmental racism, 3, 18–19, 26, 32, 36, 161, 173n70; colonialism and, 18–19, 22, 140; global capitalism and, 9–10, 18, 26, 30–32, 60, 67–68, 104, 139
Erritouni, Ali, 79
Eskom, 123
Esteve, Mary, 170n21
ethnic federalism, 76–78, 179n64
Everest, Larry, 32
Exxon Valdez, 59

Fanon, Frantz, 13–15, 102; *Black Skin, White Masks*, 102; *The Wretched of the Earth*, 8, 13–15
Farbotko, Carol, Elaine Stratford, and Heather Lazrus, 131
Farquhar, Harriet, 188n46
Felski, Rita, 161
Fortun, Kim, 29–30
fossil fuels: and climate change, 92–93, 103, 122–23, 125–26, 128–29, 142, 171n32; and climate inaction, 122, 125–26, 128–30; global economies and, 92, 125–26, 128–30
Foucault, Michel, 4, 169n12, 171n36
Fredericks, Rosalind, 171n40
Fry, Greg, 139

Gadgil, Madhav, and Ramachandra Guha, 173n75
Gandhi, Indira, 30, 174n11
Gandhi, Leela, 153
Gandhi, Rajiv, 30
Garuba, Harry, 172n59
Genocide in Nigeria (Saro-Wiwa), 64
geontology, 156
Getachew, Adom, 7
Ghana, 5
Ghosh, Amitav, 22, 177n16
Gikandi, Simon, 84, 179n70
Goodbody, Axel, 185n120
Gordin, Michael D., Helen Tilley, and Gyan Prakash, 169n6
Gordon, David M., 181n12
GraceLand (Abani), 1–2, 13
Greenpeace International, 56–57
greenwashing, 92, 128
Griswold, Wendy, 179n54
Grove, Richard, 173n73
Growth, Employment, and Redistribution Act (GEAR), 96–97, 106, 182n17
Guha, Ramchandra, and Juan Martínez-Alier, 173n75
Gulf of Mexico, 59, 125
Gupta, Akhil, 13, 171n40, 191n3

Hart, Matthew, 177n96
Hau'ofa, Epeli, 132
Heine, Hilda Cathy, 144, 189n75
Heise, Ursula K., 72, 171n39
Horner, Christopher, 142; *The Disappearing of Tuvalu: Trouble in Paradise*, 142–44

How Beautiful We Were (Mbue), 66–68, 86–91; mentioned, 22
Hull, Matthew S., 191n3
Hulme, Keri, 155–56; *The Bone People*, 156; mentioned, 23; *Stonefish*, 23, 155–59
humanitarian aid, 51, 176n78
Hurley, Jessica, 189n64

Iep Jāltok (Jetñil-Kijiner), 144–50; mentioned, 23
Iheka, Cajetan, 172n59, 178n24
Ikegami, Robin, 179n70
Indian Removal Act of 1830, 125
Indian state: bodily care and, 33–36, 39–41, 44–48; corporate accountability and, 26–28, 34–37, 49–51, 56–57; corporate collusion and, 28–30; economic liberalization and, 30–31; petitioning and, 39, 43–47; plurality of, 26–28, 57–58; welfare and, 38–41
Ingram, Forrest, 155
Innes, Catherine, 180n86
International Monetary Fund, 5
Island President, The (Shenk), 128
Isle de Jean Charles, 125–26
It Doesn't Have to Be This Way (Mackay), 121–23; mentioned, 23
Iyasere, Solomon O., 179n70

Jameson, Fredric, 11–12, 17, 171n42, 180n87; *An American Utopia*, 171n42; *Archaeologies of the Future*, 12; "Third-World Literature in the Era of Multinational Capitalism," 180n87; "Utopia as Method or, the Uses of the Future," 11–12
Jantar Mantar, 45, 176n59
Jetñil-Kijiner, Kathy, 130, 144–50; climate activism, 130, 146; *Iep Jāltok*, 144–50; mentioned, 23
Johns-Putra, Adeline, 180n88
Johnston, Barbara Rose, 189n66
Jonah Gbemre v. Shell Petroleum Development Company Nigeria Limited and Others, 72–73
Joubert, Leonie, and Gina Ziervogel, 185n117

Kailasam, Bala, 42; mentioned, 21; *Vaastu Marabu*, 42; *Where Do the Children Play?*, 42–47
Kanu, Ikechukwu Anthony, 172n59
Kaviraj, Sudipta, 6

Kenya, 5, 170n25
Keown, Michelle, 138–39, 188n55
Kerrigan, John, 172n47
Khayelitsha, 101, 111–12, 121, 184n94
Khoekhoen peoples, 103
Kiribati, 135; climate displacement, 135–38; sea level rise 23, 126. *See also* Migration with Dignity; Tong, Anote
Kissinger, Henry, 139
Klein, Naomi, 170n15
Kornbluh, Anna, 162, 191n12
Kortenaar, Neil ten, 7, 10, 79, 82–83; *Debt, Law, Realism*, 10
Kurzman, Dan, 32
Kyoto Protocol, 129

Lambourne, Tessie, 136–37
Latour, Bruno, 161, 191n6
Lauti, Toaripi, 142
Lazrus, Heather, 188n56
Lefale, Penchuro, 129–30
Lemanski, Charlotte, 97
Leton, Garrick B., 64,
Levine, Caroline, 162, 191n7
Lille, Patricia de, 117, 120
Lloyd, David, 5
Loginova, Olga, and Zak Cassel, 186n5
London, Jack, 139
Lowe, Rodney, 170n23

Madhya Pradesh, 28–29, 45; mentioned, 20
Maldives, 128, 130, 186n9. *See also* Nasheed, Mohammed
Malm, Andreas, and Alf Hornborg, 173n79
Mamdani, Mahmood, 5, 179n64
Mandela, Nelson, 96, 105
Marshall Islands, 139–42, 144–45; climate displacement, 126, 148–50; mentioned 23; nuclear militarism in, 139–40, 144–46; nuclear testing in, 139–41; and sea level rise, 126, 140–41, 146–50
Marx, John, 171n38
Marx, Karl, 4, 169n10, 191n12
Masdar, 125
Mathai, Mahesh, 31; *Bhopal Express*, 31
May, James R., and Erin Daly, 178n44
Maylam, Paul, 181n12
Mbembe, Achille, 4, 169n12
Mbue, Imbolo, 66–67, 180n101; *Behold the Dreamers*, 67; *How Beautiful We Were*, 67–68, 86–91; mentioned, 22

INDEX

McAdam, Jane, 187n36, 190n98
methyl isocyanate (MIC), 25, 29, 32, 35, 40, 43
Micronesia, 126, 189n63
Midnight's Children (Rushdie), 5, 182n35
Migration with Dignity (MWD), 135–38; mentioned, 23; as speculation, 151–54; useable past, 137–38
Millennium Drought, 116
Mitchell, Lisa, 10, 171n33
Mitchell, Timothy, 71
Moffett, Helen, 117–18
Moretti, Franco, 191n8
Movement for the Survival of the Ogoni People (MOSOP), 64, 74; mentioned, 21
Moyn, Samuel, 170n23
Mukherjee, Suroopa, 34, 39
Mukherjee, Upamanyu Pablo, 176n88
Muñoz, José Esteban, 90, 169n6

Nasheed, Mohammed, 128, 130
Nation *Ex-Situ*, 154, 187n37, 190n98
negative critique, 3–6, 11, 13–14, 161; alternatives to, 11–18, 160–64; in the humanities, 3–4, 11, 161; limits of, 8–10, 161–64
neoliberalism, 96–97, 137
Newlands suburb, 104
Niger Delta, 60–64, 66, 68, 174n19, 179n46; Ijaw people, 64, 77; Ikwerre Rescue Charter, 64; Iwherekan, 73; Kaiama Declaration, 64, 77; mentioned 1, 16, 20–22; oil drilling in, 21–22, 60–70; oil pollution in, 21–22, 60–69; Oloibiri, 63; poverty of, 3, 62–63, 74–76. *See also* Ogoni
Nigerian Civil War, 74–76
Nigerian National Petroleum Corporation (NNPC), 68
Nigerian state, 61–64, 68–78, 178n32; authoritarianism and, 64, 79–84, 86–88; corporate regulation and, 61–62, 69–73, 91; democracy and, 76–77, 84–86, 88–89; ethnic federalism and, 76–78; federal character principle and, 76–78; independence from Britain, 69, 75, 178n33; Land Use Act of 1978, 72; mentioned, 21; Petroleum Act of 1969, 69; as a petrostate, 61, 65, 68. *See also* Oil Pipelines Act of 1956 (OPA)
Nineveh (Rose-Innes), 98–101, 108–9; mentioned, 23

Nixon, Rob, 11, 19, 171n39, 174n19, 176n65
Njovane, Thando, 183n43

Ogoni, 62–64, 77–78; mentioned 21–22; Movement for the Survival of the Ogoni People (MOSOP), 21, 64, 74–78; Ogoni Bill of Rights (1990), 21, 63–64, 74–78; Ogoni Nine, 88. *See also* Saro-Wiwa, Ken
Oil Pipelines Act of 1956 (OPA), 69–72; mentioned, 21
Okpewho, Isidore, 64–65; mentioned, 21; *Tides*, 64–66, 178n21
Okri, Ben, 172n59
Oldfield, Sophie, and Saskia Greyling, 109–11
O'Loughlin, Liam, 176n78
oral narrative, 79, 80, 179n70, 180n90
Oreskes, Naomi and Erik M. Conway, 160–61
Organization of the Petroleum Exporting Countries (OPEC), 126
Osaghae, Eghosa, 75

Pacific Basin, 139–40, 188n62
Pacific extinction narratives, 138–41, 144, 147; economic unviability as, 139; fatal impact as, 138–39; nuclear testing as, 139–41, 144–46; sea level rise as, 140–41, 146–50
Pacific Rim, 139–40, 188n62
padayatra, 42–44
parens patriae, 37–38
Paris Agreement, 128, 150
Patel, Raj and Jason W. Moore, 8
Penn, Kal, 31
petrofiction, 64, 177n16
petroviolence, 60, 62
Petryna, Adriana, 41
Pierce, Steven, 179n54
Pikinni (Bikini) Atoll, 139–40
plastic pollution, 103, 122
Polynesia, 126, 131
poo wars, 97
post-apartheid South Africa, 93–98 104–14; democracy and, 94, 96–98, 105–8; economic liberalization and, 96–97; limits of, 95–102, 111–12, 124; infrastructural expansion and, 97–98, 105–14; postracialism and, 101–2; poverty alleviation and, 105–11; racial tensions

post-apartheid South Africa (*continued*) and, 96–102, 104; service delivery protests and, 97–98, 112–13. *See also* Growth, Employment, and Redistribution Act (GEAR); Reconstruction and Development Programme (RDP)

postcolonial state: in Fanon, 13–15; interventionist role of, 1–4, 6–11, 160–63, 170n19, 170n21, 171nn39–40; as Janus-faced, 1–11, 27, 61–62, 72, 111–13; violence and, 1, 4–6, 11, 13–14, 170n27, 171n39

Povinelli, Elizabeth, 156

Principle of Hope, The (Bloch), 2–3, 57, 88, 138, 154, 160

Rao, Narasimha, 30

Reconstruction and Development Programme (RDP), 96, 105–7, 109–11, 124; National Housing Subsidy Programme, 110

reparative reading, 161, 163

Ribadu, Muhammadu, 69–70

Rich, Kelly Mee, 170n21

Rickel, Jennifer, 176n78

Riddel, Juliet, 118; *Cape Town: Life without Water*, 118

Rio Declaration on Environment and Development, 56

Rising Waters: Global Warming and the Fate of the Pacific Islands (Torrice), 129–30, 140–41; mentioned, 23

Robbins, Bruce, 10; *The Beneficiary*, 170n23; *Upward Mobility and the Common Good*, 170n21

Robins, Steven, 115–16

Rodina, Lucy, and Leila M. Harris, 111–12

Rose-Innes, Henrietta, 98; mentioned, 23; *Nineveh*, 98–101, 108–9; "Poison," 98

Rosenthal, M.L., and Sally Gall, 147

Ross, Corey, 173n73

Rubenstein, Michael, 181n10

Rushdie, Salman, 5, 182n35; *Midnight's Children*, 5, 182n35

Rytz, Matthieu, 128; *Anote's Ark*, 128, 141, 153; mentioned, 23

Sackey, Edward, 180n90

Samuelson, Meg, 102, 183n44

San peoples, 103

Saro-Wiwa, Ken, 21–22, 63–64, 78, 88, 180n101; activism, 63–64, 78; execution of, 64, 88; *Genocide in Nigeria*, 64; *A Month and a Day & Letters*, 179n54; and the Ogoni Bill of Rights, 21–22, 63–64, 78; *Sozaboy*, 78

Saur International, 92–93

Scase, Wendy, 172n46

Schnitzler, Antina von, 182n15, 185n99

Sedgwick, Eve, 161, 163

Sheen, Martin, 31

Sheldon, Rebekah, 180n88

Shell, 60, 67, 68

Shenk, John, 128; *The Island President*, 128

Shephard, Nick, 94

Shortslef, Emily, 172n47

short story cycle, 155

Singh, Julietta, 176n78

Singh, Manmohan, 43–44, 47

Sinha, Indra, 47–48; *Animal's People*, 47–55, 176n65; *The Cybergypsies*, 47; *The Death of Mr. Love*, 47; mentioned, 21; work with Amnesty International, 51

slow violence, 19–20, 171n39, 174n19, 176n65

Smith, Brady, 180n91

Smith, Daniel Jordan, 76

Smith, Laila, 183n53

Smith, Neil, 181n9

Snell, Heather, 176n78

Stanley, Ben Jamieson, 185n103, 186n134

state capture, 5–6, 61, 64, 68, 86, 163, 170n16, 178n32

Stege, Tina, 128

Stevenson, Robert Louis, 139

Stoler, Ann Laura, 15–16, 90; *Duress*, 15–16

Stonefish (Hulme) 155–59; mentioned, 23

Stratford, Elaine, Carol Farbotko, and Heather Lazrus, 132

Summers, Lawrence, 18

Suvin, Darko, 152

Szalay, Michael, 170n21

Table Mountain, 103, 104

Talbot, J. F, 93

Te Kaniva, 131–35; mentioned, 23

Thames Water, 92, 181n3

Thiong'o, Ngũgĩ wa, 5

Thirteen Cents (Duiker), 101–4, 113–14, 182n37; mentioned, 23, 98

Tides (Okpewho), 64–66, 178n21; mentioned, 21

Tong, Anote, 128–30, 135–38, 141–42, 151–54, 187n38; mentioned, 23

INDEX   221

Torrice, Andrea, 129; *Rising Waters: Global Warming and the Fate of the Pacific Islands*, 23, 129–30, 140–41; mentioned, 23
Travers, Robert, 172n46
Trouble with Nigeria, The (Achebe), 79
Tuvalu, 126, 131–32, 187n28, 188n56; borrow pits, 142; climate displacement, 131–35; mentioned, 23; sea level rise, 142–44. See also *Te Kaniva*

Union Carbide Corporation, 20–21, 25–30, 48; cost-cutting and, 26, 30–32; Dow Chemical, 30; Union Carbide India Limited, 175n29; Warren Anderson, 26, 32; in West Virginia, 25
Union Carbide Corporation v. Union of India. See Bhopal settlement
Union of India v. Union Carbide Corporation. See Bhopal civil suit
Utopian method: alternative states, 16, 26–27, 32–37, 52–55, 58, 80–91, 122–23, 151–54; complaint, 12–15, 39, 41–45, 49–50, 74–76, 78, 112–13, 129; description of, 2–4, 11–18, 27–28; negativity against the grain, 13–15, 49–50, 56–58, 61–62, 91, 94–95, 104–5, 112–16, 119–20, 124, 127–28, 136–38, 148–50, 154, 160–63; political antecedents, 15–16, 32–37, 61–62, 69–72, 90–91, 105–7, 123, 135–38, 161–63; politics of fulfillment, 16–17, 36–37, 44–45, 47, 49–50, 53, 74–78, 107–14, 132, 135, 172n65; recursion, 15–16, 36–37, 50, 69–72, 89–91, 122–23, 127, 144–47; state promises, 16, 22, 37–41, 43–49, 74–78, 100, 105–6, 108–14, 132–35, 170n21. See also Jameson, Fredric
"Utopian Method or, the Uses of the Future" (Jameson), 11–12

Vaastu Marabu (Kailasam), 42
Vavae, Hilia, 143
Vlies van der, Andrew, 172n66, 184n67
Vogel, Steven K., 178n31

Water Crisis Coalition, 104
water privatization, 92–93, 95, 102, 104, 181n3, 183n53
Watts, Michael, 63, 177n6
Weber, Max, 4
welfare states, 6–7, 37–41, 56, 89, 106–7, 170n21, 170n23
Wenzel, Jennifer, 11, 79, 171n39, 174n19, 178n32
Where Do the Children Play? (Kailasam), 42–47; mentioned, 21
Wilder, Gary, 7
Williams, Daniel, 99
Williams, Raymond, 71
Wolfe, Patrick, 188n52
World Bank, 5, 18, 61, 97
World War II, 142, 145
Wretched of the Earth, The (Fanon), 13–15

Zille, Helen, 119

Rebecca Oh is Assistant Professor of English at the University of Illinois Urbana-Champaign.

www.ingramcontent.com/pod-product-compliance
Lightning Source LLC
Chambersburg PA
CBHW031148020426
42333CB00013B/561